DEVOTIONS

— *for* —

real
life

DEVOTIONS

— for —

real
life

MELODY
CARLSON

Revell

a division of Baker Publishing Group
Grand Rapids, Michigan

Published by Revell
a division of Baker Publishing Group
P.O. Box 6287, Grand Rapids, MI 49516-6287
www.revellbooks.com

Combined edition published 2012

Previously published in three separate volumes:
True © 2008
Life © 2009
Always © 2010

Printed in the United States of America

Library of Congress Cataloging-in-Publication Data
Carlson, Melody.
    Devotions for real life / Melody Carlson. — Combined ed.
        p.   cm.
    A compilation of the author's Always, Life, and True.
    ISBN 978-0-8007-2097-1 (pbk.)
    1. Christian teenagers—Prayers and devotions. 2. Bible. N.T. Gospels—Meditations.
I. Title.
BV4850.C3325 2012
242′.63—dc23   2012027351

Scripture marked CEV is taken from the Contemporary English Version © 1991, 1992, 1995 by American Bible Society. Used by permission.

Scripture marked ESV is taken from The Holy Bible, English Standard Version, copyright © 2001 by Crossway Bibles, a division of Good News Publishers. Used by permission. All rights reserved.

Scripture marked Message is taken from The Message by Eugene H. Peterson, copyright © 1993, 1994, 1995, 2000, 2001, 2002. Used by permission of NavPress Publishing Group. All rights reserved.

Scripture marked NASB is taken from the New American Standard Bible®, Copyright © 1960, 1962, 1963, 1968, 1971, 1972, 1973, 1975, 1977, 1995 by The Lockman Foundation. Used by permission.

Scripture marked NCV is taken from the New Century Version®. Copyright © 1987, 1988, 1991 by Word Publishing, a division of Thomas Nelson, Inc. Used by permission. All rights reserved.

Scripture quotations are from the Holy Bible, New International Version®. NIV®. Copyright © 1973, 1978, 1984 by Biblica, Inc.™ Used by permission of Zondervan. All rights reserved worldwide. www.zondervan.com

Scripture marked NLT is taken from the Holy Bible, New Living Translation, copyright © 1996, 2004. Used by permission of Tyndale House Publishers, Inc., Wheaton, Illinois 60189. All rights reserved.

12   13   14   15   16   17   18   7   6   5   4   3   2   1

Contents

Introduction   11

Week 1

Day 1:   More Than Food   13
Day 2:   Make God Number One   14
Day 3:   Time to Change   16
Day 4:   Follow Me   17
Day 5:   End of Your Rope   18

Week 2

Day 1:   Good Loser   20
Day 2:   Real Contentment   21
Day 3:   Hungry for God?   23
Day 4:   Tender Hearts   24
Day 5:   A Right Heart   25

Week 3

Day 1:   Making Peace   27
Day 2:   Picked On for God   28
Day 3:   Really Picked On   29
Day 4:   Salty Souls   31
Day 5:   Like a Spotlight   32

Week 4

Day 1:   More Light   33
Day 2:   The Missing Piece   35

Day 3:   Law of Love   36
Day 4:   Take It Seriously   37
Day 5:   Keeping It Real   39

Week 5

Day 1:   Watch Your Words   40
Day 2:   Clean Slate   41
Day 3:   Owning Up   43
Day 4:   Sexual Sin   44
Day 5:   Prevention   45

Week 6

Day 1:   Divorce   47
Day 2:   Empty Promises   48
Day 3:   No More Getting Even   50
Day 4:   Love Your Enemies   52
Day 5:   Feel the Love   53

Week 7

Day 1:   All Show, No Go   55
Day 2:   Secret Service   56
Day 3:   The Real Deal   58
Day 4:   Sweet Simplicity   59
Day 5:   To the Point   61

Contents

Week 8

Day 1: What Goes Around . . .   62
Day 2: Spiritual Show-offs   64
Day 3: Lasting Riches   65
Day 4: Let the Light In   66
Day 5: Choose God   68

Week 9

Day 1: No Worries   69
Day 2: Carefree and Cared For   71
Day 3: Just Relax   72
Day 4: Hang with God   73
Day 5: Here and Now   75

Week 10

Day 1: Don't Judge   76
Day 2: Hypocritical "Help"   78
Day 3: Guard Your Heart   79
Day 4: Prayer Promises   80
Day 5: Our Provider   82

Week 11

Day 1: Getting Along   83
Day 2: One Way   85
Day 3: Beware   86
Day 4: Authentic Faith   88
Day 5: Rock Solid   89

Week 12

Day 1: Priorities   91
Day 2: No-Fear Faith   92
Day 3: Power to Forgive   94
Day 4: Needy Hearts   95
Day 5: Religious Acts   96

Week 13

Day 1: Transformed Thinking   98
Day 2: Desperate Faith   99
Day 3: Faith's Reward   101
Day 4: Get Ready   102
Day 5: Start Here   104

Week 14

Day 1: Keep It Simple   105
Day 2: Reaching Out   107
Day 3: Watch Out!   108
Day 4: Persecution Problems   110
Day 5: Hang In There   111

Week 15

Day 1: Be Bold   113
Day 2: Don't Fear   114
Day 3: Your Value   116
Day 4: Stay Strong   117
Day 5: Tough Stuff   118

Week 16

Day 1: Total Trust   120
Day 2: Welcome!   121
Day 3: Team Effort   123
Day 4: Acts of Kindness   124
Day 5: Miracles   125

Week 17

Day 1: Can You Hear Me Now?   127
Day 2: Spoiled Children   128
Day 3: God's Ways   130
Day 4: Knowing God   131
Day 5: Real Rest   132

Week 18

Day 1: Religion versus Relationship   134
Day 2: Law versus Life   135
Day 3: Real Power   137
Day 4: Cling to the Holy Spirit   138
Day 5: The Power of Words   139

Week 19

Day 1: Birdseed Faith   141
Day 2: Tumbleweed Faith   143
Day 3: Weedy Faith   144
Day 4: Amazing Faith!   146
Day 5: Puzzle Pieces   147

Contents

Week 20

Day 1: Enemy Seeds 149
Day 2: In Due Time 150
Day 3: Small Beginnings 152
Day 4: Major Minors 153
Day 5: Secret Treasure 154

Week 21

Day 1: What Cost? 156
Day 2: Finders Keepers 157
Day 3: Equipped and Ready 159
Day 4: Miracle Meal 160
Day 5: Fearless Faith 162

Week 22

Day 1: Fake Faith 163
Day 2: Weight of Words 165
Day 3: Religious Traps 166
Day 4: Real Sign 167
Day 5: Who Is He? 169

Week 23

Day 1: Kingdom Keys 170
Day 2: Followers 172
Day 3: Lost and Found 173
Day 4: How Much? 175
Day 5: Real Hunger 176

Week 24

Day 1: Job Description 177
Day 2: Soul Food 179
Day 3: No Rejection 180
Day 4: Big Promise 181
Day 5: Living Bread 183

Week 25

Day 1: Life Blood 184
Day 2: Life Bread 186
Day 3: Wrong Expectations 187
Day 4: Recognize Truth 188
Day 5: Learn to Discern 190

Week 26

Day 1: The Connector 191
Day 2: Mountain Movers 193
Day 3: Three-Part Plan 194
Day 4: Taxes or Trust 195
Day 5: Small Examples 197

Week 27

Day 1: Defending the Defenseless 198
Day 2: Trip Ups 200
Day 3: Just Lose It 201
Day 4: Persistent Love 202
Day 5: Work It Out 204

Week 28

Day 1: Power Promise 205
Day 2: Forgive and Forgive 207
Day 3: Marriage Plan 208
Day 4: Hard Hearts 210
Day 5: Single Hearts 211

Week 29

Day 1: Not Enough 213
Day 2: Stumbling Block 214
Day 3: Impossible Possibilities 216
Day 4: Great Benefits 217
Day 5: First and Last 218

Week 30

Day 1: Headed to the Cross 220
Day 2: Who's on Top? 222
Day 3: Sealed Fates 223
Day 4: Thirst Quencher 225
Day 5: Throwing Stones 226

Week 31

Day 1: Life Light 228
Day 2: Earthbound Minds 229
Day 3: Seeing Jesus 231
Day 4: Who's a Pharisee? 232
Day 5: Authorized by God 233

Contents

Week 32

Day 1: Real Freedom 235
Day 2: A Slave to Sin 236
Day 3: God at Work 238
Day 4: Blinding Pride 239
Day 5: Attention! 240

Week 33

Day 1: Our Entrance 242
Day 2: Good Shepherd 244
Day 3: All for Us 245
Day 4: Safety Zone 246
Day 5: Relationship
        Reflection 248

Week 34

Day 1: Confidence 250
Day 2: Sneak Preview 251
Day 3: Total Trust 253
Day 4: Devoted Disciples 254
Day 5: Children of Light 256

Week 35

Day 1: God's Light 257
Day 2: Words of Life 259
Day 3: Servant Heart 260
Day 4: Full Disclosure 262
Day 5: Love's Brand 263

Week 36

Day 1: Second Chances 265
Day 2: Home Sweet Home 266
Day 3: Way, Truth, Life 268
Day 4: Promising Promise 269
Day 5: The Only Way 271

Week 37

Day 1: One and the Same 272
Day 2: Humble Entrances 274
Day 3: Earth-Shaking Faith 275
Day 4: Miracle Key 277
Day 5: On Second Thought 278

Week 38

Day 1: Our Helper 280
Day 2: Messes Welcome 281
Day 3: Never Alone 283
Day 4: Mismanagement 284
Day 5: Love Driven 286

Week 39

Day 1: The Cornerstone 287
Day 2: Teachable 289
Day 3: Priorities 290
Day 4: Gentle Reminders 291
Day 5: Priceless Peace 293

Week 40

Day 1: Simple Laws 294
Day 2: Love's Example 296
Day 3: The Hypocrite Trap 297
Day 4: Good Hurts 299
Day 5: Spiritual Family 300

Week 41

Day 1: Fruit Connection 302
Day 2: False Religion's
        Reward 303
Day 3: Hang Tight 305
Day 4: Wrong Expectations 306
Day 5: In Sync 307

Week 42

Day 1: Stay in Love 309
Day 2: What's Next? 310
Day 3: Real Joy 312
Day 4: Grim Warnings 313
Day 5: Sacrificial Love 314

Week 43

Day 1: Everyone's Chance 316
Day 2: True Friends 317
Day 3: Troubling Times 319
Day 4: Chosen 320
Day 5: Don't Be Tricked 321

Week 44

Day 1:   Citizens of Heaven   323
Day 2:   Earth's Final Day   324
Day 3:   Our Example   326
Day 4:   Be Aware   327
Day 5:   No Excuses   328

Week 45

Day 1:   Distractions   330
Day 2:   Forever Friend   332
Day 3:   Be Prepared   333
Day 4:   Hold On!   334
Day 5:   Always Ready   336

Week 46

Day 1:   Change Is Good   337
Day 2:   When No One's Looking   339
Day 3:   Perceptions   340
Day 4:   Timing Is Everything   342
Day 5:   Full Disclosure   343

Week 47

Day 1:   Before the Dawn   345
Day 2:   Pain to Joy   346
Day 3:   Love in Action   347
Day 4:   Just Ask   349
Day 5:   Love Connection   350

Week 48

Day 1:   Coming Back   352
Day 2:   Like a River   353

Day 3:   With Open Arms   355
Day 4:   Attention!   356
Day 5:   Jesus's Gift   357

Week 49

Day 1:   Incomprehensible   359
Day 2:   All-Out Love   360
Day 3:   Family Ties   362
Day 4:   Prayer Power   363
Day 5:   Lifetime Membership   365

Week 50

Day 1:   Communion   366
Day 2:   Betrayal   368
Day 3:   Wake Up!   369
Day 4:   Complete Joy   371
Day 5:   Safekeeping   372

Week 51

Day 1:   Rags to Riches   373
Day 2:   The Mission   375
Day 3:   Amazed by Grace   376
Day 4:   Unity   377
Day 5:   Reputation   379

Week 52

Day 1:   Heavenly Hopes   380
Day 2:   Love Letter   382
Day 3:   No Secrets   383
Day 4:   Forgiveness   384
Day 5:   Always!   386

Introduction

A few words from Melody

I've written a lot of young adult novels in the past decade. As a result I get a lot of amazing letters from my young adult readers. But I'm continually surprised at how many times I get a letter from a reader who feels totally lost when it comes to the Bible. And I wonder . . . how can that be?

Then I think back to when I was fifteen. I remember how I went from being an unchurched atheist to a sold-out believer. My life did a mind-spinning 180 turnabout, but I didn't have a clue what to do next. As far as the Bible went, I didn't know 1 Chronicles from 1 Corinthians, and being in church felt like being in a foreign country, not to mention it came with a whole new language. In other words, although I was found, I felt pretty lost.

But one of the very first things I learned as a new believer was that Jesus was not simply my new best friend, he was the foundation of my faith as well. And, trust me, I needed a foundation. I needed something strong and steady and immovable—something I could rely on even if the rest of the world was quaking and shaking. I wanted something so sturdy that I could build my entire life upon it. In other words, I needed a rock—and that Rock was Jesus.

This is a message I try to convey in my teen novels—by telling stories about contemporary people with contemporary challenges, I try to show my readers that they too need a rock to build their lives upon. And I believe that in these times, with instability all around us, we are more in need of a solid foundation than ever. We all need a rock to lean upon.

Being a young adult comes with a ton of questions. Questions like: Who am I? Why am I like this? Who can I trust? What can I expect? Who will love me? What will I do with my life? Lots and lots of question. And I believe that the Bible holds the answers to all those questions—and more. But sometimes the Bible can feel like a great big overwhelming book. So I had to ask myself, how can I help my readers to find the answers they're looking for in the Bible? How can I make the Bible more user-friendly?

So I reflected back on my own life. Remember how I went from a heathen to a Christian as a teenager? Not having gone to church (like a lot of my new Christian friends had done), I realized that I was ravenous for God's Word. As a result, I started to read and read. It was as if I was trying to devour the entire Bible. I read it from cover to cover (well, except for portions of "begetting," etc., which I didn't get). I took Bible classes, attended Bible studies, listened to teaching audios. I even memorized whole chapters of Scripture. Okay, I'll admit that I was a little obsessed—but it felt like I was starving and couldn't get enough.

As the years passed, I became more and more comfortable with the Bible. In fact, I got more comfortable with the whole Christian culture in general. Things like attending church and fellowshipping and worshiping became second nature to me. In fact, after a lot of years, it all became a little too comfortable. I knew a lot of the Bible by heart, I taught Bible studies, and I spoke nearly perfect "Christianese." As a result, I started to take spiritual things for granted. And this bothered me—a lot.

So, what did I do? I went back to Jesus. I went back to that old foundation—the Rock. Instead of trying to "become smarter" or trying to become more "theological" or trying to get a better grasp on the Bible, I decided to go back to Jesus. I got myself a redlined Bible (the kind where Jesus's words are in red type), and I only allowed myself to read the red lines—the Jesus words. And I was so blessed.

So that's the whole point of *Devotions for Real Life* (a compilation of three previously published books). This big book contains all the Jesus words—the very words that I have built my life upon. And I hope you will find these words to be foundational for your life too!

Week 1

Day 1 · More Than Food

Words from the Rock ·

> It is written: "Man does not live on bread alone, but on every word that comes from the mouth of God."
>
> Matthew 4:4 NIV

I'm sure it's no coincidence that some of Jesus's first recorded words in the New Testament were about something we can all relate to—food. And although he was addressing Satan (Jesus hadn't eaten in weeks, and the devil had been tempting him to turn stones into bread), these rock-solid words were meant for everyone.

So, imagine you're starving. You're hungrier than you've ever been in your entire life. You haven't eaten in days, and all you can think about is food, food, food. Whether it's a Big Mac and fries or a pepperoni pizza or even sushi, you are so hungry you might actually sell your soul for something to eat. That's right where Satan had Jesus—or so he thought.

But what was Jesus's response to Satan's temptation? Even in his starved and emaciated state, Jesus told Satan that it took more than food to sustain life. He said that it was God's very words that would keep him alive. But what did that mean?

Jesus was our example in that he lived his life in a very tight relationship with God. In the same way that some people must stay connected (via text messaging, cell phones, email, instant messages, etc.), Jesus related to God on an ongoing, never-ending basis. It was this tight and constant connection that gave Jesus the power and strength to do all he did. He stayed tuned to God and relied on God's communication even more than he relied on food. It was his lifeline. And that's what he wants for us too—to connect and stay tuned to him, to realize we need him even more than we need food.

My Prayer

Dear God,

It's easy to know when I need food because I hear my stomach growling, and it's all I can think about. But it's not always so obvious to know how much I need you and your words. Teach me to tune in to you—to listen to you—and to understand that your words can sustain me better and longer than my favorite meal.

Amen.

Final Word

I have hidden your word in my heart, that I might not sin against you.

Psalm 119:11 NLT

Stone for the Journey

I need God's words more than I need food.

Day 2 · Make God Number One

Words from the Rock

Go away Satan! The Scriptures say: "Worship the Lord your God and serve only him."

Matthew 4:10 CEV

This was something else Jesus said when he was out in the desert being tempted by Satan. He'd already told the devil that it took more than food to live. And when Satan tried to get Jesus to do a cheap trick to prove he was

God's Son, Jesus told that lowlife that it was wrong to use God's power just to show off. And in this verse Jesus must've been totally fed up with the devil because he simply told the loser to get lost.

Jesus also pointed out that we are to serve and worship *only God*—no one and nothing else. Seems simple, and yet how often we forget. Consider what you spend your time thinking about. Maybe it's a special someone, like your most recent crush. Or maybe it's an activity you enjoy, like a sport or shopping. The thing is, if you spend a LOT of time thinking and obsessing over this particular person or thing, it becomes a lot like worship. And you have to ask yourself, *Who am I serving?*

God wants us to put him in that *first-place position*. He wants to be the top priority in our lives. It's okay to have other loved ones beneath him, but God wants to own that number one spot. And when he does, everything else will begin to fall into place.

My Prayer

Dear God,

Thank you for showing me how important it is to keep you first and foremost in my life. Help me to remember this when other people and things try to crowd into that place. Show me how I can serve and worship you above all else!

Amen.

Final Word

The Lord is king!
 Let the earth rejoice!
 Let the farthest coastlands be glad.

Psalm 97:1 NLT

Stone for the Journey

I will keep God in the first-place position in my heart.

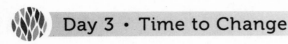

Day 3 · Time to Change

Words from the Rock · · · · · · · · · · · · · · · ·

> From that time Jesus began to preach, saying, "Change your hearts and lives, because the kingdom of heaven is near."
>
> Matthew 4:17 NCV

Although this is a short verse, it's totally power packed. After spending those long, hot, and hungry weeks in the desert, being tempted by Satan, Jesus was now starting his earthly ministry. And the first thing he told everyone listening was that it was *time for change.* He told them they needed to admit that they'd been doing things wrong, that they needed to tell God they were sorry, and that they were ready to do things differently. Jesus told the people it was time to repent!

And then he told them that the reason it was time for this kind of change was because God's kingdom was beginning—right then and there! God was going to do some amazing and wonderful things in their lives, and they needed to be ready for what was coming their way.

It's the same way with us. When we admit that we've blown it, and when we tell God we're sorry and that we really want to change, it's like we're inviting him to build his kingdom right in our hearts. It's like we're asking him to rule and reign inside us—and that's when things really begin to change. And here's the cool deal—it's not really a one-time-only thing; it's something we can and need to do on a regular basis. We need to tell God when we mess up. We need to say we're sorry. And we need to want to change. Then he comes into our lives and helps us to do that.

My Prayer · · · · · · · · · · · · · · · · · · ·

> *Dear God,*
>
> *I admit that I blow it a lot. Help me to remember to come directly to you each time I do. And then help me to change, so you can take up residence inside me. Thank you!*
>
> *Amen.*

Final Word ·

Get rid of these evil thoughts and ask God to forgive you.

Acts 8:22 CEV

Stone for the Journey ·

I will turn from my mistakes and put them behind me.

 # Day 4 · Follow Me

Words from the Rock ·

Come with me! I will teach you how to bring in people instead of fish.

Matthew 4:19 CEV

When Jesus gave this invitation to follow him, he was talking to some fishermen along the Sea of Galilee. They were going about their normal business, which was actually very hard labor, and Jesus paused to tell them that if they would leave their boats and nets, he would teach them to do something much better than fish for bass and perch. He would transform them into men who fished for the souls of men and women.

Now, you'd think those tough, crusty fishermen would've been shocked by that crazy-weird invitation, but they weren't. They stepped away from their boats and the life they knew like it was no big deal. They walked away from what had been their livelihood, and they simply followed Jesus. And everything Jesus promised them eventually came true.

Jesus invites you to follow him in a very similar way. He promises that he has better ways of doing things. He has a better kind of work for you to do. He has something really special and amazing in store . . . *if you will just follow him*. But sometimes that sounds crazy-weird—like how do you step away from your life and just follow him? Here's the secret—you don't have to figure it all out. You simply follow where he leads.

My Prayer ·

> *Dear God,*
>
> > *I want to follow you. I want to believe you have a unique plan for me, just as you did for those fishermen. But I know believing that requires a lot of trust on my part. Help me to have that kind of faith.*
> >
> > *Amen.*

Final Word ·

> I did this as an example so that you should do as I have done for you.
>
> John 13:15 NCV

Stone for the Journey · · · · · · · · · · · · · · · · · ·

> I choose to follow God wherever he leads.

 ## Day 5 · End of Your Rope

Words from the Rock · · · · · · · · · · · · · · · · · · ·

> You're blessed when you're at the end of your rope. With less of you there is more of God and his rule.
>
> Matthew 5:3 Message

Sometimes Jesus said things that didn't make complete sense to everyone, at least at first. Hopefully the truth soaked in later. But sometimes Jesus said things that sounded like an oxymoron—like "you're a *lucky loser*" or "isn't that a *great disaster*." Okay, those weren't Jesus's exact words, but sometimes the things he said made people scratch their heads and wonder.

When Jesus taught the Sermon on the Mount (Matthew 5–7), he spoke of a variety of ways that people were blessed. And the first one he described was how we'd be blessed when we reached the end of our rope. Huh? Was he saying we should be glad when we have nothing left to give, when we're spent, worn-out, or beaten? Seriously, who feels happy about that?

But Jesus knew something we didn't. He knew that as soon as we figured out that we'd done all we could and still failed—that was when we might begin to look to God for assistance. When we hit an impossibly tough spot, we'd cry out for help. Because, unfortunately, most of us have to be exhausted and beaten up and backed into a corner before we realize that God is just waiting for us to invite him to help.

So Jesus was saying that if we can figure out that truth sooner in our everyday lives—if we can grasp and accept that we're not strong enough, smart enough, or quick enough—*then life will get better.* When we step aside and allow God to be our strength, our wisdom, and our protection, that's when we'll be blessed!

My Prayer

Dear God,

Sometimes I forget just how weak I really am. Teach me to figure it out sooner. I try to do things on my own, and I make a total mess. Help me to remember how much I need you as I recognize how inadequate I really am. And then I can be glad you made me like this—just so you can bless me with more of you!

Amen.

Final Word

He [the Lord] replied, "My kindness is all you need. My power is strongest when you are weak." So if Christ keeps giving me his power, I will gladly brag about how weak I am.

2 Corinthians 12:9 CEV

Stone for the Journey

I give God my weakness in exchange for his strength.

Week 2

 Day 1 · Good Loser

Words from the Rock · · · · · · · · · · · · · · ·

> You're blessed when you feel you've lost what is most dear to you.
> Only then can you be embraced by the One most dear to you.
>
> Matthew 5:4 Message

The next blessing Jesus described in his mountaintop sermon is similar to the first one—meaning it sounds a bit like an oxymoron. Remember the "lucky loser" line? Well, this particular blessing involves personal loss. Admit it, it's hard to get excited about losing someone or something you love. But Jesus said you'd be blessed when you lose whatever is most valuable to you.

And that's a little scary. I mean, think about it. What is so precious to you that you cannot imagine living on the planet without it? Is it a person—like your best friend, a family member, your latest crush? Or maybe it's a thing—a great car, your computer, your cell phone, or a pet. How would you feel if it was suddenly taken from you?

Okay, maybe that's something you'd rather not think about right now. Or maybe you've already experienced that loss in some form. Whatever the case, Jesus is saying that when you know what it's like to lose whatever you love the most, you will then understand what it means to be gathered up into God's arms and loved like you've *never been loved before*. It's not that God doesn't love you now, but this is his guarantee that if you suffer a painful loss, he has a very special way of comforting you.

If you think about it, that's an amazing promise. And if you believe it and take it seriously, that promise can give you the confidence to go bravely through life, because you'll know that no matter what happens, even if what you love most is taken, God will be there ready to love you in a way that will blow your socks off—a way that's beyond any earthly form of love. That's an awesome blessing!

My Prayer ·

Dear God,

Help me to understand how huge your love for me really is. Whether or not I've experienced a big loss in my life, help me to realize that you are able to make up for it in ways I cannot begin to imagine. I want my faith to grow as I choose to trust you with whatever loss has come or will come into my life. Help me to reach the place where I know I am blessed no matter what.

Amen.

Final Word ·

If you want to save your life, you will destroy it. But if you give up your life for me, you will save it.

Luke 9:24 CEV

Stone for the Journey ·

I can trust God with my loss.

Day 2 · Real Contentment

Words from the Rock ·

You're blessed when you're content with just who you are—no more, no less. That's the moment you find yourselves proud owners of everything that can't be bought.

Matthew 5:5 Message

How many people do you know who can honestly say, "I like who I am and how I look, and I like my mind and my abilities . . . and I wouldn't change a thing about myself"? Yeah, right. It's just not that easy, is it?

Not that we don't wish we could live in that happy place and have that kind of positive attitude. But it just seems impossible—at least in a 24-7 kind of way. And maybe we even try. But get real—how many of us jump out of bed every single morning and look in the mirror and say, "Wow, awesome"?

Something about the human condition seems to have destined us for discontent and comparisons. We might not like to admit that we sometimes long for more, but most of us have been there, done that—whether it's wishing we looked like some hot celebrity or simply had straight hair and a different eye color. And, whether we wish we had as much money as Donald Trump or just enough money to buy an old used car, we know we're not always satisfied with the status quo.

Yet Jesus said we'd be blessed when we're able to see ourselves as we really are and go, "Yeah, all right . . . I'm cool with that." When we get to the place in life where we're truly content with ourselves and the way God made us, we will finally be free of the comparison game, petty jealousy, and general discontent. And, seriously, what a blessing that would be!

My Prayer · · · · · · · · · · · · · · · · · ·

> *Dear God,*
>
> *I confess that I'm not always content with who I am. Okay, that might be an understatement. But I pray that you'll help me see myself the way you see me. I pray that you'll remind me that you made me like this for a reason and that I can trust you with that. I give all that I am to you, and I ask for your help in finding a place of contentment—because I can't get there without you. Thank you!*
>
> *Amen.*

Final Word · · · · · · · · · · · · · · · · · · ·

A devout life does bring wealth, but it's the rich simplicity of being yourself before God. Since we entered the world penniless and will leave it penniless, if we have bread on the table and shoes on our feet, that's enough.

1 Timothy 6:6–8 Message

Stone for the Journey · · · · · · · · · · · · · ·

I choose to be happy with the way God made me.

Day 3 • Hungry for God?

Words from the Rock · · · · · · · · · · · ·

You're blessed when you've worked up a good appetite for God.
He's food and drink in the best meal you'll ever eat.

Matthew 5:6 Message

This might be one of the more obvious blessings from Jesus's Sermon on the Mount. Jesus was simply pointing out that we'll be blessed when we hunger and thirst for God as much as we do for food and drink. Simple enough . . . and yet most of us don't live our lives like that on a daily basis. Usually our stomachs growl for food a whole lot more quickly than our hearts cry out for God.

But have you ever noticed how many Bible verses compare God and Jesus to food and drink? And do you wonder why that is? Okay, maybe that's obvious too. Food and drink are things we all enjoy on a pretty regular basis. They're a part of life and things that healthy people aren't willing to give up. Think about it. It doesn't take more than, say, six hours without eating or drinking before we wonder when the next meal is coming.

Jesus was saying that if we desire God the way we long for our next hot meal, we will be really blessed. That's because we will have more and more of God in our lives—we'll be filled up with his love, his goodness, his mercy . . . all sorts of amazing things. And that would be an enormous blessing not just for us but for everyone around us.

My Prayer · · · · · · · · · · · · · · · · ·

Dear God,

Please make my heart hungry for you. Make me thirst for you the way I'd thirst for water in a hot, arid desert. Remind me that I can never get too full of you—and that I need to come to you just as regularly as I head for the lunch line or dinner table.

Amen.

Final Word · · · · · · · · · · · · · · · · · · ·

> As the deer pants for streams of water,
> so my soul pants for you, O God.
>
> Psalm 42:1 NIV

Stone for the Journey ·

> I am hungry and thirsty for more of God in my life.

 ## Day 4 · Tender Hearts

Words from the Rock ·

> God blesses those people who are merciful.
> They will be treated with mercy!
>
> Matthew 5:7 CEV

How often do you hear someone say, "I don't care"? How often do you say it yourself? Sometimes it seems the world is full of people who simply don't give a rip. But Jesus is saying that you will be blessed when you care—*when you care enough to take care of others.*

Jesus wants you to learn to look outside yourself and see that others are in need. He wants you to learn to put aside your selfishness and roll up your sleeves to help someone else. But do you know why? Is it because God's too busy to take care of everyone? No, of course not. God made the universe—he can easily take care of everyone and everything connected to it. And he does. But his plan is bigger than that. He wants to partner with you.

God knows that you are changed when you help someone else. You grow up a little, and you begin to look more like God. Not only that, but when you care for others, it gets attention. People take notice when someone does something kind or generous or unselfish—because it's a little outside the norm. And when people observe you helping or caring for someone else, they have to scratch their heads and ponder it—like, "What's up with that?" And perhaps someone will be curious enough to ask you—and you can say it's because of God and what he's doing in your life. That'll make 'em wonder.

My Prayer ·

> *Dear God,*
>
> *Teach me to be more caring of others around me. Help me to see when someone is in need. Show me ways I can help. And if anyone asks, let me give the credit to you.*
> *Amen.*

Final Word ·

> Love must be sincere. Hate what is evil; cling to what is good.
>
> Romans 12:9 NIV

Stone for the Journey ·

> I will keep my eyes peeled for someone who needs my help.

 # Day 5 • A Right Heart

Words from the Rock ·

> They are blessed whose thoughts are pure,
>   for they will see God.
>
> Matthew 5:8 NCV

Jesus said you'll be blessed when your heart, that hidden inner place only God can see, becomes clean and pure. But how do you purify a heart? It's not like you can take Lysol and bleach and give it a good scrub. Even if you could clean it yourself, it would only get dirty again. Because the moment you have bad thoughts toward someone, or feel jealous, or get angry, or lie, or cheat, or hurt someone, your heart gets messed up again. Oh, you can pretend like everything's nice and neat because no one besides you knows just what your heart looks like inside . . . well, except for God. He knows.

And God is the only one who can clean your heart. He did this once and for all by sending his love and forgiveness to earth in the form of Jesus. When you invite Jesus to live in your heart, he's the one who starts cleaning things up. Your job is to cooperate and let him. You can do this by being honest with him, by asking him to help you with areas of your life that need cleaning.

Just as a house needs to be cleaned on a regular basis, so does your heart. It's one of those daily things—a job that must be done again and again. But the good news is that when your heart is clean, you see God in a whole new way—kind of like looking through a freshly cleaned window. And the more you see him, the more you start to look like him.

My Prayer

Dear God,

I invite you to do some deep cleaning inside my heart. I know that you're the only one who can really make my heart pure, and I agree to cooperate. Show me the messy spots I need to turn over to you—and help me allow you to clean them in your own way. I want to see you more clearly. I want to know you better. Thank you! Amen.

Final Word

The purpose of this command is for people to have love, a love that comes from a pure heart and a good conscience and a true faith.

1 Timothy 1:5 NCV

Stone for the Journey

I choose to keep my heart clean by focusing on God.

Week 3

 ## Day 1 • Making Peace

Words from the Rock · · · · · · · · · · · · ·

> You're blessed when you can show people how to cooperate instead of compete or fight. That's when you discover who you really are, and your place in God's family.
>
> Matthew 5:9 Message

We hear a lot of talk about world peace—and that's a great goal for everyone to adopt. But how about making peace right where we live? Sometimes the hardest place to keep peace is right under our own roof.

Jesus said that when we learn how to get along peacefully with others, and when we make an effort to help others get along peacefully as well, we begin to experience what being an integral part of God's family is about. Not only that, but people who are watching us can't help but notice that something is different—because all we need to do is look around to see that peace doesn't just happen.

So, next time you sense tension or hear voices rising in anger, say a quick prayer and ask God to lead you, then do your part to encourage cooperation, consideration, understanding—whatever it takes to prevent a fight. Whether it's offering a kind word or a gentle reminder, or simply urging a person to walk away, your efforts will show others that you really are God's child—and you will be blessed.

My Prayer · · · · · · · · · · · · · · · · ·

Dear God,

I confess that sometimes it feels exciting to witness a heated argument—especially if I'm not the one in the middle of it. But I know that's wrong. Please help me be an instrument of peace. Help me remember to place myself in your hands and to be ready to be used for healing instead of hurting.

Amen.

Final Word ·

People who work for peace in a peaceful way plant a good crop of right-living.

James 3:18 NCV

Stone for the Journey ·

I will be on the lookout for ways to bring peace to those around me.

Day 2 · Picked On for God

Words from the Rock · · · · · · · · · · · · · · · · · ·

You're blessed when your commitment to God provokes persecution. The persecution drives you even deeper into God's kingdom.

Matthew 5:10 Message

Because we live in a country with religious freedom, we don't worry that we might be put to death because of what we believe. And yet there are quiet, subtle forms of persecution that happen fairly regularly. Maybe someone makes fun of you for standing up for your convictions. Or maybe you've been teased for saying a blessing over your lunch or carrying a Bible or attending youth group.

Jesus said you'll be blessed when your faith—that is, your commitment to God—makes others want to persecute you. So perhaps the question is, are you being persecuted because you're doing what God has called you to do? Or are you being persecuted because you're being an in-your-face, Bible-thumping Christian, begging for negative attention? If it's the latter, watch out. That kind of "persecution" won't come with a blessing attached.

Blessing comes as a result of the relationship you have with God. In other words, when you're simply doing what God has asked you to do and, as a result, someone picks on you, God will bless you by increasing his presence in your life. You will feel more connected to him and his kingdom than ever before.

My Prayer

Dear God,

> *Show me how to serve and love you more. Not in a showy way but in a way that is genuine and humble. And if, while doing that, I get picked on, help me to remember that you are blessing me with more of you and your kingdom.*
>
> *Amen.*

Final Word

Consider it pure joy, my brothers, whenever you face trials of many kinds, because you know that the testing of your faith develops perseverance.

James 1:2–3 NIV

Stone for the Journey

I'll consider it a blessing if I am picked on for my faith.

 ## Day 3 • Really Picked On

Words from the Rock

Not only that—count yourselves blessed every time people put you down or throw you out or speak lies about you to discredit me. What it means is that the truth is too close for comfort and they are uncomfortable. You can be glad when that happens— give a cheer, even!—for though they don't like it, I do! And all heaven applauds. And know that you are in good company. My prophets and witnesses have always gotten into this kind of trouble.

Matthew 5:11–12 Message

Now, the sort of persecution Jesus describes in these verses is not the everyday variety. At least not in our country. Jesus was warning his followers that their persecution might be extreme and severe—they would be locked up, tortured, and even executed for their faith. And that's just what happened. Since then, many more generations of Christians have gone through persecution. And in some countries it still happens today.

It's hard to imagine that we could be persecuted for our faith like that in the United States, but if we were, we could be assured that God would bless us in a huge way. And we could also know that we wouldn't be alone. In a very real sense, we'd have Jesus and all the others who have suffered for their faith standing alongside us, cheering and encouraging us as we remained firm in our commitment to God. Perhaps best of all, we'd know that we really belonged to God—because we'd be enduring the same kind of persecution as his own Son.

My Prayer

Dear God,

It's hard to imagine that the world would ever change so drastically that I would be seriously persecuted for my faith. But if that's ever the case, I pray that you would be my strength and that I would stand firm and remember you are standing right beside me.

Amen.

Final Word

But it is no shame to suffer for being a Christian. Praise God for the privilege of being called by his name!

1 Peter 4:16 NLT

Stone for the Journey

I'll hang on tighter to God if the going gets really rough.

Day 4 • Salty Souls

Words from the Rock

> You are the salt of the earth. But if the salt loses its salty taste, it cannot be made salty again. It is good for nothing, except to be thrown out and walked on.
>
> Matthew 5:13 NCV

When Jesus described his followers as "salt," they probably got it. Or at least they understood that he was saying something good. Although we don't think much of salt today—it's cheap and available everywhere—salt was a highly prized commodity back when Jesus said this. And for his followers to be compared to salt meant they had value too.

I remember a time when my husband's parents were on a salt-free diet. They invited us to dinner, which was some kind of a stew with parsnips and some other vegetables, all without salt. And there was no salt to be had in the house either. That stew was so bland that it was difficult to eat more than a bite or two. In fact, I think I can honestly say it was the worst meal I'd ever eaten. Okay, I'm not crazy about parsnips, but I might've been able to eat them with a bit of salt. That night I realized how valuable salt is.

When Jesus says we're to be salt, it's no small thing. He's saying that our lives, our hearts, our commitment to him should be so savory and flavorful that people will smack their lips and ask for more. Okay, maybe that's stretching the metaphor a bit. But he is saying that he wants us to make a difference. He wants us to be a tasty sample of his love, his forgiveness, his kindness, so that people around us will want seconds.

My Prayer

Dear God,

Help me to be a flavorful sample of what you have to offer for everyone. Show me how to live my life in a way that makes others hungry for you.

Amen.

Final Word ·

Be pleasant and hold their interest when you speak the message. Choose your words carefully and be ready to give answers to anyone who asks questions.

Colossians 4:6 CEV

Stone for the Journey · · · · · · · · · · · · · · · · · · ·

I want to add zest and seasoning to the world around me.

 ## Day 5 · Like a Spotlight

Words from the Rock · · · · · · · · · · · · · · · · · · ·

You are the light of the world. A city on a hill cannot be hidden.

Matthew 5:14 NIV

That's a tall order, isn't it? Jesus said he wants us to be like a bright light that's set on the hilltop of a big city, a beam so bright it can guide people toward the city even when it's pitch black outside. That sounds cool, but what does it mean?

Well, if you know anything about lights, you know that they need something to power them. What good is a flashlight without batteries? What good is a table lamp without electricity? What good is a kerosene lamp without kerosene? I think what Jesus is saying is that we're supposed to be the flashlight or lamp or spotlight, but he will be what powers and fuels the actual light. In other words, it's not up to us to provide the energy to run. We just need to be ready and willing and in the right place at the right time. And we need to be fully connected to him—because even a lamp that's plugged in to a power outlet is useless if it's not turned on. We need his power to flow through us.

So when we say to Jesus, "Here I am; use me however you like," he is able to be that endless power supply that shoots his energy through us, making our lights bright and clear. And that's when people around us will stop and take notice. That light will illuminate things that need to be seen. And who knows, some might even use our light to find their way home—back to God.

My Prayer

Dear God,

I do want to be your light. I want to make myself available to you, connected to you, so that your energy will gush through me and create a light that will help me and others find the way to you.

Amen.

Final Word

He [Jesus] said, "I am the light for the world! Follow me, and you won't be walking in the dark. You will have the light that gives life."

John 8:12 CEV

Stone for the Journey

I'll stay connected to God, my power source, so that my light shines brightly.

Week 4

Day 1 • More Light

Words from the Rock

No one would light a lamp and put it under a clay pot. A lamp is placed on a lampstand, where it can give light to everyone in the house. Make your light shine, so that others will see the good that you do and will praise your Father in heaven.

Matthew 5:15–16 CEV

Light is such a great metaphor for how God works. It's no surprise that the Bible uses it over and over. But in these two verses, when Jesus speaks of light, he's bringing it to a whole new level. He's talking about lighting up the home. He starts out by saying that we wouldn't turn on a table lamp, then throw a tarp over it. That would be pretty dumb—not to mention "ungreen" and unsafe.

Jesus is saying that when we're in our homes and living our everyday lives, *we still need to let our light shine.* We still need to remain connected to him and to have his energy flowing through us, because he wants our families, relatives, and close friends to see his light too.

Okay, to be fair, sometimes home is the hardest place to let our light shine. It's easy to want to conceal what God is doing in our lives when we're around parents or siblings—people who have seen the very worst of us, people who might even make fun of us or question our beliefs. But Jesus makes it very clear that he wants us to shine around our family just as much as we shine around others. And he sums it up by saying that when we let our light shine in our homes, the loved ones around us will eventually turn their eyes to God. And, really, what could be better than that?

My Prayer

> *Dear God,*
>
> *I confess that sometimes I feel like hiding my faith when I'm at home. And I confess that it's my own family that often brings out the worst in me. Please help me be connected to you, my power source, so I can shine your light in my home. And help those around me see that it's you providing the power!*
>
> *Amen.*

Final Word

> Whatever I say to you in the dark, you must tell in the light. And you must announce from the housetops whatever I have whispered to you.
>
> Matthew 10:27 CEV

Stone for the Journey

> I won't hide what God is doing in my life.

Day 2 • The Missing Piece

Words from the Rock

> Don't suppose for a minute that I have come to demolish the Scriptures—either God's Law or the Prophets. I'm not here to demolish but to complete. I am going to put it all together, pull it all together in a vast panorama.
>
> Matthew 5:17 Message

Some of Jesus's followers had gotten the wrong idea about Jesus. They were so eager for change (political, religious, and personal) that they thought he was going to toss out everything they'd been taught, including God's commandments and Old Testament prophecies, many of which specifically foretold Jesus's life and ministry.

What Jesus wanted them, and everyone, to grasp was that God had a much bigger plan—a plan that had been in place since the beginning of time. Jesus wanted his followers to respect that he was part of God's plan; in fact, he was the most important part. He was like the missing puzzle piece—when he was put into place, they would begin to see the whole picture and get it. And Jesus didn't intend to pull apart all that God had already put together. Instead he was going to do something so amazing (dying on a cross and then rising from the dead) that everything would finally begin to make sense.

It's a lot like that in our lives too. God has put some things together (like who we are, who our parents are, where we live), and he has a purpose in those things. He doesn't want us to toss them aside. But it will take Jesus's involvement in our lives to make that purpose happen. When we partner with him, it's like we finally have the missing pieces to the puzzle, and life actually starts to make sense.

My Prayer

Dear God,

Help me to trust your plans, both for the universe and for my own life. Help me to realize that you've already put some things into place—things I need to accept. And then teach me how to obey and cooperate with you so that my life works out the way you planned it.

Amen.

Final Word · · · · · · · · · · · ·

> Trust in the LORD with all your heart
>   and lean not on your own understanding;
> in all your ways acknowledge him,
>   and he will make your paths straight.
>
> Proverbs 3:5–6 NIV

Stone for the Journey ·

> I will trust God with the blueprint of my life.

 ## Day 3 · Law of Love

Words from the Rock ·

> God's Law is more real and lasting than the stars in the sky and the ground at your feet. Long after stars burn out and earth wears out, God's Law will be alive and working.
>
> Matthew 5:18 Message

God's law may seem big and intimidating, but it's actually pretty simple and straightforward. Despite how religious people have tried to complicate God's law during the past several thousand years, Jesus summed it up in a couple of concise sentences. Here's the nutshell version: (1) Love God. (2) Love your neighbor. Simple, right?

Okay, maybe it's simple, but as you know, simple isn't always easy. Perhaps that's why some religious people try to complicate the law by adding to it and making it tricky—maybe it's a way to distract themselves and others from what God's law really is and from actually doing it.

God's law is simply the ultimate *law of love*. And, as Jesus pointed out, God's law will last forever. So what's the purpose of laws? They are made for us to obey—meaning we have a choice. And not just a onetime choice either—it's a daily choice, sometimes a minute-by-minute choice. And if we choose to love God first of all, wholeheartedly and intentionally, then he will help us to do the next part—to love others (even the unlovable ones). That's how God's law works and how it becomes a living law—and one that lasts forever.

My Prayer ·

> *Dear God,*
>   *I want to obey your law, but I know I need your help. First, let me choose to love you with all that I am. Then remind me to come to you when I need help in loving others.*
>   *Amen.*

Final Word ·

> Love the Lord your God with all your heart, soul, and mind.
>
> Matthew 22:37 CEV

Stone for the Journey ·

> I choose to fulfill God's law by loving him and others.

Day 4 • Take It Seriously

Words from the Rock ·

> Trivialize even the smallest item in God's Law and you will only have trivialized yourself. But take it seriously, show the way for others, and you will find honor in the kingdom.
>
> Matthew 5:19 Message

If you really believe that God's law is the law of love, if you truly embrace it and want to obey it, you need to take it seriously. But sometimes that's hard. Not everyone is easy to love. Sometimes it would be way easier just to look the other way and pretend like you momentarily forgot that God wants you to love everyone. Or maybe you could cover it up with something else—like a good deed.

But that would be trivializing God's law. It would be like saying, "Hey, God, you didn't really mean it. I don't have to take it seriously . . . no big deal."

Take a moment to think of a person you really don't like—someone you don't even want to love. Maybe it's a sibling who knows how to jab at you when you're already bummed. Maybe it's a bully or a mean girl at school. Maybe there's a certain teacher who doesn't like you, someone who's treated you unfairly. Maybe it's a parent or a grandparent or the next-door neighbor.

And maybe that person has really done you wrong—so much so that you feel justified in your feelings toward them, feelings that have nothing to do with love. That means you are not taking God's law seriously. And it's a putdown to him—and, as a result, it's a putdown to you. You see, you can't slam God without slamming yourself too. That's why he's there, ready to help you to love the most challenging people.

My Prayer

> *Dear God,*
>
> *I confess that I have trivialized your law. I know that by not loving [name], I'm not taking you seriously. I know that I'm belittling you, which only makes me a smaller person. Please help me to love everyone. And when I think I can't, please remind me to come to you for help.*
>
> *Amen.*

Final Word

> Oh, how I love your law!
>   I meditate on it all day long.
> Your commands make me wiser than my enemies,
>   for they are ever with me.
>
> Psalm 119:97–98 NIV

Stone for the Journey

I will take God seriously and obey his commands.

Day 5 • Keeping It Real

Words from the Rock · · · · · · · · · · ·

> Unless you do far better than the Pharisees in the matters of right living, you won't know the first thing about entering the kingdom.
>
> Matthew 5:20 Message

The Pharisees were the religious leaders during Jesus's earthly ministry, and unfortunately, many of them were corrupt. Imagine a really, really bad TV evangelist—he's all dressed up and preaching to his faithful listeners about how God is not happy with them, but if they'll just send him a big fat check, he'll help make things okay between them and God. Yeah, right.

Pretty disgusting, isn't it? But in some ways, that's not a lot different from the Pharisees. It's like they put on a good show, they wore expensive clothes, and they acted a certain way. They probably even seemed to be serving God, but all the while they were making God less accessible than ever before. They pretended to be godly, but underneath their big act, many of them were hypocrites.

That's the last thing Jesus wants to see in us. He doesn't want us to become spiritual hypocrites, falling into the trap of looking good, acting good, saying the right things—while underneath it all we're a mess. Instead, he wants us to remain in a thriving relationship with him. He wants us to be real, not phony. And that's when we experience his kingdom—right here and now!

My Prayer · · · · · · · · · · ·

Dear God,

I don't ever want to be like a Pharisee. Help me to keep it real. Help me to stay close to you so that your life flows through me. And help me to draw people closer to you instead of pushing them away.

Amen.

Final Word · · · · · · · · · · ·

> Blessed is the man
> who does not walk in the counsel of the wicked
> or stand in the way of sinners

or sit in the seat of mockers.
But his delight is in the law of the LORD,
    and on his law he meditates day and night.

Psalm 1:1–2 NIV

Stone for the Journey

I will honor God by being real.

Week 5

Day 1 • Watch Your Words

Words from the Rock

You know that our ancestors were told, "Do not murder" and "A murderer must be brought to trial." But I promise you that if you are angry with someone, you will have to stand trial. If you call someone a fool, you will be taken to court. And if you say that someone is worthless, you will be in danger of the fires of hell.

Matthew 5:21–22 CEV

Wow, this is a really strong warning about how powerful words can be. Has it ever occurred to you that you can say things that are as lethal as committing murder? Or maybe you've been severely wounded by someone else's thoughtless words toward you. Jesus is commanding you to take the power of your tongue much more seriously. He wants you to understand that wounds from insults and putdowns can sometimes take a lifetime to heal. And some cut so deeply that they can be life threatening.

Think about it. How often have you replayed in your mind something mean that someone has said to or about you? How many times have you felt pain when you remembered some harsh words directed at you? Is it possible that you've inflicted that same kind of pain on someone else? If so, you'd better do whatever it takes to make it right. And although you can't undo the words that were said, you might remember to *think before you speak* next time.

The old adage "If you can't say anything nice, don't say anything at all" may sound trite, but the truth is, it would be much better to keep your mouth shut than to have to stand before Jesus and confess to having murdered someone with your tongue.

My Prayer

> *Dear God,*
>
> *Help me to be more careful with my words. Remind me of the poison that can be slipped into a seemingly small insult. I need your help to control this tongue of mine. Please show me when it's time to keep my mouth shut.*
> *Amen.*

Final Word

> My tongue will speak of your righteousness
> and of your praises all day long.
>
> Psalm 35:28 NIV

Stone for the Journey

> I will control my tongue or keep my mouth shut.

 ## Day 2 • Clean Slate

Words from the Rock

> This is how I want you to conduct yourself in these matters. If you enter your place of worship and, about to make an offering, you suddenly remember a grudge a friend has against you, abandon your offering, leave immediately, go to this friend and

. make things right. Then and only then, come back and work things out with God.

Matthew 5:23–24 Message

Jesus tells us that we need to keep a clean slate between ourselves and others so that we can avoid hypocrisy. Specifically, he warns that we need to be especially careful when we're going someplace to worship God. Whether it's a Sunday service at church or youth group or a Bible study, we need to make sure we're not taking any unfinished business with us when we're getting ready to praise God with others.

If we attempt to worship, knowing full well that we've offended someone without making it right, we're putting ourselves at serious risk for becoming just like one of those hypocritical Pharisees or that phony-baloney TV evangelist—people who pretend to serve God but have turned into fakers and takers. Seriously, who wants to end up like that?

Jesus isn't saying that we have to be perfect and somehow manage to live our lives without offending anyone. That's not even possible. What he *is* saying is that we need to make things right with others—we need to say we're sorry and to ask forgiveness—quickly. And especially before we start singing the praises of the one who died on the cross for the very purpose of forgiveness. Then, once the slate is clean, we can come back and worship God without being distracted and without feeling like hypocrites. And, really, isn't that way better?

My Prayer

Dear God,

Help me to remember this important warning. I want to keep a clean slate with everyone so I can worship you with honor and truth. Help me to stay on track.

Amen.

Final Word

Peter came to Jesus and asked, "Lord, how many times shall I forgive my brother when he sins against me? Up to seven times?"

Jesus answered, "I tell you, not seven times, but seventy-seven times."

Matthew 18:21–22 NIV

Stone for the Journey ·

I will go make things right with others before I go worship God.

 ## Day 3 • Owning Up

Words from the Rock ·

If your enemy is taking you to court, become friends quickly, before you go to court. Otherwise, your enemy might turn you over to the judge, and the judge might give you to a guard to put you in jail. I tell you the truth, you will not leave there until you have paid everything you owe.

Matthew 5:25-26 NCV

Okay, you probably don't have anyone who's ready to haul you into court, but you never know. What Jesus is saying is that you need to own up to any past wrongs you may have done—back before you were trying to follow Jesus and live according to his rules. (Remember "love God, love your neighbors"?) In the same way you want a clean slate before you go to worship, you want to clear up any past offenses with others as well.

So at any given opportunity, you need to step up and own up. Look that person in the eye and say, "I was wrong, and I am sorry. Please forgive me." And offer to do whatever is necessary to set things right. You just might catch that offended person so off guard that she will simply nod and say, "Okay, no hard feelings."

Do you know why Jesus takes time to say these seemingly basic and obvious things? Because he knows you're human. He knows that you've blown it and that you'll blow it again. But he wants you to clean up your act, so you don't walk around beneath a cloud of guilt and regret and so he can use you to help others. Pretty simple—as long as you cooperate.

My Prayer ·

> *Dear God,*
>
> > *Please forgive me for the times I've hurt others. And help me to find the opportunities to make things right. Give me the strength to own up to my messes, to apologize, and to come clean.*
> > *Amen.*

Final Word ·

> If you have sinned, you should tell each other what you have done. Then you can pray for one another and be healed. The prayer of an innocent person is powerful, and it can help a lot.
>
> > James 5:16 CEV

Stone for the Journey ·

> I will do all I can to restore messed-up relationships.

 ## Day 4 · Sexual Sin

Words from the Rock ·

> You know the commandment which says, "Be faithful in marriage." But I tell you that if you look at another woman and want her, you are already unfaithful in your thoughts.
>
> > Matthew 5:27–28 CEV

Okay, this is a touchy subject (no pun intended) for many people. What was Jesus really saying? Obviously he was talking about sex. And he was stating that sex outside of a marriage relationship is wrong. Nothing new about that. But at the same time he was saying more—much, much more.

He was saying that sexual sin begins long before two people engage in a sexual act. He was saying that when you focus on unmarried sex, when you daydream about it, and when you obsess over it, even if you're not technically having sex, you are still stepping over the line—and you are playing with fire.

Whether it's reading a book that's too graphic, visiting a website that's too skanky, or going too far with your crush, it's wrong. And that's what Jesus was trying to say.

Ironically, this day and age isn't that much different from when Jesus walked the earth. Even then people got caught up in sexual sin. And Jesus knew it was harmful. He knew that it could wound a person's spirit and conscience in a way that nothing else could. He wanted to prevent that. And so he didn't simply say, "Don't have sex outside of marriage." He said, "Don't do all those things that lead up to that." He was basically telling people to protect themselves—and their hearts.

My Prayer

Dear God,

Help me to know where to draw the line. Whether it's in regard to my thought life or to someone I'm dating, please show me what's in my best interest and what's not. And then help me to stay firm in my decision to obey you and put you first in all things.

Amen.

Final Word

Sin pays off with death. But God's gift is eternal life given by Jesus Christ our Lord.

Romans 6:23 CEV

Stone for the Journey

I commit myself to obey God in all things—even dating!

 # Day 5 • Prevention

Words from the Rock

Let's not pretend this is easier than it really is. If you want to live a morally pure life, here's what you have to do: You have to blind your right eye the moment you catch it in a lustful leer. You have to choose to live one-eyed or else be dumped on a moral trash pile. And you have to chop off your right hand the moment you notice it raised threateningly. Better a bloody stump than your entire being discarded for good in the dump.

Matthew 5:29–30 Message

Upon first hearing this, it can seem like a pretty extreme warning. Is Jesus saying we should become blinded or become amputees to avoid sinning? Or is he simply suggesting that we can't blame wrongdoing on a single piece of our lives? That we can't play the victim and pretend that it is an addiction to [fill in the blank] that causes us to sin?

If we selectively blame one thing (especially something outside of our control), we will never own up to the fact that we have the ability to choose between right and wrong. And we will never get better.

So maybe Jesus is being ironic or satiric when he says we should pluck out an eye or cut off a hand to avoid sinning. Maybe what he really means is that we need to get control of ourselves and to admit we're sinful, and then roll up our sleeves to do something about it. Something besides whining and complaining and blaming someone or something else for all our problems. And if we can't handle that, well, maybe we should consider blindfolds and handcuffs first—just to see if they make any difference.

My Prayer ·

Dear God,

Help me to take control of my life by admitting my weaknesses and confronting my own mistakes. Teach me to make right choices. And most of all, help me to go directly to you for guidance and help.

Amen.

Final Word ·

But the Law no longer rules over us. We are like dead people, and it cannot have any power over us. Now we can serve God in a new way by obeying his Spirit, and not in the old way by obeying the written Law.

Romans 7:6 CEV

Stone for the Journey · · · · · · · · · · ·

I will do whatever I can to avoid making bad choices that hurt me and others.

Week 6

Day 1 · Divorce

Words from the Rock ·

You have been taught that a man who divorces his wife must write out divorce papers for her. But I tell you not to divorce your wife unless she has committed some terrible sexual sin. If you divorce her, you will cause her to be unfaithful, just as any man who marries her is guilty of taking another man's wife.

Matthew 5:31–32 CEV

In Jesus's day, there were some men (mostly wealthy ones) who decided they'd grown weary of their wives, and, as a result, they went through the legal, "religious" steps to be free of their wives so they could marry another (maybe a younger, prettier model). Naturally, this practice disgusted Jesus, and he decided to make a statement about it. He took this position not only to put the brakes on divorce in general but for several other good reasons as well.

For one thing, Jesus had real empathy for the cast-off wife because he knew that life could be hard on a divorced woman back then. Without alimony or Social Security, she might end up begging on the streets. But besides that, Jesus knew that everyone related to her would suffer. He knew that divorce would divide a family. He also knew that a "religious" divorce was really a masquerade for hypocrisy. He knew that a line needed to be drawn—and he was willing to draw it.

Does that mean Jesus believed all divorce is wrong? That's not what he was saying. He was only pointing out that some "religious" types were using legal divorce as a cover-up for their own personal sin. He wanted to put a stop to that. In some cases, divorce was the right, just, and kind thing to do—but not usually.

My Prayer

Dear God,

Help me to understand your heart when it comes to confusing issues like divorce and remarriage. Remind me that you are loving and forgiving. But also help me to remember that you want the very best for me and my life. Let me build my life on you and avoid some of these pitfalls that you warn against.

Amen.

Final Word

And so, each of us must give an account to God for what we do. We must stop judging others. We must also make up our minds not to upset anyone's faith.

Romans 14:12–13 CEV

Stone for the Journey

I will strive to do things God's way instead of looking for the easy way out.

Day 2 · Empty Promises

Words from the Rock

And don't say anything you don't mean. This counsel is embedded deep in our traditions. You only make things worse when you lay down a smoke screen of pious talk, saying, "I'll pray for you," and never doing it, or saying, "God be with you," and not meaning it. You don't make your words true by embellishing them with religious lace. In making your speech sound more religious, it becomes less true. Just say "yes" and "no." When you manipulate words to get your own way, you go wrong.

Matthew 5:33–37 Message

Jesus is talking about our words again. He seems to dwell on this a lot—and for good reason. Seriously, isn't it the dumb things we say that get us into the most trouble?

This time Jesus is warning about making promises you don't intend to keep. Or maybe you think you'll keep them, but you can't, because you didn't really consider what you were saying. Maybe you just wanted to sound good, so you made that promise lightly or flippantly—you were blowing hot air. And Jesus says that's wrong.

Do you know why it's wrong? Remember that old hypocrisy thing? Well, when you're standing around in your youth group and you promise to pray for something or someone, sure, you sound like a pretty cool person—a really good Christian. And some might even look up to you because of it. But when you don't really mean it or you don't really do it, aren't you just acting like one of those Pharisees? Aren't you just faking it?

That's why Jesus wants you to keep it simple—and why he says just say yes when you mean it and no when you don't. Jesus doesn't want you to put yourself in a compromising position. The same goes for saying, "God told me to do such and such," when you know it's not true. That's no different than promising something you can't deliver. In other words, it's a lie, and it puts you right back in the hypocrite's chair.

My Prayer ·

Dear God,

Help me to see that words are crucial—not just to people who hear me speaking but to my own heart as well. Teach me to keep it simple—to say yes when I mean it and no when I don't. Thanks for keeping it simple!

Amen.

Final Word ·

> LORD, who may dwell in your sanctuary?
>   Who may live on your holy hill?
> He whose walk is blameless
>   and who does what is righteous,
>   who speaks the truth from his heart.
>
> Psalm 15:1–2 NIV

Stone for the Journey ·

> I will say what I mean and mean what I say.

Day 3 · No More Getting Even

Words from the Rock ·

> You have heard that it was said, "An eye for an eye, and a tooth
> for a tooth." But I tell you, don't stand up against an evil person.
> If someone slaps you on the right cheek, turn to him the other
> cheek also. If someone wants to sue you in court and take your
> shirt, let him have your coat also. If someone forces you to go
> with him one mile, go with him two miles. If a person asks you
> for something, give it to him. Don't refuse to give to someone
> who wants to borrow from you.
>
> Matthew 5:38–42 NCV

It seems to be part of human nature to want justice, fairness, and equality. And while those aren't bad values, we often drag them down and corrupt them. We use them as an excuse for battle. Being human, we get territorial, and we want what's ours. We get mad, and we want others to get what they deserve. Someone lashes out at us, and we want to lash back. It's called *getting even*.

But Jesus changed the rules. He said if someone hits us, we're to stand there and take it. No more hitting back. That's a hard one, isn't it? Everything in us demands our right to defend ourselves—why should we take that kind of abuse from anyone? Surely, we rationalize, Jesus didn't mean this literally.

But what if he did? What if he is telling us to live peacefully simply because he is ready to step in for us? What if he's waiting to be our advocate? What if he has a plan to ultimately make things right for us? Maybe not today, but in his time. What if he just wants us to trust him more?

It takes huge trust to step out of a conflict—especially when we've been wronged. It takes enormous faith to let something go and believe that God will look out for our best interests. And we can do that only when we turn to God and ask for his help. When we find ourselves in tough spots, times when we feel threatened, afraid, or abused—that's when it's time to call out to God. And that's when he steps in and begins to change things and do miracles.

My Prayer

Dear God,

I confess that I don't like being wronged. I want to fight back and defend myself. Please help me to understand that you have a better way. Help me to trust you more and ask for your help when my back is against the wall.

Amen.

Final Word

Love your enemies and be good to them. Lend without expecting to be paid back. Then you will get a great reward, and you will be the true children of God in heaven. He is good even to people who are unthankful and cruel.

Luke 6:35 CEV

Stone for the Journey

I won't try to get even—I will trust God instead.

Day 4 • Love Your Enemies

Words from the Rock · · · · · · · · · · · · · · · · · · ·

> You have heard that it was said, "Love your neighbor and hate your enemy." But I tell you: Love your enemies and pray for those who persecute you, that you may be sons of your Father in heaven. He causes his sun to rise on the evil and the good, and sends rain on the righteous and the unrighteous.
>
> Matthew 5:43–45 NIV

Jesus knows that we can relate to loving our friends. Who doesn't love their friends? And for the most part our friends love us back. That's a nice little comfort zone. But Jesus is asking us to step out of our comfort zones. He's telling us that *it's time to love our enemies*. Yikes!

Imagine the person you like the very least, that certain someone you would go out of your way to avoid. Now imagine walking up and throwing your arms around that person and proclaiming your love for him or her. You'd probably both fall over from the shock of it.

Yet Jesus is telling us to love our enemies. He is reminding us that God shares good gifts with all of mankind. Have you ever noticed that when the sun shines, it's not selective about where it sheds its warmth and cheer? Or that on a hot, parched day when the rain finally comes, it will fall on your grumpy neighbor's brown lawn as much as it falls on your own? That's just how God works.

Then Jesus takes us a step further by telling us to pray for people who feel like enemies—people who are mean to us. And maybe that's the best place to start, because something happens to our hearts when we pray for others. *We begin to care.* Of course, Jesus knows this will be the case. He also knows that when we begin to love our enemies, we will begin to look more like God. And he knows that will get people's attention, and, as a result, they might begin to see God in a whole new way.

My Prayer ·

Dear God,
I confess that I don't want to love my enemies—not really. Teach me to understand the way your love works—how your kindness

*stretches out toward everyone—and then help me to love others
like that.*

Amen.

Final Word ·

Jesus, overhearing, shot back, "Who needs a doctor: the healthy
or the sick? Go figure out what this Scripture means: 'I'm after
mercy, not religion.' I'm here to invite outsiders, not coddle
insiders."

Matthew 9:12–13 Message

Stone for the Journey ·

I will look for opportunities to show love to and pray for my
enemies.

 # Day 5 · Feel the Love

Words from the Rock ·

If all you do is love the lovable, do you expect a bonus? Anybody
can do that. If you simply say hello to those who greet you, do
you expect a medal? Any run-of-the-mill sinner does that.

In a word, what I'm saying is, Grow up. You're kingdom sub-
jects. Now live like it. Live out your God-created identity. Live
generously and graciously toward others, the way God lives
toward you.

Matthew 5:46–48 Message

Okay, this might sound like more of the "love your enemy" commandment,
but it's actually different. Jesus is reminding us to *love the unlovely*. But
what does that really mean? Because now he's not talking about the people
we hate. He's talking more about the people we are uncomfortable with—like
people we can't relate to, or shirk away from, or maybe just ignore.

Who is the unlovely person in your life? Perhaps there's more than just one. For starters, that person is probably very different from you—or so you assume. Perhaps he is different ethnically, and you don't understand why he talks or acts the way he does. Or maybe it's a girl who dresses weird. Or a boy who farts in geometry. Or someone who's mentally challenged. Or an elderly person who smells like sauerkraut. Or someone who's unattractive or simply obnoxious. Take your pick.

But Jesus says to love them anyway. He doesn't mince words either. Jesus tells us to "grow up." He points out that it's no big deal to be nice to people who are nice to us. Anyone can do that. But he reminds us once again that we show others that we belong to God when we imitate the way he loves everyone—regardless of how they look, act, talk, or smell!

My Prayer

Dear God,

I confess that I need to learn how to love the kind of people who make me uncomfortable. But I know that I need your help to do this. Please show me someone who I can be kind to today.

Amen.

Final Word

What if I could speak all languages of humans and of angels?
If I did not love others, I would be nothing more than a noisy gong or a clanging cymbal.

1 Corinthians 13:1 CEV

Stone for the Journey

I will keep my eyes and heart open for "unlovely" people, and then I will show them God's love at work.

Week 7

 ## Day 1 • All Show, No Go

Words from the Rock ·

> Be especially careful when you are trying to be good so that you don't make a performance out of it. It might be good theater, but the God who made you won't be applauding.
>
> When you do something for someone else, don't call attention to yourself. You've seen them in action, I'm sure—"playactors" I call them—treating prayer meeting and street corner alike as a stage, acting compassionate as long as someone is watching, playing to the crowds. They get applause, true, but that's all they get.
>
> Matthew 6:1-2 Message

It's no coincidence that Jesus's next warning (after pointing out the good things we should be doing) is a reminder that we need to be sincere and genuine in all we do. Jesus is no fool. He knows there are fakers and takers—people who do acts of goodness for nothing but show and a pat on the back. He describes them as theatrical and hypocritical. They may draw attention to themselves, but God isn't pleased.

Okay, we're only human—and for that reason we all like to be appreciated. It feels good to be approved and even applauded sometimes. But when that becomes our goal, and when we attempt to draw attention to ourselves while serving God, we'd better watch out. When we go around talking about all the amazing things we're doing for God, or when we act more generous, kind, and loving all because we know others are watching . . . well, we might as well forget about it. *God isn't impressed.* For that matter, the people looking on probably aren't either. Oh, they might smile or say, "Good job," but they can probably see right through our little act.

God wants our goodness to come from the heart. He rejoices when we do something for someone else when no one is looking. He loves when we do good deeds secretly—when our only reward is that sweet feeling deep inside ourselves, knowing that God is pleased.

My Prayer · · · · · · · · · · · · · · · · · ·

> *Dear God,*
>
> *I confess that I do like approval and appreciation. But I don't want that to be my motivation in serving you. Please show me special ways I can do good things for others without drawing attention to myself.*
>
> *Amen.*

Final Word ·

> Pure and genuine religion in the sight of God the Father means caring for orphans and widows in their distress and refusing to let the world corrupt you.
>
> James 1:27 NLT

Stone for the Journey · · · · · · · · · · · · · · · · · ·

> I will be genuine before God and others—he gets the credit, not me.

 ## Day 2 · Secret Service

Words from the Rock · · · · · · · · · · · · · · · · ·

> When you help someone out, don't think about how it looks. Just do it—quietly and unobtrusively. That is the way your God, who conceived you in love, working behind the scenes, helps you out.
>
> Matthew 6:3-4 Message

In a way, Jesus is asking us to join the Secret Service. Okay, he's not asking us to become underworld spies, but he does want us to learn how to *serve others secretly*. Do you ever wonder why that is? Why does he want us to do good deeds without drawing attention to ourselves? Why does he want us to sneak around to help others? Why not just let everyone see what we're up to?

The answer is because that's just how God does it. Again and again, God is quietly at work in our lives—giving us what we need to live, protecting us from unseen dangers, guiding us through the maze of our lives . . . and most of the time we don't even notice. And why does he do it like that? Simply because he loves us. He loves us so much that he quietly cares for us just like a loving parent. God doesn't have a rock-star mentality. He doesn't need to make a lot of noise and expect a standing ovation. Certainly, he's glad when we do praise and thank him, but that's not why he loves us. He just simply loves us.

And that's what he wants us to learn to do for others: to simply and quietly and unobtrusively love them. So if you see someone in need and you have what it takes to help them, remember you're in the Secret Service, and do it secretly.

My Prayer

Dear God,

Thank you for loving me so much that you take care of me—unobtrusively and without drawing attention to yourself. Help me to learn from you as I attempt to reach out to others in a similar way. Show me opportunities to put your love into quiet action.

Amen.

Final Word

But among you it will be different. Whoever wants to be a leader among you must be your servant, and whoever wants to be first among you must be the slave of everyone else.

Mark 10:43–44 NLT

Stone for the Journey

I will do good deeds quietly, without drawing attention to myself.

Day 3 · The Real Deal

Words from the Rock ·

And when you come before God, don't turn that into a theatrical production either. All these people making a regular show out of their prayers, hoping for stardom! Do you think God sits in a box seat?

Here's what I want you to do: Find a quiet, secluded place so you won't be tempted to role-play before God. Just be there as simply and honestly as you can manage. The focus will shift from you to God, and you will begin to sense his grace.

Matthew 6:5–6 Message

Once again, Jesus is telling us to *keep it down* and *keep it real*. He's teaching us how to come before God, and he wants us to do it in an appropriate and genuine way. *That means without drama.* Jesus is well aware that some "religious" types like to make a big deal of praying to God. They act like they're starring in *The Ten Commandments* with a packed theater of starstruck fans. They speak loudly and dramatically and put on quite a show. But Jesus says not to.

Instead Jesus gives us a simple plan. He says to find a quiet and private place—a secluded spot where no one is watching. Like a closet. Or maybe your bedroom if you don't share it. Or maybe outside beneath a big old tree. Then you focus on God. Without fanfare or fancy words, you simply be yourself and come before God with all the honesty you can muster.

All he wants is *to be with you* and to have a vital, loving relationship with you. He wants you to converse with him openly, to tell him about your innermost secrets and desires and fears. He wants you to ask him for whatever you need. He wants you to pray for others in your life. And he wants you to be thankful. The best way to communicate with God is to keep it sincere, simple, and straightforward. And if anyone tells you otherwise, you'd better not fall for it.

My Prayer ·

Dear God,

Thank you for showing me how to come to you. It's a relief to know that I don't need fancy words or dramatic gestures to get your attention. Help me to pray to you as often as possible—and help me to keep it real!

Amen.

Final Word · · · · · · · · · · · · · · · · · ·

Then if my people who are called by my name will humble themselves and pray and seek my face and turn from their wicked ways, I will hear from heaven and will forgive their sins and restore their land.

2 Chronicles 7:14 NLT

Stone for the Journey ·

I will look for private places and quiet opportunities to spend time with God.

 # Day 4 • Sweet Simplicity

Words from the Rock ·

The world is full of so-called prayer warriors who are prayer-ignorant. They're full of formulas and programs and advice, peddling techniques for getting what you want from God. Don't fall for that nonsense. This is your Father you are dealing with, and he knows better than you what you need.

Matthew 6:7–8 Message

The longer we're Christians and around other Christians, the greater the chance that we'll hear about all kinds of tricky techniques for living the "Christian life." We can attend seminars or purchase all sorts of how-to books and CDs and charts and formulas and gadgets and stuff. It's no secret that there's always something new in "Christian" merchandise. That isn't to say that some ideas aren't worthwhile, but in this verse, Jesus reminds us to *keep it simple.*

That's because he doesn't want us to get caught up in a lot of nonsense that might sidetrack us from what's really important—drawing near to God. Jesus saw firsthand how difficult the Pharisees made it for regular people to get close to God. And Jesus doesn't want to see that happen with us.

That's why Jesus warns us that some "prayer techniques" could actually be harmful because they might pull us away from God. He knows our human nature and how we can easily get caught up in fads like "name it and claim it" prayers or "the seven-day prayer plan to a perfect life." And he knows those fads don't really work. Oh, they might seem to at first, but eventually we all need to get back to the basics of keeping it simple.

My Prayer

Dear God,

Help me to understand that praying is simply you and me spending time together in earnest conversation. It's my time to talk with you, to ask you for what I need, to pray for others, to praise you, and to thank you. Sweet and simple.

Amen.

Final Word

When you go without eating, don't try to look gloomy as those show-offs do when they go without eating. I can assure you that they already have their reward.

Matthew 6:16 CEV

Stone for the Journey

I will keep my prayers sincere and simple—just the way God likes them.

Day 5 • To the Point

Words from the Rock · · · · · · · · · · · · ·

You should pray like this:
> *Our Father in heaven,*
> *help us to honor*
> *your name.*
> *Come and set up*
> *your kingdom,*
> *so that everyone on earth*
> *will obey you,*
> *as you are obeyed*
> *in heaven.*
> *Give us our food for today.*
> *Forgive us for doing wrong,*
> > *as we forgive others.*
> *Keep us from being tempted*
> > *and protect us from evil.*
>
> Matthew 6:9–13 CEV

Jesus wants to make things about prayer perfectly clear. He wants to show us how to get right to the point. And that's why he taught his followers this short, simple, yet all-inclusive prayer. You may have heard it called the Lord's Prayer. And you might even have it memorized in another translation. But what you can't help but notice is that it's very simple and relatively short.

Does Jesus mean that this is the only prayer we should pray, or that we shouldn't expand it or change it? Not at all. He simply wants to show us how prayer is done. He wants to give us some guidelines—something we can both imitate and be inspired by.

Basically, this prayer consists of seven elements. When we pray like Jesus suggests, we acknowledge that (1) God is our heavenly Father, (2) God is in control of heaven, (3) God wants us to obey him on earth, (4) God wants us to ask for our daily needs (like food), (5) God wants us to ask for forgiveness, (6) God wants us to forgive others, and (7) God wants us to ask him for help so we won't be led astray.

This kind of prayer was revolutionary in its simplicity. Unlike the religious leaders of Jesus's day who could go on and on, Jesus got right to the point. And he wants us to do the same.

My Prayer ·

> *Dear God,*
>
> *Thank you for teaching me how to pray. Help me to do it on a regular basis. But help me to keep it personal and real. Remind me that prayer is my lifeline, connecting me directly to you!*
> *Amen.*

Final Word ·

> Call to me and I will answer you and tell you great and unsearchable things you do not know.
>
> Jeremiah 33:3 NIV

Stone for the Journey · · · · · · · · · · · · · · ·

> I will pray to God on a regular basis.

Week 8

 Day 1 · What Goes Around . . .

Words from the Rock · · · · · · · · · · · · · · · ·

> In prayer there is a connection between what God does and what you do. You can't get forgiveness from God, for instance, without also forgiving others. If you refuse to do your part, you cut yourself off from God's part.
>
> Matthew 6:14–15 Message

Jesus is making an important point in these two short verses. He wants us to grasp a vital concept—so vital that it's even included in the Lord's Prayer. And yet it's a principle that many Christians struggle to accept.

Jesus puts it right out there, pulling no punches—he states that *we can't be forgiven by God if we refuse to forgive others*. Period. Simple, right? And yet that might be one of the most misunderstood concepts in Christian living. Does the verse mean that God will take away our forgiveness, that he'll undo what Jesus did on the cross, if we don't forgive someone who really, really hurt us? That seems a little harsh, maybe even unfair. Why would a loving, merciful God do that?

But that's where we need to back up. Because it's not God who does that—it's us. When we refuse to forgive someone (no matter how badly we've been hurt), we immediately begin constructing a wall between us and God. And the longer we hang on to our bitterness, the bigger this wall becomes. It's like we add on another stone as each day passes. And finally, the wall is so huge that there is no getting beyond it. But was that wall God's fault? No, of course not. He didn't build it. All he asks is that we imitate him by forgiving others, whether they deserve it or not. And then—with God's help—that wall comes down.

My Prayer

> *Dear God,*
>
> *Help me to wrap my head around this. You want me to forgive others so I don't start building a wall that will separate me from you. I don't want to lose out on your forgiveness. I will choose to forgive others as you forgave me.*
>
> *Amen.*

Final Word

> Be kind and compassionate to one another, forgiving each other, just as in Christ God forgave you.
>
> Ephesians 4:32 NIV

Stone for the Journey

> I will forgive others just as God has forgiven me—completely.

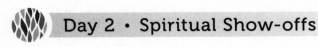 Day 2 · Spiritual Show-offs

Words from the Rock · · · · · · · · · · · · · · · · · ·

> When you practice some appetite-denying discipline to better concentrate on God, don't make a production out of it. It might turn you into a small-time celebrity but it won't make you a saint. If you "go into training" inwardly, act normal outwardly. Shampoo and comb your hair, brush your teeth, wash your face. God doesn't require attention-getting devices. He won't overlook what you are doing; he'll reward you well.
>
> Matthew 6:16–18 Message

Once again, Jesus is warning against showmanship and hypocrisy. Do you wonder why he makes this point so much? Perhaps it's because he understands human nature. Jesus knows that *people like to show off*. And the last way he wants to see anyone showing off is in regard to their relationship with God.

In these verses, Jesus is talking about fasting (the "appetite-denying discipline"). Skipping meals was a popular way for religious people to show their "devotion" to God. Many of them would go around with unwashed bodies and with their heads hanging, acting all pathetic and deprived just so others would notice and be impressed by their "holiness." But as Jesus mentioned before, God wasn't impressed. Neither was Jesus.

Jesus says that if you want to do something like fasting to enhance your spiritual life, go for it—just don't advertise it for the world to see. Otherwise, what's the point? Doesn't it simply turn into a circus with everyone putting on their own sideshow of false spirituality? Who needs that?

My Prayer ·

> *Dear God,*
>
> *Thank you for reminding me again to keep it real. I want to be devoted to you, but not in a way that draws attention to me. Show me how and what I can do to serve you best.*
>
> *Amen.*

Final Word

The eyes of the LORD range throughout the earth to strengthen those whose hearts are fully committed to him.

2 Chronicles 16:9 NIV

Stone for the Journey

I will serve God with honesty and devotion.

Day 3 • Lasting Riches

Words from the Rock

Don't hoard treasure down here where it gets eaten by moths and corroded by rust or—worse!—stolen by burglars. Stockpile treasure in heaven, where it's safe from moth and rust and burglars. It's obvious, isn't it? The place where your treasure is, is the place you will most want to be, and end up being.

Matthew 6:19–21 Message

It's so easy to worry about *things*. It seems to be the American way to be consumed with always "needing" more. Perhaps it's because we live in such a consumer culture—we get bombarded daily by commercial ads that lead us to think that what we have right now is not enough. We need something bigger, better, newer, faster, cooler. But even when we get it, *it's not enough*.

Did you know that one of the most thriving enterprises in our country is the mini storage warehouse—that place where people store their junk after their garages are too stuffed to hold anything else? And then that stuff piled high in the warehouse usually ends up mildewed, ruined by mice or moths, or whatever. What's up with that?

So Jesus reminds us that we need to set our sights much higher than getting the latest, greatest electronic gadget. He says we need to view our spiritual lives and serving him as *the real treasure*. When we do that, it's like having a heavenly bank account. We obey God by loving, forgiving, and helping—and he keeps track. So when we get to heaven, we not only have lots of loved ones to hang with, we have a lasting treasure as well.

My Prayer ·

Dear God,

Help me to remember that earthly treasures don't last. I want to value what you value—I want to be loving, forgiving, and involved with others. That's where real treasure lies. Help me to find it!
Amen.

Final Word ·

If you give to others, you will be given a full amount in return. It will be packed down, shaken together, and spilling over into your lap. The way you treat others is the way you will be treated.

Luke 6:38 CEV

Stone for the Journey ·

I will treasure what God has in store for me more than material stuff.

 ## Day 4 · Let the Light In

Words from the Rock ·

Your eyes are like a window for your body. When they are good, you have all the light you need. But when your eyes are bad, everything is dark. If the light inside you is dark, you surely are in the dark.

Matthew 6:22–23 CEV

Have you ever noticed how we naturally look toward light? Whether it's a brightly lit sign, a string of colorful Christmas lights, a bonfire, or a full moon, our eyes are drawn to light. Maybe God made us that way to remind us that we need to stay focused on him—his light, his goodness, his loving-kindness—rather than staring into darkness.

Jesus says that our eyes are like windows (or peepholes) that can illuminate our inner lives. But that's only if we keep our eyes opened and focused on God and all his goodness. Then our hearts feel warm and illuminated, and life is good.

But if we focus on things that aren't of God (like self-pity, fear, or hatred), it's as if we've pulled the shades down over our windows. Consequently, our inner self becomes dark and sad and lonely. And if we stay like that too long, it can impair not only how we see things but how we think as well. We need to pull up that shade and get back into the light. That's why Jesus reminds us to keep our eyes lit up by looking at him—since he is, after all, the Light of the World. And when we focus on his goodness, his mercy, and his unconditional love, our hearts are well lit and warm and happy.

My Prayer

Dear God,

I want my eyes to be windows looking straight to you. I want your light to flow through me and to illuminate things I might not otherwise understand. Thank you for filling my heart and my life with your warmth and light.

Amen.

Final Word

The LORD is my light and my salvation—
whom shall I fear?
The LORD is the stronghold of my life—
of whom shall I be afraid?

Psalm 27:1 NIV

Stone for the Journey

I will keep my eyes on God, focusing on his goodness and light.

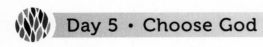

Day 5 · Choose God

Words from the Rock· · · · · · · · · · · · · · · · ·

No one can serve two masters. The person will hate one master and love the other, or will follow one master and refuse to follow the other. You cannot serve both God and worldly riches.

Matthew 6:24 NCV

This is another pretty strong warning. But you have to appreciate how Jesus gets right to the point. He's not mincing words. He says you can either serve God or serve money. Not both. You can either love God or love money. Not both.

So where does that put you? Do you love money? Do you love God? Now, be honest. Do you want to admit that perhaps you love them both? Okay, sure, you might say that you love God more. But are you certain? Jesus is saying you need to choose. You need to draw the line in the sand and place God on one side, money on the other. Then choose which side you'll take. You can't take both. If you try to, you'll end up hating either God or money. And there's a good chance it would be God. Because, like it or not, money is a powerful force. In some ways, it rules the world. But do you want it to rule your life?

The good news is that if you choose God, you will be taken care of no matter what, because, unlike the mighty dollar, God's resources are limitless. So if you choose him, your resources will be limitless too. Not that he wants you to choose him just because he has deep pockets. No, he wants you to choose him because you really do love him more than money.

My Prayer ·

Dear God,

I confess that money sometimes seems to have a hold on me. I mean, who doesn't want more? But I choose you, God. I want you, not money, to be my master. I want to love you and put you first in everything.

Amen.

Final Word ·

The kingdom of heaven is like what happens when someone finds a treasure hidden in a field and buries it again. A person like that is happy and goes and sells everything in order to buy that field.

Matthew 13:44 CEV

Stone for the Journey ·

I choose to serve God first and foremost and put everything else below him.

Week 9

Day 1 · No Worries

Words from the Rock ·

That is why I tell you not to worry about everyday life—whether you have enough food and drink, or enough clothes to wear. Isn't life more than food, and your body more than clothing?

Matthew 6:25 NLT

Jesus definitely got the big picture. He knew without a doubt that his Father, God, was providing for his every need—big or small, he was covered. No worries. But Jesus also understood that faith like that is not so easy for the rest of us. So he started with simple things, basic things. He said don't worry about food. Don't worry about clothes. There are better ways to spend our time.

Sounds simple—and, really, who likes feeling worried and anxious? But like so many of those other simple-sounding things, it's not always easy to pull it off. For instance, fashion can seem very important sometimes. So important that you might feel anxious about it. And, hey, when you're hungry—you're hungry! But Jesus wasn't saying to just forget about food or clothes or to act like they don't exist. He didn't suggest we run around naked and hungry. All he was saying was *don't worry about them*. Don't get all anxious and fretful and consumed over things like clothes and food. No big deal.

But how do you do that? How do you *not* fret over your clothes when you really want to look cool for a special reason? How do you not feel concerned when you're away from home and broke and starving? You learn to trust God. You learn to *lean on him for everything*. And when you feel anxious about something—whether it's needing a new pair of shoes or it's your growling stomach—tell God what's going on. Ask him to help you. Then see what he can do!

My Prayer

> *Dear God,*
> *I confess that sometimes it's hard to have faith with everyday things like food and clothes. But I want to trust you more. Remind me to come to you if I feel worried or anxious. I know that you are there to help me. Thanks!*
> *Amen.*

Final Word

> For day and night
> your hand was heavy upon me;
> my strength was sapped
> as in the heat of summer.
>
> Psalm 32:4 NIV

Stone for the Journey

I won't freak over material things—instead I will trust that God will provide.

Day 2 • Carefree and Cared For

Words from the Rock

Look at the birds. They don't plant or harvest or store food in barns, for your heavenly Father feeds them. And aren't you far more valuable to him than they are?

Matthew 6:26 NLT

To further make his previous point about not worrying, Jesus tells us to look at the birds. He uses their carefree lives as an example of how we should live. Have you watched birds or listened to them? It seems like they have a pretty good time. They sing happily when they know the sun is coming up. They fly and dart around—sometimes it seems just for the fun of it. Seriously, birds don't have it too bad.

Something else I've noticed about birds is that they are always eating, or snacking, or whatever birds call it. And I'd think they'd run out of food—especially in the heart of winter. Yet they get by just fine. And even on the frostiest day, they still sing as the sun comes up. Even with snow on the ground and food scarce, they still sing and flit and fly like life is good. Why is that?

Because, like Jesus said, they're not worrying about where their next meal is coming from. Somehow God has wired their little birdbrains with the kind of faith that tells them that they'll be okay—there will be food because God will provide. And so they just go about their business—and they have fun while they're doing it. We could learn a lot from the birds.

My Prayer

Dear God,

Okay, sometimes I might feel like a birdbrain, but I admit I don't have a bird's kind of faith. Please help me to trust you more. Help me not to worry about my daily needs. Instead, let me focus on you and all the ways you continue to provide for me. Thank you!

Amen.

Final Word · · · · · · · · · · · · · · ·

> When that time comes, you won't have to ask me about anything.
> I tell you for certain that the Father will give you whatever you
> ask for in my name.
>
> John 16:23 CEV

Stone for the Journey ·

> I will set aside anxiety, replacing it with trust and faith.

 ## Day 3 · Just Relax

Words from the Rock ·

> Has anyone by fussing in front of the mirror ever gotten taller
> by so much as an inch? All this time and money wasted on
> fashion—do you think it makes that much difference? Instead
> of looking at the fashions, walk out into the fields and look at
> the wildflowers. They never primp or shop, but have you ever
> seen color and design quite like it? The ten best-dressed men
> and women in the country look shabby alongside them. If God
> gives such attention to the appearance of wildflowers—most of
> which are never even seen—don't you think he'll attend to you,
> take pride in you, do his best for you?
>
> Matthew 6:27-30 Message

Do you suppose there's a reason Jesus continues to talk about not worrying? Do you think he suspects it might take hearing all this a time or two, or ten thousand, before you get it?

This time he's talking about flowers and how lovely they look—delicate wildflowers, which are sometimes here today and gone tomorrow. Yet he describes them as if they were royalty. Then he points out that you are much more important to God than flowers. So why wouldn't God want you to look great too? That's kind of reassuring. Especially if you like looking nice. You see, God wants you to look nice too!

But here's the deal. He doesn't want you to obsess over your looks. He doesn't want you to fret over your clothing. He doesn't want you to stay up late at night trying to decide what to wear the next day. He wants you to just relax. Give yourself a break. Instead of worrying, why not spend time with God? Why not tell him about what's troubling you and ask for his advice? He might even have a fashion tip or two to share. The main thing is to quit worrying. Worrying won't change anything. Give your cares and concerns to God, and who knows? Maybe you'll avoid a few worry wrinkles or frown lines.

My Prayer

Dear God,

I admit that I do worry about my appearance and how I'm dressed. But I want to let it go. I want to just relax. And to do that, I know I have to trust you. Show me how to turn my cares over to you. Thanks!

Amen.

Final Word

I will lie down and sleep in peace,
   for you alone, O LORD,
   make me dwell in safety.

Psalm 4:8 NIV

Stone for the Journey

I will trust God to give me what I need—even when it comes to clothes.

Day 4 • Hang with God

Words from the Rock

What I'm trying to do here is to get you to relax, to not be so preoccupied with getting, so you can respond to God's giving.

People who don't know God and the way he works fuss over these things, but you know both God and how he works. Steep your life in God-reality, God-initiative, God-provisions. Don't worry about missing out. You'll find all your everyday human concerns will be met.

Matthew 6:31–33 Message

More than anything, Jesus wants you to get connected to God. He wants you to know God intimately and to love God completely—just like Jesus does. He says that if you didn't know God, you'd have reason to be worried. But because you do know God, you should know that he is caring for you. And for that reason, you shouldn't be concerned about having what you need. God will provide!

But maybe you're still wondering, *How do I get to know God?* The answer is: the same way you get to know anyone. Say you meet a guy that you really like, but you don't really know him—what do you do? Assuming this guy likes you too, you would probably begin spending time together. You would talk and do things together, and before long you would know each other.

It's no different with God. You spend time with him. You talk to him. You listen. You tell him your secrets. You find out his likes and dislikes. You begin to care about the same things he cares about. In time, you and God are best friends, and you wonder how you ever got along without him. And guess what? While you're doing all this—focusing your attention and energy on getting to know God—he is quietly taking care of everything you need.

My Prayer · · · · · · · · · · · · · · · · ·

Dear God,

I know that I need to know you better. Show me how I can spend more time with you. Help me to talk to you openly, even in those moments when I think I don't want to. Thank you for taking care of all that I need.

Amen.

Final Word · · · · · · · · · · · · · · · · ·

I will bless you with a future filled with hope—a future of success, not of suffering.

Jeremiah 29:11 CEV

Stone for the Journey ·

I will spend time with God, knowing that he is taking care of what I need.

 # Day 5 · Here and Now

Words from the Rock ·

Give your entire attention to what God is doing right now, and don't get worked up about what may or may not happen tomorrow. God will help you deal with whatever hard things come up when the time comes.

Matthew 6:34 Message

This is one of my all-time favorite Rock verses. Honestly, I could just about build my whole life on this one. This is a fairly short and succinct Bible verse, but in it Jesus tells us three extremely important things. First of all, he says to *give God our full attention*. He doesn't say it's okay to do it later—he says to do it RIGHT NOW. And that means do it ALWAYS and every day. Get it? Does it get any clearer?

Second, Jesus tells us not to freak over tomorrow or what we think may or may not happen. In other words, *don't worry*, don't be anxious, and don't stress over things that haven't even happened yet. *Okay*, you might be thinking, *that's easier said than done*. How does a person go about doing that? How is it possible NOT to worry? Especially if your life, like most people's, doesn't travel down a nice, smooth road.

And that's where the third part of this verse comes in handy. Jesus tells us that *God will help us handle whatever tough stuff comes*. And since this is life on earth (not heaven), we can plan on plenty of hard things heading our way. But Jesus's promise is that when we need it, when the time comes, God will help us. We just need to believe him, have faith, stand on the Rock, and trust that he can do it.

My Prayer ·

Dear God,

You are my Rock. Help me to keep my eyes on you, not tomorrow or next week, but RIGHT NOW. And help me not to worry about what's going to happen next but believe that you are going to help me handle whatever life sends my way—because you are my Rock, and I can trust in you!

Amen.

Final Word ·

I've commanded you to be strong and brave. Don't ever be afraid or discouraged! I am the LORD your God, and I will be there to help you wherever you go.

Joshua 1:9 CEV

Stone for the Journey ·

I will trust God for everything—no matter how bad things look.

Week 10

 Day 1 · Don't Judge

Words from the Rock ·

Do not judge others, and you will not be judged. For you will be treated as you treat others. The standard you use in judging is the standard by which you will be judged.

Matthew 7:1–2 NLT

This is probably one of the most explicit and to-the-point statements that Jesus ever made. And, like many of his other important teachings, he didn't speak about judgment only once. He made this same point numerous times—and always with passion. Not only that, but he lived out this teaching in his actions and choices—often taking flak from religious leaders as a result. It's like he wanted to ensure there was no wiggle room in his words. He wanted us to get it!

And yet judging others is something that many Christians do. In fact, there are many nonbelievers who feel that Christians are among the most judgmental people on the planet. Can you imagine how that must make Jesus feel? Here we are, the people who bear his name by claiming to be Christians, and yet sometimes we throw his words right back in his face by choosing to judge or criticize or put down others.

Why is that? Where does judgment come from? Maybe you've heard the old quote, "Don't criticize someone until you've walked a mile in his moccasins"—meaning we don't know what other people go through because we're not them. Ignorance is often the source of judgment. Let's say there's a guy at school who walks around like Mr. Snooty and seems so full of himself. But what if he's been really hurt by someone? What if he's wearing superiority like a protective overcoat to keep from being hurt again? If you assume he's just stuck-up, you are guilty of both ignorance and judgment. So wise up and try to understand others on a deeper level—and see if your judgments don't slowly evaporate.

My Prayer

> *Dear God,*
> *Help me look beneath the rough exteriors of others. Help me to get rid of my ignorance and to see people as you see them.*
> *Amen.*

Final Word

> We must stop judging others. We must also make up our minds not to upset anyone's faith.
>
> Romans 14:13 CEV

Stone for the Journey

> Judging or criticizing others only reveals my own ignorance.

Day 2 · Hypocritical "Help"

Words from the Rock ·

> Why do you look at the speck of sawdust in your brother's eye
> and pay no attention to the plank in your own eye? How can
> you say to your brother, "Let me take the speck out of your eye,"
> when all the time there is a plank in your own eye? You hypo-
> crite, first take the plank out of your own eye, and then you will
> see clearly to remove the speck from your brother's eye.
>
> Matthew 7:3–5 NIV

Once again, Jesus is warning against hypocrisy as well as judgment. Only this time he's exposing a tendency to disguise insincere opinions as helpfulness. Obviously he has reasons for making this point. He knows that humans, being flawed, might try to invent ways to appear innocent while annihilating others.

Say you have an overweight friend who's struggling to stay on her diet. Maybe she's even asked for your help. So you walk into the cafeteria and catch her snarfing down some fries, so you say something "helpful" like, "Hey, if you don't want to be a cow, why are you eating like a pig?" So maybe she gets mad and tosses the fries in the trash, then stomps out. And you hold your hands up like, "What did I do? She said she wanted my help."

The point is, that wasn't helpful. It was hurtful. And even if she has a problem with what she's putting into her mouth, you might have a problem with what's coming out of yours. And, really, which is worse? Her choice to fudge on her diet hurts only her. But your choice to say something mean is hurtful and humiliating and wrong. Your "helpfulness" will probably make your friend's problem worse, plus you'll end up looking like a jerk. And how does that make God look?

My Prayer ·

Dear God,

I sometimes do or say things in the pretense of helpfulness, but I know in my heart that they aren't helpful. Teach me to help others from motives that are pure. Show me ways to encourage others through kindness and love.

Amen.

Final Word · · · · · · · · ·

Some of you accuse others of doing wrong. But there is no excuse for what you do. When you judge others, you condemn yourselves, because you are guilty of doing the very same things.

Romans 2:1 CEV

Stone for the Journey · · · · · · · · · · · · · · · ·

I will examine my own heart—and my own motives—before I attempt to straighten out someone else.

 # Day 3 · Guard Your Heart

Words from the Rock · · · · · · · · · · · · · · ·

Don't give to dogs what belongs to God. They will only turn and attack you. Don't throw pearls down in front of pigs. They will trample all over them.

Matthew 7:6 CEV

The translation of the Greek for this Scripture is basically, "Don't give the sacred to the dogs." That might not make much sense in itself, at least in our culture. But in Jesus's time, dogs and pigs were pretty low on the animal importance scale. Dogs were more like scavengers than pets. And pigs were considered "unclean"—not an animal a Jewish person would own. So what is Jesus saying?

I think he's warning us to protect our hearts by not going around and telling anyone and everyone about what God is doing in our lives. Sure, there are times when God wants you to share your faith with others—and often he'll make it clear when it's the right time. But there are other times when you might be tempted to tell someone (a person who couldn't care less about God or faith or even you) about something important and miraculous that God is doing in your life. And that person might, in effect, spit on what you're saying. He might argue with you or put down God. And, in the end, not only does it make you feel sad, but it's also useless since the person obviously doesn't get it. It's like taking a diamond ring and flushing it down the toilet. Pointless and wasteful.

God wants you to value what he's doing in your heart and in your life. He wants you to treat his words and his work in you as something precious and wonderful—and not to toss them around lightly.

My Prayer

Dear God,

I know you're at work in me. You're doing some amazing things in my heart. Give me the wisdom to know when it's best to keep these things to myself and when it's okay to tell others.

Amen.

Final Word

Be prepared. You're up against far more than you can handle on your own. Take all the help you can get, every weapon God has issued, so that when it's all over but the shouting you'll still be on your feet.

Ephesians 6:13 Message

Stone for the Journey

I will treasure God's work in my life so much that I won't flippantly show off my spirituality to others.

 ## Day 4 · Prayer Promises

Words from the Rock

Ask, and it will be given to you; seek, and you will find; knock, and it will be opened to you. For everyone who asks receives, and he who seeks finds, and to him who knocks it will be opened.

Matthew 7:7-8 NASB

Jesus makes us an incredible promise in these verses. In fact, this promise sounds almost too good to be true. And yet it is totally legit—we just need to have the faith to believe and embrace it. But most of all, we need to really wrap our heads and hearts around it. It takes some insight to fully grasp and understand what this promise actually means. Unfortunately, a common human response is to assume that this verse is the "magic formula." That if you simply pray those words—presto chango—you should get whatever it is you want. Kind of like a genie lamp, right? Wrong.

For starters, Jesus isn't promising he'll give us material things like money or cars or designer shoes, and he's not even saying he'll hand over desired things like success or romance. He's primarily talking about the most important elements in life. In other words, he's saying that when we seek him out and ask him to meet our spiritual needs, he will absolutely deliver the goods—*the spiritual goods*.

Oh, he might not deliver exactly what we expect. Say we pray for patience, and all we get are more challenges (which eventually teach us patience). Also, God's timing often differs from ours (we usually think in terms of fast food—here and now!), and sometimes he says, "Later." But when we knock on spiritual doors, when we ask Jesus to meet us, and when we seek God's guidance—doors will open, Jesus will be there, and we will definitely receive. We can count on it!

My Prayer

Dear God,
Show me how to seek you more, to knock on more doors, and to expect some life-changing answers from you.
Amen.

Final Word

He will give us whatever we ask, because we obey him and do what pleases him.

1 John 3:22 CEV

Stone for the Journey

I will ask and seek and knock with the expectation that God will answer.

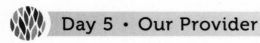

Day 5 · Our Provider

Words from the Rock · · · · · · · · · · · · · · · · · · ·

> You parents—if your children ask for a loaf of bread, do you give them a stone instead? Or if they ask for a fish, do you give them a snake? Of course not! So if you sinful people know how to give good gifts to your children, how much more will your heavenly Father give good gifts to those who ask him.
>
> Matthew 7:9–11 NLT

It might not always seem like it, especially to a teenager, but most parents want the best for their kids. They want to give them nice things and make sure all their needs are met. That's just part of being a good parent. And even when parents have to sacrifice to provide, they're usually glad to do it—because they love their kids. And yet these are earthly parents, and they are just human—and, as you probably know, they are not perfect.

But God, on the other hand, is perfect. And he is the most loving parent in the universe. So loving, in fact, that he provides abundantly for all his creation—whether they believe in him or not. He's designed the planet to provide our basic needs (like food, water, oxygen, and sunlight), as well as making it extremely scenic with beautiful sights (like lakes, oceans, mountains, and forests) for our pleasure and enjoyment.

And that's just the beginning. Because there is much more that he is ready to share. He has life-impacting gifts (like peace, joy, and love) that he wants to pour on us. Our heavenly Father is able to do much more than what any earthly parent can dream of. But he needs us to be ready—*ready to receive.* Jesus is trying to help us grasp this concept—to understand that God, the perfect and loving heavenly Father, is ready to give every good and perfect gift to us. But first he wants us to come to him—and ask.

My Prayer ·

> *Dear God,*
>
> *Help me to understand how much you love me. Help me to come to you for all my needs, knowing that you want to give only the very best to me.*
>
> *Amen.*

Final Word ·

> Our LORD and our God,
> you are like the sun
> and also like a shield.
> You treat us with kindness
> and with honor,
> never denying any good thing
> to those who live right.
>
> Psalm 84:11 CEV

Stone for the Journey ·

> My heavenly Father is ready to give me more good things than
> I can begin to imagine.

Week 11

Day 1 · Getting Along

Words from the Rock · · · · · · · · · · · · · · · · · · ·

> Treat others as you want them to treat you. This is what the Law
> and the Prophets are all about.
>
> Matthew 7:12 CEV

You might have heard this often-quoted Scripture called the Golden Rule before. Maybe you recall a version like this: "Do unto others as you would have them do unto you." Perhaps your third grade teacher posted it on the bulletin board to remind kids to be nice. And if you had to choose only one rule for interacting with others, this would be an excellent one.

Perhaps the most mind-boggling thing about this rule is that it's so simple. Of course, just because it's simple doesn't mean it's easy. But it's nothing short of amazing that Jesus is able to sum up, in one sentence, what generations of Jewish scribes and Pharisees had taken thousands of years and thousands of words to explain. They had made lists and lists of cumbersome laws and rules and sacrifices and atonements—yet they never really got it. It's like they were incapable of treating others with the respect they demanded for themselves. Instead of exhibiting kindness and love, they focused on outward legalities to force people into "good behavior." But Jesus focuses on the heart—when the heart changes, good actions simply follow.

Jesus says to treat others the way you want to be treated—period. If you want to be respected, show some respect. If you want to be loved, love others. If you want people to share with you, be generous toward them. In other words, whatever it is that you feel you're not getting, try giving it first. Then see what happens.

My Prayer

Dear God,
   Remind me that my own needs and wants are like a mirror, reflecting what it is that I should be giving to others. Show me new ways to do this.
   Amen.

Final Word

For the whole Law is fulfilled in one word, in the statement, "You shall love your neighbor as yourself."

Galatians 5:14 NASB

Stone for the Journey

I will treat others how I want to be treated.

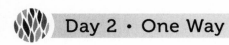

Day 2 • One Way

Words from the Rock · · · · · · · · · · · · · · ·

> Go in through the narrow gate. The gate to destruction is
> wide, and the road that leads there is easy to follow. A lot of
> people go through that gate. But the gate to life is very nar-
> row. The road that leads there is so hard to follow that only a
> few people find it.
>
> Matthew 7:13–14 CEV

Some people assume that when Jesus teaches about the "narrow gate," he is talking only about what happens after you die. But Jesus had made it clear right from the start that he came to bring life—here and now—and he came to make our earthly lives bigger and better than they've ever been before. And yet, he says, we have to go through a narrow gate. So what does that mean?

In other Scriptures, Jesus is called "the door" and "the way." As you can see, both these metaphors are similar to a gate in that they are types of entryways. That's because Jesus is the entrance to God. He's the guy who welcomes us with arms outstretched, saying, "Come on in!" He's our living invitation to enter into God's kingdom—not after we're dead but right here in this very life. He wants us to experience all the wonders and gifts and satisfaction of God's kingdom right here on earth. And he's not only our ticket, he's the gateway to enter.

Does that suggest that Jesus is "narrow" or "small" or "tight"? Or is he simply comparing his very specific entryway to the thousands of other "options" out there? Unbelievers will say things like, "Do whatever feels good," "Any way is the right way," "It's all relative," "There are no absolutes," or "Hey, whatever." But Jesus, in essence, says, "Come through my gate. It might seem harder to get through initially, but it'll be so worth it!" And, seriously, think about it. Which road sounds more interesting—a narrow, winding mountain path that weaves past trees and rivers and fields and waterfalls, leading up to the summit, or a long, wide asphalt highway that goes straight and flat and leads nowhere?

My Prayer · · · · · · · · · · · · · ·

Dear God,

Help me to continually choose Jesus as my entrance to you. And if the path seems hard or challenging, remind me where that flat highway goes.

Amen.

Final Word · · · · · · · · · · · · · · · · · · ·

Work hard to enter the narrow door to God's Kingdom, for many will try to enter but will fail.

Luke 13:24 NLT

Stone for the Journey · · · · · · · · · · · · · ·

My real life begins when I enter it through Jesus—he is my gateway to fulfillment.

Day 3 · Beware

Words from the Rock · · · · · · · · · · · · · · · ·

Be wary of false preachers who smile a lot, dripping with practiced sincerity. Chances are they are out to rip you off some way or other. Don't be impressed with charisma; look for character. Who preachers are is the main thing, not what they say. A genuine leader will never exploit your emotions or your pocketbook. These diseased trees with their bad apples are going to be chopped down and burned.

Matthew 7:15–20 Message

Jesus, being one with God and supernatural, knew that lots of false teachers and preachers would come after his earthly ministry ended. He knew that many would attempt to lead people astray in "the name of Jesus." Whether they did it for money or prestige or power, or simply because they were mixed up,

Jesus knew that those teachers and preachers would be around for a long time. Just like he predicted, there were many that came shortly after his death and resurrection. And now, more than two thousand years later, they're still around.

But how do you know whether a spiritual leader is the real deal? Unfortunately, it's not always easy to figure out—at first. Most false preachers have natural charm and charisma. They have the kind of traits that draw people in. They seem well spoken and smart. They appear to be warm and friendly and personable—just like a legitimate preacher. So how do you know who's who?

For one thing, a false teacher or preacher places a lot of focus on money—particularly yours. Too much pressure to give financially is not a good sign. Also, a false teacher might jerk you around emotionally, pushing you to places far beyond your comfort zone and not even healthy. Also, they may have a bad track record—a history of hurting others, moving around a lot, broken marriages, money problems. All are signs that something's wrong. Does that mean preachers and teachers can't make mistakes? Of course not. Everyone makes mistakes. But a legitimate leader will admit his failures and change his ways. A false leader won't.

My Prayer

> *Dear God,*
>   *Please help me to know the difference between a false leader and someone who truly loves and serves you. Help me to be part of a healthy church.*
>   *Amen.*

Final Word

> Dear friends, do not believe everyone who claims to speak by the Spirit. You must test them to see if the spirit they have comes from God. For there are many false prophets in the world.
>
> 1 John 4:1 NLT

Stone for the Journey

> Don't be so impressed with outward appearances that you miss what lies beneath.

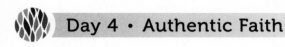

Day 4 · Authentic Faith

Words from the Rock ·

> Not everyone who calls me their Lord will get into the kingdom
> of heaven. Only the ones who obey my Father in heaven will
> get in. On the day of judgment many will call me their Lord.
> They will say, "We preached in your name, and in your name
> we forced out demons and worked many miracles." But I will
> tell them, "I will have nothing to do with you! Get out of my
> sight, you evil people!"
>
> Matthew 7:21–23 CEV

These passionate and angry words of Jesus come directly after what he says about false teachers and fake preachers and lying prophets. Can you understand why Jesus would be so aggravated and irritated at people who were passing themselves off as his servants in order to take advantage of others? Why wouldn't he be enraged?

Imagine how you would feel if someone pretended to be your good friend in order to rip off some poor, innocent person who knew and trusted you. What would you do if the victim came to you in tears and said, "Why did you send that thief to my house? Why did you tell that rapist to introduce himself as your friend?" You'd be shocked and sorry and probably furious. That's what Jesus's reaction will be to anyone who uses his name as a pretense to falsely "minister" to others while picking their pockets. And unless they have confessed their sins and repented, those predators and spiritual fakes will not be welcome in heaven.

Jesus states that only the ones who "obey my Father" will be allowed into heaven. A strong warning, to be sure, but Jesus has strong feelings about those who would fake their ministry and use his name not only to cheat his followers out of money, but also to cheat them out of experiencing things like love, joy, peace, honesty, happiness, and all the spiritual fruits that would be the result of a legitimate ministry.

My Prayer

Dear God,

Help me to always obey you so I'll never be accused of being a false anything. And help me to be quick to sniff out any false leaders who might be attempting to recruit me.

Amen.

Final Word

Depart from me, all you workers of evil,
for the LORD has heard the sound of my weeping.

Psalm 6:8 ESV

Stone for the Journey

Just because someone claims to serve God does not mean they do.

 ## Day 5 • Rock Solid

Words from the Rock

Anyone who listens to my teaching and follows it is wise, like a person who builds a house on solid rock. Though the rain comes in torrents and the floodwaters rise and the winds beat against that house, it won't collapse because it is built on bedrock. But anyone who hears my teaching and doesn't obey it is foolish, like a person who builds a house on sand. When the rains and floods come and the winds beat against that house, it will collapse with a mighty crash.

Matthew 7:24–27 NLT

Jesus didn't have TV or movies to assist in his teachings, but he did know how to create vivid images—ones that would remain indelibly printed on the minds of millions over the next two thousand years—through his gift of storytelling. And this particular parable (meaning a story with a lesson) is a great visual aid for understanding how Jesus is our rock-solid foundation.

Everyone likes the idea of a beach house, right? Imagine these two surfer dudes who decide to build their seaside dream homes. One guy can't wait to get into his house—he's imagining something very cool and something great for parties, and he wants it done fast. So he buys the cheapest ocean-view lot and quickly builds his dream home right on the sand near the water. But the other guy does some research and pays more money to buy a lot a little higher—same great view, but the lot is on stone, and the house doesn't go up as quickly since it takes time to do things right. Finally both houses are complete—and then a hurricane hits. Guess which guy is suddenly homeless?

That's how people feel when their lives aren't built on Jesus. He's the Rock that anchors us through the worst storms—and they do come eventually. Sure, it might seem faster or easier to just plant a house on the beach and kick back, but that house won't get us through the storms. Jesus, the Rock, will.

My Prayer

Dear God,

I want my life to be firmly grounded on you. Help me to hold fast to your truth and your words so my "house" will withstand the worst of storms.

Amen.

Final Word

Live under the protection
of God Most High
and stay in the shadow
of God All-Powerful.
Then you will say to the LORD,
"You are my fortress,
my place of safety;
you are my God,
and I trust you."

Psalm 91:1-2 CEV

Stone for the Journey ·

> Only a rock-solid foundation on Jesus will keep you safe during life's hurricanes.

Week 12

Day 1 • Priorities

Words from the Rock ·

> Another disciple said to Jesus, "Lord, let me wait till I bury my father." Jesus answered, "Come with me, and let the dead bury their dead."
>
> Matthew 8:21–22 CEV

In Jewish tradition, there was almost nothing that took precedence over the death of a loved one. And although the body was buried quickly, sometimes it took several days to handle the responsibilities of seeing to the widow, the inheritance, and other details. Under normal circumstances, a devoted son wouldn't dream of taking off during that time. In fact, his friends and neighbors would probably label him as a no-good loser if he did such a thing.

But Jesus, the Messiah, was inviting this man to *follow* him. Jesus was offering him the privilege to come and listen and learn from the Son of God. This was an opportunity that came around, well, only once in eternity. Others had left jobs, spouses, children, families, neighbors, and livelihoods in order to follow Jesus during his brief earthly ministry. And you can bet that none of them regretted their choice when all was said and done.

When Jesus said, "Let the dead bury their dead," he was in essence saying, "Come and experience life." If that man had gone with Jesus, if he'd taken the time to discover what Jesus had to offer, he could have eventually gone back to his family (who were spiritually dead) and shared Jesus's words of life with them. But he declined the invitation.

The good news is that Jesus extends this invitation to everyone. He invites you to step away from the land of the dead and to experience the fullness of life.

My Prayer

Dear God,

Thank you for the opportunity of a lifetime—to follow you and to live my life to the fullest. Help me to always choose life over death.

Amen.

Final Word

Jesus said to him, "Come with me!" So he got up and went with Jesus.

Mark 2:14 CEV

Stone for the Journey

Saying no to Jesus is like climbing into a casket and closing the lid.

 ## Day 2 • No-Fear Faith

Words from the Rock

After Jesus left in a boat with his disciples, a terrible storm suddenly struck the lake, and waves started splashing into their boat. Jesus was sound asleep, so the disciples went over to him and woke him up. They said, "Lord, save us! We're going to drown!" But Jesus replied, "Why are you so afraid? You surely don't have much faith." Then he got up and ordered the wind and the waves to calm down. And everything was calm. The men in the boat were amazed and said, "Who is this? Even the wind and the waves obey him."

Matthew 8:23–27 CEV

Most people would freak if they were in a small boat out in the middle of the sea and a big squall began. Think about it. The sky grows dark with clouds, the rain comes down in a cold deluge, the wind whips up waves that are taller than the boat, and—this is a big one—you know you're going down. Who wouldn't be scared?

Well, everyone would be—except Jesus, that is. Jesus was sleeping soundly in the boat. The disciples, certain they were doomed, felt they had to wake him. But what do you suppose would've happened if they hadn't awakened him? Would the boat have sunk and everyone in it have drowned at sea? (So much for God's plan to save the world.) Of course not. And that's exactly why Jesus was able to sleep. He knew they were going to be just fine. That's also probably why he was slightly aggravated at his disciples for waking him. And that's probably why he reprimanded them by saying, "Why are you so afraid? You surely don't have much faith."

They had already seen Jesus perform all kinds of miracles—up close and personal. They already knew him well, and they knew that he had come from God. And yet their faith was small. What hope is there for us?

The hope comes later, when Jesus empowers them and us by sending the Holy Spirit to help us, to guide us, and to remind us (again and again) that God knows what he's up to. And if we're where we should be (even in a huge storm), God will keep us safe.

My Prayer

Dear God,

    Help my faith to grow stronger. Remind me that you really are in control and that as long as I'm leaning on you, I'll be fine. Amen.

Final Word

If you have faith the size of a mustard seed, you will say to this mountain, "Move from here to there," and it will move; and nothing will be impossible to you.

Matthew 17:20 NASB

Stone for the Journey

I will trust Jesus to keep my boat afloat and to keep me safe throughout my storms.

Day 3 · Power to Forgive

Words from the Rock · · · · · · · · · · · · · · · ·

> "Take courage, son; your sins are forgiven. . . .
>
> "Which is easier, to say, 'Your sins are forgiven,' or to say, 'Get up, and walk'? But so that you may know that the Son of Man has authority on earth to forgive sins"—then He said to the paralytic, "Get up, pick up your bed and go home."
>
> Matthew 9:2, 5–6 NASB

Word of Jesus's incredible ministry spread quickly, and more people came to him, hoping for miracles. This was the case when he arrived in his hometown and a paralyzed man was brought to him for healing. But when Jesus bent down and kindly told the sick man that his sins were forgiven, some of the Jewish leaders took offense. In their opinion, forgiveness wasn't something a person could just hand out. According to their laws, it had to be purchased.

Jesus knew what they were thinking (and saying behind his back), so he used this opportunity to make an important point. He made it clear that not only did he have the authority to forgive sins, but he also had the power to heal. And this authority and power came from the same source—his Father God. Now, it was one thing for the religious leaders to be upset when Jesus forgave someone's sins, but can you imagine how shocked they must've been when Jesus healed that paralyzed man?

But Jesus wasn't simply showcasing God's authority that day. Maybe that's why he linked the power of forgiveness with the miracle of healing. Today, more than two thousand years later, medical professionals are admitting that forgiveness and physical and emotional wellness go hand in hand. In other words, if we reject forgiveness, our bodies and minds will probably suffer for it.

My Prayer ·

> *Dear God,*
>
> *Remind me that I need to experience your forgiveness on an ongoing basis. Help me to see how it impacts all areas of my life—including my health and wholeness.*
>
> *Amen.*

Final Word ·

And he has given him the authority, simply because he is the Son of Man, to decide and carry out matters of Judgment.

John 5:27 Message

Stone for the Journey ·

Jesus's forgiveness is vital to my physical and emotional health.

Day 4 • Needy Hearts

Words from the Rock ·

Healthy people don't need a doctor—sick people do. . . . Now go and learn the meaning of this Scripture: "I want you to show mercy, not offer sacrifices." For I have come to call not those who think they are righteous, but those who know they are sinners.

Matthew 9:12–13 NLT

Shortly after healing the paralyzed man, Jesus met a tax collector named Matthew who later invited Jesus to dine at his house. Now to get this, you have to understand that tax collectors were like the bottom-feeders in Jewish society. In fact, they weren't much different from thieves, since they collected exorbitant taxes from the locals, then pocketed the profits from their take before handing the remainder over to the oppressive Roman government. In other words, they got rich at the expense of their neighbors.

When the local religious leaders (the same ones who complained about Jesus's forgiveness) observed Jesus going to dine with this low-life tax collector, they were shocked. And if Matthew wasn't scandalous enough, didn't Jesus realize that that crook hung out with other thugs and even a few hookers? What man in his right mind would want to be connected with a crowd like that, let alone eat dinner with them?

But that's exactly what Jesus wanted to do—and exactly what he did. When Jesus said, "Healthy people don't need a doctor," he was in essence saying that Matthew and his mixed-up friends did need a doctor. They were despised by their neighbors, their lives were going sideways, and they were probably miserable. And yet they welcomed Jesus into their homes—and eventually into their hearts. They were eager to receive forgiveness and healing—they were ready for a fresh start.

My Prayer

Dear God,

Help me to realize how much I need you. I want to welcome you into my heart and into my life the same way Matthew did. Thank you for forgiving me!

Amen.

Final Word

But the tax collector stood at a distance and dared not even lift his eyes to heaven as he prayed. Instead, he beat his chest in sorrow, saying, "O God, be merciful to me, for I am a sinner."

Luke 18:13 NLT

Stone for the Journey

When we admit our neediness, we are ready to receive help.

 ## Day 5 · Religious Acts

Words from the Rock

One day some followers of John the Baptist came and asked Jesus, "Why do we and the Pharisees often go without eating, while your disciples never do?" Jesus answered: The friends of a bridegroom don't go without eating while he is still with them. But the time will come when he will be taken from them. Then they will go without eating.

Matthew 9:14–15 CEV

Our modern American culture sometimes has difficulty understanding cultures that are bound up in religious rules and traditions. It's like another world. But that was the world Jesus entered when he came to earth. And it was that world Jesus wanted to transform. Still, it wasn't easy to break through thousands of years of religion.

The ultimate goal behind all the religious rules and laws and dogma was supposedly for people to get connected to God. Unfortunately, that wasn't working. If anything, people were farther away from God than ever. That's why Jesus came—to show everyone that there was a better way to connect to God. But they still weren't getting it. Some people, even those who were trying to follow Jesus, were still caught up in the trappings of religion. For instance, fasting (going without food) seemed like an impressive religious act, and one that was sure to get attention. Why didn't Jesus fast too?

What Jesus was trying to tell and show the people was that they didn't need to fast to connect with God. God was right there with them, in the form of Jesus! Couldn't they see it? Couldn't they feel it? They'd witnessed miracles. They'd heard teaching. And yet they were still stuck in the thinking that it was up to them to connect to God.

Sometimes we do the same thing. We go through steps that we think look good. We do religious acts that are meant to impress. And yet what we fail to see is that God is right there with us! All we need to do is take Jesus's hand—and we're connected to God.

My Prayer

Dear God,

I don't want to put on a religious act for you. I don't want to try to impress anyone. Help me to remember that you are right here with me. Help me to stay connected.

Amen.

Final Word

In certain ways we are weak, but the Spirit is here to help us. For example, when we don't know what to pray for, the Spirit prays for us in ways that cannot be put into words.

Romans 8:26 CEV

Stone for the Journey · · · · · · · · · · · · · ·

God wants us not to jump through hoops but to bring our open hearts to him.

Week 13

Day 1 · Transformed Thinking

Words from the Rock ·

Besides, who would patch old clothing with new cloth? For the new patch would shrink and rip away from the old cloth, leaving an even bigger tear than before.

And no one puts new wine into old wineskins. For the old skins would burst from the pressure, spilling the wine and ruining the skins. New wine is stored in new wineskins so that both are preserved.

Matthew 9:16–17 NLT

Jesus is speaking in metaphors again—using parables to make a point. But what is he really saying? First of all, he makes this statement right after he tells his followers that they don't need to do a "religious" act to connect to God—because God is right there among them in the form of Jesus! But he wants to drive this point home further by speaking their language. Unfortunately, it's not really our language or the language of modern culture.

What Jesus is saying is that he's got something fresh and new, and it will be useless if it's stored in an old container. To put this into modern-day words, imagine that all you have is this really old computer (from the previous century), and you're trying to download a brand-new, state-of-the-art, totally cool video game on it. No matter how much you want to play that video game, it ain't gonna work. You need a new computer.

That's what Jesus is saying. You can't use your old rules and ways of practicing religion and try to fit Jesus into them. It's like trying to download a new song from the Internet onto your grandma's old stereo. No way, José.

So what does this mean to you personally? Is it possible you have some old ways of thinking? Some myths that you've adhered to? Perhaps you've created some distorted religious traditions of your own. Maybe you're superstitious about something. Let Jesus transform you (make you new) in order to fill you with himself. Come to him and say, "Okay, do what you want with me." And then let him do it.

My Prayer

Dear God,

I don't want to be like an old computer—unable to contain the latest and greatest thing that you want to do in me. Help me to change. Make me new.

Amen.

Final Word

"For I know the plans I have for you," says the LORD. "They are plans for good and not for disaster, to give you a future and a hope."

Jeremiah 29:11 NLT

Stone for the Journey

Change is good—when God is the one in charge of it.

 ## Day 2 • Desperate Faith

Words from the Rock

Just then a woman who had hemorrhaged for twelve years slipped in from behind and lightly touched his robe. She was thinking to herself, "If I can just put a finger on his robe, I'll get well." Jesus turned—caught her at it. Then he reassured her: "Courage, daughter. You took a risk of faith, and now you're well." The woman was well from then on.

Matthew 9:20–22 Message

It's hard to imagine what it would've been like to have a serious illness two thousand years ago. And without modern medicine or modern conveniences, even something like a common cold could be miserable. So it's easy to understand how people were drawn to Jesus simply because of his power to heal. Without good doctors, medication, or hospitals, they were desperate for miracles.

And the woman who had suffered from hemorrhaging for twelve years must've been truly miserable. To complicate matters, in her culture a woman was considered "unclean" while having her period, and, as a result, she had all kinds of rules to follow—as well as having a stigma attached—until she was "clean" again. And this poor woman hadn't stopped bleeding for years. Her condition (probably a result of tumors, cysts, or even cancer) wasn't only hurting her physically, but it had to be hard on her everyday life as well. It's no wonder she snuck up behind Jesus—she probably didn't want anyone to know that an "unclean" woman was in the crowd. But Jesus knew.

Can you imagine her surprise when he turned and smiled at her? And then he told her that she'd been brave to come, and that her step of faith had made her well. In other words, there's nothing wrong with desperate faith. Jesus loves it when we come to him needing and expecting his help. He wants us to be like that desperate woman, reaching out to touch him and hoping for a miracle.

My Prayer

Dear God,

Help me to take risks with my faith—and teach me to come to you with all my problems and concerns and with the high expectation that you will help me.

Amen.

Final Word

And he said to her, "Daughter, your faith has made you well. Go in peace. Your suffering is over."

Mark 5:34 NLT

Stone for the Journey · · · · · · · · · · · · · · ·

Risks are not so risky when your faith is in God and he's the one leading you.

Day 3 • Faith's Reward

Words from the Rock · · · · · · · · · · · · · · · ·

When he had gone indoors, the blind men came to him, and he asked them, "Do you believe that I am able to do this?"

"Yes, Lord," they replied.

Then he touched their eyes and said, "According to your faith will it be done to you."

Matthew 9:28–29 NIV

Do you ever wonder why Jesus didn't just lift up his arms and do one great big mega miracle that healed everyone all at the same time? He certainly had the power. And that sure would've saved a lot of time, not to mention travel (mostly by foot). And yet he didn't want to do it like that. He had another plan.

Jesus knew there was much more at stake in his ministry than simply making people well again. He knew that health alone was not enough. He also knew that when he touched and healed people on a one-on-one basis, he entered into a partnership with them. A partnership that required something from them as well. For starters, the sick person (or their loved one) was usually the one who asked Jesus for help. That meant the person in need of healing was forced to make an effort to step out of their comfort zone, come before Jesus, admit to a problem, and then humbly ask for assistance. In other words, they were putting their trust and their lives in his hands. He had the power, and they had the need. A partnership was formed.

And when Jesus healed them, it was like the partnership was sealed. Oh, maybe that person didn't totally get it right in the moment. For sure, there must've been people who were so overjoyed with their ability to walk, see, or hear that they may have temporarily forgotten how it happened. But later on, they had to appreciate what had taken place. They must've valued the gift they'd been given. And, as a result, wouldn't they have become followers? Wouldn't they have taken that partnership to a new level of relationship by committing the rest of their lives to Jesus? Because that was his goal.

And that's still his goal with us today. He wants us to take that step of faith toward him, and then he will partner with us.

My Prayer

Dear God,

Maybe I'm not physically blind, but sometimes I'm blind in other ways. Help me to have enough faith to come to you and ask for healing. Then remind me that we are partners in this—my faith combined with your power means nothing is impossible.

Amen.

Final Word

Faith makes us sure of what we hope for and gives us proof of what we cannot see.

Hebrews 11:1 CEV

Stone for the Journey

When we believe, God is able to do anything.

 ## Day 4 · Get Ready

Words from the Rock

The harvest is great, but the workers are few. So pray to the Lord who is in charge of the harvest; ask him to send more workers into his fields.

Matthew 9:37–38 NLT

Jesus's earthly ministry (less than four years) was relatively short. Think about it. Most people spend more time than that in college. Yet Jesus was trying to give the world a much larger education than any four-year degree could. And as his ministry increased and the word spread as to who he was and what he could do, the crowds and their needs grew to an overwhelming number. Okay, Jesus probably wasn't a bit overwhelmed. He was God. He could handle it. But he knew that he wasn't going to be around long enough to take care of all those people himself.

There was a need for that partnership thing again. Only this time he wanted people to partner with him on an even higher level. He wanted them to help spread the Good News (forgiveness, salvation, and a relationship with God) to everyone who was waiting to hear about it. And there were a lot of people waiting—in fact, it seemed there were more people ready and waiting to hear it than there were people ready to go out and share it. That's the meaning behind his words, "The harvest is great, but the workers are few."

So what did Jesus do? He didn't tell the people to go out and gather the harvest. Instead, he told them to *pray about it*. He told them to ask God (the one in charge of the harvest) to send people out to gather his harvest and to do his work. And again, that's our invitation to partner with him. Are we praying about this? Do we remember to ask God to send missionaries to places like Sudan or India, or even around the corner? Because there's still a "harvest" out there. What will you do about it?

My Prayer

Dear God,
Show me specific ways that I can be praying for those who are still waiting to hear about you. Remind me to pray for people to go out and collect the harvest.
Amen.

Final Word

Don't act like them. If you want to be great, you must be the servant of all the others. And if you want to be first, you must be the slave of the rest.

Matthew 20:26–27 CEV

Stone for the Journey ·

Though many need to hear, few are willing to go, so pray that
God sends more.

 ## Day 5 · Start Here

Words from the Rock ·

Don't begin by traveling to some far-off place to convert unbelievers. And don't try to be dramatic by tackling some public
enemy. Go to the lost, confused people right here in the neighborhood. Tell them that the kingdom is here. Bring health to
the sick. Raise the dead. Touch the untouchables. Kick out the
demons. You have been treated generously, so live generously.

Matthew 10:5–8 Message

Jesus knew that when he challenged his followers to pray for God to send out
people to gather his harvest, their own hearts would be changed. Meaning
that it's hard to pray for something and not become open to the possibility
that God could be asking you to be part of the answer.

As a result, Jesus's disciples and other followers were suddenly willing to
go out and spread the Good News themselves. And, in case you've forgotten,
they lived in an era of no TV, radio, Internet, or telephone—consequently, the
only way to let people know what was going on was through word of mouth.
And that meant some traveling (by foot), which required time and energy. No
easy task. But they were up for the challenge. And they were ready to head
off in every direction. Imagine them poring over maps, making plans, getting
excited, packing their bags, resoling their sandals.

But Jesus said, "Wait." He told them to share this Good News with their
own family and friends first and to start this thing right where they lived—in
their own towns and neighborhoods. Because Jesus knew that those "nearby"
people were just as lost and confused as those who lived hundreds of miles away.
He also knew that people are sometimes more willing to listen to someone if
they already have a relationship with that person. For instance, if a stranger
comes to you and says, "Hey, you should buy this new CD," you might be
skeptical. But if a trusted friend says the same thing, you'd probably get the

CD. And Jesus says it's similar with us—before we pack our bags to go help people in Nepal, we should reach out to those around us first.

My Prayer

Dear God,

I want to be willing to share your Good News. But I know I need your help. If you really want me to start with people I know, please lead the way. Show me who and how—and give me the courage to share.

Amen.

Final Word

Do not withhold good from those who deserve it when it's in your power to help them.

Proverbs 3:27 NLT

Stone for the Journey

Before you can love the whole world, you need to love your neighbor.

Week 14

Day 1 • Keep It Simple

Words from the Rock

Don't think you have to put on a fund-raising campaign before you start. You don't need a lot of equipment. You are the equipment, and all you need to keep that going is three meals a day. Travel light.

Matthew 10:9-10 Message

Jesus was still talking to his followers in this verse, giving them some tips for the adventures they were about to begin—whether it meant returning to their hometowns or returning to someplace else. And it makes sense that some of them would be concerned about all the various details involved. Because many of them had given up jobs—they lived with Jesus and trusted him for their provision while they were on the road—they suddenly got a little worried about how things would go when they stepped out on their own without Jesus. How would they fund their traveling expenses? Where would they stay? What would they eat? What did they need to take with them?

But Jesus was very casual about the whole thing. He told them not to fuss about money or what they thought they might need because he knew they already had what they needed. They'd been listening to Jesus teach and preach for some time now, and they'd seen him do miracles. The most important part of their mission was right with them, hidden safely in their hearts. Jesus had already seen to that. And he had been trying to teach them by example that God would provide them with food and take care of their basic needs. They just needed to have faith—and to go.

That's the most important thing for us to keep in mind too. When God sends us to tell someone something, he will give us what we need to do it. That means we don't need to have a Bible in hand. We don't need a little booklet or bracelet or button to give the person. We just need to have a ready and willing heart—and trust God to do the rest.

My Prayer

Dear God,

Thank you for teaching me so many good things. Thank you for changing me from the inside. And I know that if you want me to tell someone about what you're doing, you will give me what it takes to do it.

Amen.

Final Word ·············

And this same God who takes care of me will supply all your needs from his glorious riches, which have been given to us in Christ Jesus.

Philippians 4:19 NLT

Stone for the Journey ···············

God will not send you where he hasn't already equipped you to go.

Day 2 • Reaching Out

Words from the Rock ·············

When you enter a town or village, don't insist on staying in a luxury inn. Get a modest place with some modest people, and be content there until you leave.

When you knock on a door, be courteous in your greeting. If they welcome you, be gentle in your conversation. If they don't welcome you, quietly withdraw. Don't make a scene. Shrug your shoulders and be on your way. You can be sure that on Judgment Day they'll be mighty sorry—but it's no concern of yours now.

Matthew 10:11–15 Message

Jesus was giving even more instructions for this new outreach ministry. But the counsel he gave his disciples and followers then is no different than what he would say today. For starters, Jesus points out that you don't have to seek out the best or the fanciest accommodations. That's because he doesn't want you to put yourself in places where you'll appear superior to the ones he's called you to reach out to. He doesn't want you to be out of touch with those who are in serious need.

Then he encourages you to be courteous as you speak to people. Now, that doesn't seem like a big deal, except that almost everyone has heard stories of "Christians" who attempt to "minister" in bossy, know-it-all, smug ways. And what does that accomplish? Jesus says to be thoughtful and kind, and if the person you're speaking with responds and asks you to, say, have a cup of coffee, don't turn them down. As you talk, be compassionate in your words. Instead of pointing out that person's problems, show how Jesus is loving and merciful. And then see what happens. Most people will warm up and want to hear more.

But if the person gets mad or doesn't want to listen or attempts to engage you in some ridiculous religious argument, don't make a scene. Just smile and shrug your shoulders and head on your way. It's not your fault that they don't get it. Besides, it might just be a matter of timing with that person—they might not be ready to hear the truth. But maybe you've planted some seeds of truth in them. And by you not reacting or getting mad, those seeds have a greater chance of growing someday. Remember that God is in charge of the outcome of the harvest. You're more like a tool in his hand.

My Prayer

> Dear God,
>   There's so much to learn about telling others about you. Please teach me and show me so I can do my part.
>   Amen.

Final Word

> Peace and prosperity to you, your family, and everything you own!
>
>   1 Samuel 25:6 NLT

Stone for the Journey

> Even the toughest customer finds it hard to reject honesty, kindness, and love.

 ## Day 3 · Watch Out!

Words from the Rock

> Stay alert. This is hazardous work I'm assigning you. You're going to be like sheep running through a wolf pack, so don't

call attention to yourselves. Be as cunning as a snake, inoffensive as a dove.

Matthew 10:16 Message

Jesus was fully aware of the serious dangers his followers would face. It was a frightening time when Christians were routinely beaten, imprisoned, or even murdered as a result of their faith. Obviously this warning was extremely relevant to them. And yet Jesus's words weren't meant only for that era—there's a warning here that still applies today.

While it's unlikely you'll be locked up or executed for your beliefs, at least in America, there are plenty of pitfalls to trip you up. The tricky part is that our modern-day challenges are a lot more subtle than the challenges of the early church were. Their opposition was blatant and threatening and in-your-face deadly. Ours is sneaky and quiet—yet just as lethal in the spiritual sense. Compare an enemy with a loaded machine gun aimed directly at your head to an enemy disguised as a friend who slips arsenic into your water. Both are out to destroy.

That's why Jesus warns you to "stay alert." He wants you to keep your eyes open and be fully aware. He wants you to realize that you will have spiritual opposition and to be on guard against it. Your enemy might hit you with the temptation to cheat on a math test or to have premarital sex or to lie to your parents. These are just some of the subtle ways your spiritual integrity can be eroded so that you are separated from God and ultimately destroyed. But Jesus wants you to be smart—to comprehend what you're up against so that you don't fall into those traps. Because although Jesus is always ready to rescue you, he knows that the more times you get caught in those traps, the harder it becomes to get out.

My Prayer ·

> *Dear God,*
>
> *Help me to be alert enough to see any dangers that are lurking around the corner. But at the same time, keep me from obsessing over these things, and help me focus my attention on you.*
>
> *Amen.*

Final Word · · · · · · · · · · · · · · · ·

I am glad that everyone knows how well you obey the Lord.
But still, I want you to understand what is good and not have
anything to do with evil.

Romans 16:19 CEV

Stone for the Journey ·

Keep your spiritual eyes open, because the most destructive
enemy is sneaky and quiet and tricky.

 ## Day 4 · Persecution Problems

Words from the Rock ·

Don't be naive. Some people will impugn your motives, others
will smear your reputation—just because you believe in me.
Don't be upset when they haul you before the civil authorities.
Without knowing it, they've done you—and me—a favor, given
you a platform for preaching the kingdom news! And don't worry
about what you'll say or how you'll say it. The right words will
be there; the Spirit of your Father will supply the words.

Matthew 10:17–20 Message

Jesus wants you to know that situations will come up where you are put
on the spot because of your faith. That's just part of being a Christian.
Whether it's a friend challenging your personal convictions, a teacher questioning your beliefs, or maybe even someone who makes false accusations just
to get to you, you can expect that life won't always go smoothly. In fact, if
your life is going too smoothly, you might want to wonder what that means.
Because it's usually the ones who are making their best effort to follow Jesus
that get hit the hardest—like a spiritual smackdown.

But Jesus is saying not to be concerned when this happens to you. In fact,
he takes it a step further by saying that it's a positive thing when you meet this
kind of opposition, because it gives you the opportunity to speak out about
what God's doing in your life. It's like that person (the one picking on you

because of your faith) has just given you the stage, the spotlight is on you, and now you get to tell anyone within hearing distance that you belong to God and that he's doing some very cool things in your life. And it's likely that some observer is going to be hugely impacted by your statement.

Okay, the idea of being the center of attention might make some people nervous. Especially ones with a phobia of public speaking. (By the way, that's the number one fear in our country.) But Jesus says not to worry about what you'll say. He promises that God will give you the right words at the time you need them. All you need to do is trust him to do that. Just don't forget that it's all about him—not you.

My Prayer

Dear God,

Prepare me for times when I get smacked down because I'm living my life for you. Help me to trust you for just the right words to answer my opposition.

Amen.

Final Word

This should prove to you that I am speaking for Christ. When he corrects you, he won't be weak. He will be powerful!

2 Corinthians 13:3 CEV

Stone for the Journey

When you live all-out for God, you should expect some opposition.

Day 5 • Hang In There

Words from the Rock

When people realize it is the living God you are presenting and not some idol that makes them feel good, they are going to turn on you, even people in your own family. There is a great irony here: proclaiming so much love, experiencing so much hate! But don't quit. Don't cave in. It is all well worth it in the end. It is not success you are after in such times but survival. Be survivors! Before you've run out of options, the Son of Man will have arrived.

Matthew 10:21–23 Message

People who aren't living for God sometimes feel threatened by those who are. For instance, if you're seen doing something that shows you have a different moral code (say, you're trying to obey God by not drinking alcohol), it might make someone (the guy who thinks it's cool to drink alcohol) feel uncomfortable. As a result, you might have to take some flak. There's also a chance that someone in your own family or maybe a friend will turn against you if you stand up for what you believe (and it's not what they believe). Jesus said to expect this.

He also said that even if you handle a tough situation in a really kind and nonjudgmental way—like you show a person you love them despite your differences—the person might still turn on you. In fact, they might return your kindness with hostility and hatred. But don't let that stop you from being loving and patient with that person, because that's how hearts are changed. At the very least, *you* will be changed. When you love someone who's picking on you, it's like you're loving with a very pure, godly love—and, as a result, you become more like him.

Jesus says even if it gets really, really hard, don't give up. Hang in there. And be assured that God will never ask more than you (with his power) are able to take. Just when it feels hopeless, he'll step in and intervene.

My Prayer

Dear God,
   Help me to remember that I will be picked on because of you—and that that's a good thing. Please love others through me.
   Amen.

Final Word

Everyone will hate you because of me. But if you keep on being faithful right to the end, you will be saved.

Mark 13:13 CEV

Stone for the Journey ·

Don't be surprised when God's goodness threatens nonbelievers.

Week 15

 ## Day 1 · Be Bold

Words from the Rock ·

Don't be afraid of anyone! Everything that is hidden will be found out, and every secret will be known. Whatever I say to you in the dark, you must tell in the light. And you must announce from the housetops whatever I have whispered to you.

Matthew 10:26–27 CEV

Jesus knows it's not easy living a Christian life in a world that doesn't always get it. Even so, he wants you to have total confidence in him. He wants your faith to be so rock solid that you will reach that place where you realize you can't be frightened or intimidated by anyone. Where you accept that God is bigger and stronger—and you're assured that he's looking out for you.

Does that mean you can swagger down the halls at school like you own the place, like no one or nothing can hurt you? Probably not. And why would you even want to? Think about it. How did Jesus act when he walked the earth? In spite of the fact that he knew he was one with God, that he had all the power and authority of his Father, and that he could call down lightning bolts to wipe out all his enemies with one swift blow, he didn't. In fact, he eventually allowed himself to be beaten and ridiculed and nailed to a cross. Yet the whole while, he knew that he had far more power and authority than the ones who killed him.

It's that quiet kind of confidence that gets people's attention. It's that calm attitude of humble faith that stands out in a crowd full of boasters. It's that knowledge that you are linked to the power of the universe. Even if you look like a nobody to some people, your Father in heaven will eventually set things straight. He'll make it known that you are valuable because you belong to him.

My Prayer

> Dear God,
> I want a rock-solid kind of faith. Help me to get to that place where my trust in you is so strong that I'm not afraid and I know you are taking care of me.
> Amen.

Final Word

> Whatever you have said in the dark will be heard in the light, and what you have whispered behind closed doors will be shouted from the housetops for all to hear!
>
> Luke 12:3 NLT

Stone for the Journey

> Where faith lives strong, there is no room for fear.

 ## Day 2 · Don't Fear

Words from the Rock

> Don't be bluffed into silence by the threats of bullies. There's nothing they can do to your soul, your core being. Save your fear for God, who holds your entire life—body and soul—in his hands.
>
> Matthew 10:28 Message

In this verse, Jesus encourages you to take your rock-solid faith to an even deeper level. Instead of simply being free from fear, he challenges you to speak up for him while surrounded by nonbelievers. And not just those quiet, apathetic nonbelievers either. He's talking about those antagonistic kind of nonbelievers, those bully types with an ax to grind.

Okay, that sounds a little intimidating, doesn't it? Who would want to stumble into a satanic street meeting wearing a WWJD T-shirt? And, seriously, if God wasn't the one prompting you to do this, you probably shouldn't. But if you find yourself in a dicey situation and you sincerely believe God is nudging you to speak for him, you can do it with the bold confidence that he's backing you. And as Jesus has pointed out, he will give you the words. Chances are, the outcome will be amazing—even if it doesn't seem that way at the time—and you can be assured that God is up to something big.

But here's the main point of this verse: Jesus is saying not to be afraid of someone who can physically hurt or even kill you, because doing that gives that person power over you, power that really doesn't belong to them. The only one you should give that kind of power to is God—because he's the ruler of the universe and has all power and authority, and he's the one responsible for every important part of your life. In other words, you're in good hands.

My Prayer

Dear God,

Help me not to be intimidated by anyone. Let me be assured that only you have real power over me. And remind me that you only want the best for me.

Amen.

Final Word

He was quite explicit: "Vengeance is mine, and I won't overlook a thing" and "God will judge his people." Nobody's getting by with anything, believe me.

Hebrews 10:30–31 Message

Stone for the Journey

Humans might try to bluff through intimidation, but God holds all the cards.

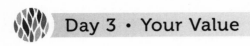

Day 3 · Your Value

Words from the Rock

What's the price of a pet canary? Some loose change, right?
And God cares what happens to it even more than you do. He
pays even greater attention to you, down to the last detail—even
numbering the hairs on your head! So don't be intimidated by
all this bully talk. You're worth more than a million canaries.

Matthew 10:29–31 Message

Although we need to understand and respect that God is the greatest su-
perpower of the universe, Jesus also wants us to remember how valuable
we are to him. And this isn't an easy concept to grasp, because our human way
of thinking suggests that the more significant and influential a person is (like
the president or a celebrity), the more likely it is that person wouldn't give us
the time of day. And yet God is way more powerful and way more important
than any person on the planet.

It's hard to imagine how small we are compared to God—we're like one tiny
droplet, and he is the entire ocean. And yet God knows every single thing about
us clear down to how many hairs are on our heads (and that number changes
daily). So perhaps you wonder, *How can God be so huge and so mighty and
care about someone as insignificant as me?* Because he is God—it's just who he
is. And it's impossible for us to wrap our earthly minds around that concept.

But Jesus is reminding us that God is intimately involved in our lives and
that God loves us more than we can imagine. And for that reason we should
rest assured that he will take care of us—and that he will see us through life's
hardest challenges.

My Prayer

Dear God,
Help me to comprehend how powerful and amazing you are.
Thank you for placing such great value in me.
Amen.

Final Word ·

> How much more valuable is a man than a sheep! Therefore it
> is lawful to do good on the Sabbath.
>
> Matthew 12:12 NIV

Stone for the Journey ·

> God knows everything about me, and yet he loves me.

 # Day 4 • Stay Strong

Words from the Rock ·

> Whoever acknowledges me before men, I will also acknowledge
> him before my Father in heaven. But whoever disowns me before
> men, I will disown him before my Father in heaven.
>
> Matthew 10:32–33 NIV

It's good to have a private relationship with God. Those intimate times when you go one-on-one with your heavenly Father help you to grow. And those quiet moments draw you closer to God as well as strengthen your faith. But if you always keep your faith private, if you keep your beliefs to yourself and your lips sealed, something is wrong.

What if you fell in love and were planning to get married, but you never told anyone about it? Maybe your fiancé asked if you wanted to put an announcement in the local paper, but you said, "No, that's too embarrassing." Would your fiancé think you were ashamed? Maybe he would question your commitment. Because most newly engaged people can't wait to tell everyone. Wouldn't keeping quiet be cause for concern?

That might be similar to how Jesus feels when you're unwilling to talk about him. He might wonder about your commitment level or think that you're ashamed to be in a relationship with him. And it would probably make him sad.

Jesus wants you to speak freely about his involvement in your life. He wants you to be open about what he's doing and what he's done for you. It's one of the main ways he draws others to himself. But if you keep your mouth shut or act like you don't know him, it's a serious concern. In fact, doing that suggests that maybe you don't really know him at all. And if that's the case, how will he know you? How will he present you to his Father?

My Prayer

> *Dear God,*
>
> *Help me to speak freely about you to anyone who wants to hear. Show me natural ways to bring up what you're doing in my life without shoving it down someone's throat.*
>
> *Amen.*

Final Word

> And I say to you, everyone who confesses Me before men, the Son of Man will confess him also before the angels of God.
>
> Luke 12:8 NASB

Stone for the Journey

> I won't hide my relationship with Jesus from anyone.

 ## Day 5 · Tough Stuff

Words from the Rock

> Don't think I've come to make life cozy. I've come to cut—make a sharp knife-cut between son and father, daughter and mother, bride and mother-in-law—cut through these cozy domestic arrangements and free you for God. Well-meaning family members can be your worst enemies. If you prefer father or mother over me, you don't deserve me. If you prefer son or daughter over me, you don't deserve me.
>
> Matthew 10:34–37 Message

Again, Jesus was encouraging his disciples and followers to brace themselves for some tough times ahead. And, for sure, the disciples were about to enter into some pretty treacherous territory. Jesus didn't want to deceive them, and he wasn't about to tell them that following him would be just a walk in the park. More like a walk through a minefield.

While your life probably won't be threatened as a result of your faith, it's possible that you could endure some challenges that were similar to those of the disciples. For instance, it's likely that not all your family members will share your beliefs. In fact, there might be some who will criticize you for your faith. They might even ridicule you or try to talk you out of it. There might be some who will cut you off or freeze you out. It could be the price you will pay for following Jesus. But does that mean you should back down? Should you set aside your faith in order to please your family? Of course not.

Jesus makes it clear that if you choose your family (even your parents) over him, you are making a serious mistake. If you allow even the most loving family member to convince you to abandon your faith, you will be sorry. And you won't be sorry only for your own sake, but you will also be sorry for theirs—when you realize that if you'd stuck to your beliefs, perhaps they would've joined you eventually. So, even if it's tough, hold firm to your faith. Trust God more than family or friends or anyone—and in the end you will not regret it.

My Prayer

> Dear God,
>   I choose to put you first in my life. Even if my family doesn't support my faith, I will follow you. Please help them to see your work in me and to want you to be first in their lives too.
>   Amen.

Final Word

> Do you think that I came to bring peace to earth? No indeed! I came to make people choose sides.
>
> Luke 12:51 CEV

Stone for the Journey

> Even if it's hard and I feel alone, I will stick with God—and he will stick with me.

119

Week 16

Day 1 · Total Trust

Words from the Rock

> And unless you are willing to take up your cross and come with me, you are not fit to be my disciples. If you try to save your life, you will lose it. But if you give it up for me, you will surely find it.
>
> Matthew 10:38–39 CEV

Some people think the image of a cross is lovely. You see artistic versions of it in churches, on walls, even around people's necks. But back when Jesus made this statement, the cross was equivalent to a hangman's noose or an electric chair. It was the symbol of death. To "take up your cross" meant being ready to die for something—or someone. It was a total commitment—no backing down, all the way.

And that's the "invitation" Jesus was offering his disciples? Death? As devoted as they were to him, it must've been fairly startling to hear those words. Imagine these guys scratching their heads and glancing nervously at each other. Was Jesus really asking them to die for him? If so, was that a price they were willing to pay? Perhaps at the time of hearing this, they weren't too sure. But before their lives ended (mostly by painful executions), Jesus's disciples would not only come to grips with this invitation, they would gladly accept it.

What does that mean for you? Is Jesus asking you to die for him too? Maybe. But more than that, he's asking you *to live for him*. He's asking you to put aside personal goals and selfish dreams and to come to him for direction. He's inviting you to trust him so completely that you're willing to put your life in his hands. Because he knows if you try to live life your way, it will only disappoint you. But the way to a real life—one that's fulfilling and rewarding and genuine—is by receiving it from him.

My Prayer

Dear God,

Help me to accept your invitation to a real life. Show me how to set aside my ways in exchange for your ways.

Amen.

Final Word

In the same way, anyone who holds on to life just as it is destroys that life. But if you let it go, reckless in your love, you'll have it forever, real and eternal.

John 12:25 Message

Stone for the Journey

If I cling to my life, it will vanish, but in God's hands it will flourish.

Day 2 • Welcome!

Words from the Rock

Anyone who welcomes you welcomes me. And anyone who welcomes me also welcomes the one who sent me.

Matthew 10:40 CEV

This straightforward Scripture is actually rather profound in its simplicity. And for a relatively short verse, it holds a whopper of a promise. Jesus says that if someone welcomes you, they are likewise welcoming him—and not only him, but his Father as well. In other words, he's saying that you're like an ambassador of salvation to the people you interact with. They welcome you . . . they welcome God. But what does that really mean?

Is Jesus saying that if you knock on a friend's door and your friend says, "Hey, welcome, come on in," that means they're saying the same thing to God? Maybe so. But does that mean your friend, who doesn't claim to be a

Christian, really is one? Maybe not. Or maybe not yet. It could just be a question of timing. So perhaps the bigger question here is, how do you get someone to welcome you? What does that entail?

Think about it. What causes you to accept others? What makes you want to welcome someone into your world? What does a good friend do that encourages you to open up and talk? That's not hard to answer. It's usually because of the way you're treated. When someone shows you genuine love and respect, when they're sincere and kind and caring, you can't help but want to be around that person. And when you're like that to others, they suddenly become open to what you have to say—even if you want to tell them about what God is doing in your life.

My Prayer

Dear God,

Help me to be the kind of person that people welcome into their lives. Let my words and actions be motivated by love so that my friends will see you in me.

Amen.

Final Word

In a loud voice Jesus said: Everyone who has faith in me also has faith in the one who sent me.

John 12:44 CEV

Stone for the Journey

When I'm caring, loving, and kind, I show that God is caring, loving, and kind.

Day 3 • Team Effort

Words from the Rock ·

> Accepting a messenger of God is as good as being God's messenger. Accepting someone's help is as good as giving someone help. This is a large work I've called you into, but don't be overwhelmed by it.
>
> Matthew 10:41 Message

God made you unique—as a result, he doesn't expect you to live the same life or do the same things as someone else. And although the previous few verses focused on spreading the good news about connecting others to God, not everyone has the same abilities and gifts to get the job done. Fortunately, God doesn't want everyone to be an evangelist or a missionary—and the world would be a crazy place if everyone wanted to be a preacher or teacher or leader. It really takes all kinds.

That's why God chose something special for each of us to do, a distinct way we can each do our part to assist in his big plans. And being that God is God and infinitely creative, he's created you with specific gifts, gifts that he wants you to put to good use. Maybe it's the gift of being a loyal friend. Maybe you're good at listening. Maybe you like to help people. Maybe you're a good encourager. Those are all gifts—and all are useful as long as we're using them to help each other. God wants us to learn how to be team players. He wants us to cooperate with each other, to value our individual gifts, and to be willing to put them to good use.

So if you have a friend who's really good at sharing his faith, you might be gifted at encouraging him. Or maybe you have a friend with a knack for teaching from the Bible, but she's not very organized, so you help to keep her on track. Even when you're behind the scenes, what you are doing is valuable. Jesus said it is equally as valuable as what the person out in front is doing. So whatever it is, do your part!

My Prayer ·

Dear God,

Help me to recognize what my gifts are—and then to use them. I want to be a committed team player, helping my teammates, with you as the captain.

Amen.

Final Word · · · · · · · · · · · · · ·

> By this we know that we love the children of God, when we love
> God and observe His commandments.
>
> 1 John 5:2 NASB

Stone for the Journey · · · · · · · · · · · · · · · · ·

> When we appreciate our individual gifts and work as a team,
> God gets the glory.

 ## Day 4 · Acts of Kindness

Words from the Rock · · · · · · · · · · · · · · ·

> And anyone who gives one of my most humble followers a cup
> of cool water, just because that person is my follower, will surely
> be rewarded.
>
> Matthew 10:42 CEV

Getting someone a drink of water doesn't seem like a big deal, but Jesus said that if someone does something that seemingly insignificant for one of his followers, that person will be rewarded.

This suggests two things. For starters, Jesus is making a statement about how devoted he is to his followers. He's saying that they are so valued to him, so important, so dearly loved, that it gets his attention whenever someone treats them with kindness. Jesus is also saying he cares deeply about the person who shows kindness. And he doesn't say that the person has to be a believer either. He simply states that he will reward the person who shows kindness.

But here are some questions for you: What if you're serving Jesus and a nonbeliever offers to do something kind for you—and you reject their kindness? What if you just shrug and say, "No thanks, I don't need your help"? Does that rob that person of a reward? According to this verse, that could be the case. So think about it. The next time someone tries to help you or does something for you or shows you some kindness, why not accept it and say thank you—and know that by doing so, you are helping that person to be rewarded. Perhaps the real reward is that a relationship has begun—which hopefully, in time, will help that person to discover God loves him or her just as much as he loves you.

My Prayer

Dear God,

Help me to be a good receiver. Don't let my pride get in the way if a person offers help. Remind me that you want to reward that person through me.

Amen.

Final Word

For whoever gives you a cup of water to drink because of your name as followers of Christ, truly I say to you, he will not lose his reward.

Mark 9:41 NASB

Stone for the Journey

When I accept help from nonbelievers, I allow them to be blessed.

Day 5 • Miracles

Words from the Rock

Go back and tell . . .

The blind see,
The lame walk,
Lepers are cleansed,
The deaf hear,
The dead are raised,
The wretched of the earth learn that God is on their side.

Is this what you were expecting? Then count yourselves most blessed!

Matthew 11:4–6 Message

Probably the most amazing, mind-blowing, and crowd-gathering part of Jesus's short but intense ministry was when he performed miracles. And why not? After all, he was God's Son, and he wanted to get the world's attention. What better way to get people to sit up and take notice? But that wasn't his only reason for doing miracles. Otherwise he could've done wonders like parting the Sea of Galilee. He could've made mountains walk or pigs fly. But Jesus chose to do personal miracles. He touched people with his own two hands, reaching right down to where people lived—and then he made them whole.

That's because Jesus had enormous compassion for the people he'd come to help—and especially those who were in great need. Rather than wanting to impress or entertain them, he wanted to change their lives. And, naturally, the word got around that something was going on. But think about it. What if you had been blind and Jesus touched you, and you could suddenly see? What would you do? Well, you'd probably run around and see everything you'd been missing, but you'd also tell people. And so Jesus's plan worked. He performed personal miracles for people, and they performed word-of-mouth advertising for him.

In many ways, it's not much different today. Jesus comes into your life. He does something amazing, and you want to tell others about it. Okay, maybe he doesn't raise you from the dead literally, but maybe he gives you a life unlike anything you've had before. That's something to talk about!

My Prayer

Dear God,

Thank you for being personal in my life. Just knowing you is a miracle. Show me new ways to tell others about what you're doing in me.

Amen.

Final Word

The blind will see,
and the ears of the deaf
will be healed.

Isaiah 35:5 CEV

Stone for the Journey

God's miracles in my life can have a big impact on those around me.

Week 17

Day 1 • Can You Hear Me Now?

Words from the Rock ·

> Are you listening to me? Really listening?
>> Matthew 11:15 Message

> If you have ears, pay attention!
>> Matthew 11:15 CEV

> He who has ears, let him hear.
>> Matthew 11:15 NIV

Have you ever considered what a distractingly noisy world you live in? And not just when you're out doing things, but even when you're alone. Whether it's from a cell phone, an iPod, a TV, websites, video games, or whatever, some people never really experience a real sense of silence. In fact, some people get extremely uncomfortable when it gets too quiet. Have you ever noticed how some people walk into a room and immediately turn on the TV or radio or CD player? Maybe you're one of those people.

Jesus is asking, "Can you hear me now? Are you even listening? Do you know how to tune in to my voice?" If the volume of everything else in your life is turned up full blast, how can you possibly hear God speaking to you? How can you even hear yourself? And what happens when you turn the volume down? Are your ears still ringing? Have your ears grown hard of hearing because of the constant chatter that's usually going on? Maybe you just need to give yourself some quiet time—turn off everything around you and practice the art of just listening. See if you can learn how to really hear.

God's voice is described as a gentle whisper . . . so quiet that you won't hear it unless you're really focused. So quiet that you won't hear it if there's noise all around you—or if there's noise inside you. So give yourself some time to learn how to listen. Allow yourself the privilege of experiencing the rare commodity of golden silence. And see if God doesn't speak to you.

My Prayer

Dear God,
Show me the value of being quiet. Help me to get comfortable without constant noise. Teach me to tune in to you and really listen.
Amen.

Final Word

If you have ears, listen to what the Spirit says to the churches. I will let everyone who wins the victory eat from the life-giving tree in God's wonderful garden.

Revelation 2:7 CEV

Stone for the Journey

When my world is too noisy, it's difficult to hear God.

 ## Day 2 • Spoiled Children

Words from the Rock

How can I account for this generation? The people have been like spoiled children whining to their parents, "We wanted to skip rope, and you were always too tired; we wanted to talk, but you were always too busy." John came fasting and they called him crazy. I came feasting and they called me a lush, a friend of the riffraff. Opinion polls don't count for much, do they? The proof of the pudding is in the eating.

Matthew 11:16–19 Message

Most of us don't really seem to know what we want. Oh, we might know what we want to eat for lunch or recognize some other immediate need, but when it comes to the larger picture, many of us aren't too sure. Maybe it's because we don't take the time to really think about our lives and where they're headed. Or maybe we're just generally distracted.

But Jesus came to earth with a very specific plan. A plan that a lot of people just didn't get—at least while he was in their midst. Later on, after Jesus was no longer with them, they began to grasp what he had been up to. Through the help of the Holy Spirit, people finally understood that Jesus's plan had been to connect himself with people—all people—and to reunite them to God. It was actually fairly simple.

And it's just that simple today. Jesus's plan hasn't changed a bit. He still wants to connect with us and reunite us to God. But some people refuse to accept this. They want it their way. They want to play "religious" games that confuse and complicate things so that Jesus's plan starts to look murky and eventually gets lost by the wayside. Jesus compares those people to spoiled children—because they want everything *their* way. It's as if they are determined not to figure out that God has a better way. And so they don't. But Jesus wants us to focus on him, to separate his way from all the games and distractions that might try to trip us. And then we won't be like spoiled children, whining because they didn't get their own way.

My Prayer

Dear God,

Don't let me be like a spoiled kid, throwing a tantrum because things aren't going my way. Help me to understand that your way is best. I want your way for my life.

Amen.

Final Word

So you have not received a spirit that makes you fearful slaves. Instead, you received God's Spirit when he adopted you as his own children. Now we call him, "Abba, Father."

Romans 8:15 NLT

Stone for the Journey

When I demand my own way, I end up lost . . . but God's way leads me back.

Day 3 · God's Ways

Words from the Rock

> Abruptly Jesus broke into prayer: "Thank you, Father, Lord of heaven and earth. You've concealed your ways from sophisticates and know-it-alls, but spelled them out clearly to ordinary people. Yes, Father, that's the way you like to work."
>
> Matthew 11:25–26 Message

The wiser you get, the more you know how little you know. Okay, maybe that sounds confusing, but it's true. People who think they know everything usually have closed minds and consequently never learn anything new. It's like they live in a little metal box that nothing can penetrate. But people who admit they don't know it all are open to learning and will naturally become wiser. Those people are like sponges, able to soak up knowledge like water.

Jesus's prayer in these verses was related to the reception he'd received from "impressive" cities where he'd ministered and done miracles. Places where the religious, educated people had rejected him and refused to believe he'd been sent by God. In comparison, Jesus did similar miracles in some of the more rural and "less sophisticated" regions, and that's where people listened and got excited. These ordinary people were open to Jesus. They wanted to learn new things, and they were ready to receive.

But not much has changed more than two thousand years later. When you think you know all there is to know (which is impossible), you allow pride to take over, and you shut yourself down. On the other hand, if you admit and accept that you'll never know all there is to know, and if you're eager to experience more of Jesus, you open yourself up for all he has for you. You put yourself in a position to grow and learn to become the best you can possibly be.

My Prayer

Dear God,
Please help me to remember that I'll never know it all. Keep my heart humble and eager to learn more from you.
Amen.

Final Word ·

> With praises from children
> and from tiny infants,
> you have built a fortress.
> It makes your enemies silent,
> and all who turn against you
> are left speechless.
>
> Psalm 8:2 CEV

Stone for the Journey ·

> When I assume I have all the answers, I forget where to go with
> my questions.

 # Day 4 • Knowing God

Words from the Rock ·

> My Father has given me everything, and he is the only one who
> knows the Son. The only one who truly knows the Father is the
> Son. But the Son wants to tell others about the Father, so that
> they can know him too.
>
> Matthew 11:27 CEV

As you've heard, the primary goal of Jesus's ministry was to connect people to God. Plain and simple. And yet it was never easy. Not because Jesus wasn't equipped for the task, since he obviously had all the power and authority. It was difficult because so many people didn't want to listen. They were so entrenched in their old religion and binding laws and confining traditions that it became a huge challenge for Jesus to break through to them. It's like their culture was a huge obstacle.

Unfortunately, that can still happen today. The culture can be a barrier between you and God. Maybe it's not old religious laws that hold you back. But perhaps you have some contemporary obstacle that stands between you and knowing God. It could be a way of thinking, some activity, or an ideal—something that builds a big wall between you and God. Maybe you even know exactly what it is.

In the same way that Jesus wanted to break through those barriers during his earthly ministry so long ago, he wants to break through them with you today. Because he knows God and God knows him, he wants to knock down any walls that would keep you outside of that inner circle. He wants to connect you to himself and, as a result, connect you to God.

My Prayer

Dear God,

Show me what stands as a barrier between me and you. Then help me to knock it down. I don't want anything to separate me from you and your love.

Amen.

Final Word

You gave him [Jesus] power over all people, so that he would give eternal life to everyone you give him. Eternal life is to know you, the only true God, and to know Jesus Christ, the one you sent.

John 17:2–3 CEV

Stone for the Journey

When I know Jesus, I know God.

 ## Day 5 • Real Rest

Words from the Rock

Are you tired? Worn out? Burned out on religion? Come to me. Get away with me and you'll recover your life. I'll show you how to take a real rest. Walk with me and work with me—watch how I do it. Learn the unforced rhythms of grace. I won't lay anything heavy or ill-fitting on you. Keep company with me and you'll learn to live freely and lightly.

Matthew 11:28–30 Message

Religion can really wear a person out. Back when Jesus was ministering, there were a lot of people who felt totally burned out by it. They were weary from jumping through all the religious hoops. They were sick and tired of feeling guilty for being unable to obey all the tedious and often ridiculous laws, and they were fed up with being fined when they didn't. Yet, when Jesus offered them a break from it all, they were hesitant to accept. And maybe understandably so.

Because they were accustomed to such religious bondage, they were probably worried that they'd be in big trouble if they "strayed" from the religious norm and followed Jesus. They knew that local religious leaders and family members could ostracize them for doing something so *radical*. And yet eventually many did. And when they followed Jesus, it was like a breath of fresh air. It was like taking off a scratchy woolen jacket on a warm summer day. Or removing a backpack loaded with bricks and leaving it behind.

Jesus offers the same thing to us. He invites us to set down the heavy loads we sometimes carry—whether someone has laid them on us or we just happened to pick them up. Jesus wants us to be unencumbered and to live in a place of rest with him. Does that mean we'll just sit around and do nothing? Of course not. But what he invites us to do won't beat us down and wear us out. Instead it will energize and invigorate us.

My Prayer

Dear God,

I do want to give my heavy load to you. I want to learn how to walk with you without being weighed down. Please show me how.

Amen.

Final Word

Those who feel tired and worn out will find new life and energy, and when they sleep, they will wake up refreshed.

Jeremiah 31:25–26 CEV

Stone for the Journey · · · · · · · · · · · · · · · · · ·

Jesus won't load me down with useless baggage.

Week 18

Day 1 · Religion versus Relationship

Words from the Rock · · · · · · · · · · · · · · · · · ·

> I tell you that there is something here greater than the temple.
> Don't you know what the Scriptures mean when they say, "Instead of offering sacrifices to me, I want you to be merciful to others?" If you knew what this means, you would not condemn these innocent disciples of mine. So the Son of Man is Lord over the Sabbath.
>
> Matthew 12:6–8 CEV

Jesus really was a radical. Almost everything he said and did upset the local Jewish leaders. But it was about time someone rocked their world. And Jesus was the only one who could do it. At first the pompous leaders merely tolerated Jesus as a fanatic who would eventually fade away. But as his popularity grew, they made attempts to trip him up, hoping he'd fall on his face. As a result, it was the arrogant religious leaders themselves who wound up looking silly.

And when these leaders questioned the disciples' respect for the Sabbath, Jesus came back with a challenge straight from their Scriptures. He reminded them that God would rather have merciful hearts than sacrifices. Then he pointed out that they didn't even understand what that meant.

Not only did Jesus understand what that Scripture meant, he lived it out right before their very eyes. He publicly displayed kindness and mercy and forgiveness by reaching out to anyone and everyone. He showed them, through his actions, how God wanted them all to live. Not with the same old stodgy focus on religion and rules, but with a fresh commitment to love each other and to show mercy. Now that was radical!

And that's what Jesus wants from you. He wants you to imitate him by loving and forgiving others, by building relationships instead of playing at religion.

My Prayer

Dear God,

I don't want to be religious. Help me to be like you—to love and forgive and build relationships.

Amen.

Final Word

I'd rather for you to be faithful
and to know me
than to offer sacrifices.

Hosea 6:6 CEV

Stone for the Journey

Religion ties your hands, but relationship opens them.

 # Day 2: Law versus Life

Words from the Rock

He replied, "Is there a person here who, finding one of your lambs fallen into a ravine, wouldn't, even though it was a Sabbath, pull it out? Surely kindness to people is as legal as kindness to animals!" Then he said to the man, "Hold out your hand." He held it out and it was healed. The Pharisees walked out furious, sputtering about how they were going to ruin Jesus.

Matthew 12:11-14 Message

Once again, the Pharisees were challenging Jesus. They told him it was unlawful to heal on the Sabbath. The original law was to respect the Sabbath as a day of rest and to keep it holy. But over the years, there had been hundreds of restrictive legal addenda to that law, stating things like how far people were allowed to travel (not far) or what they were allowed to carry (not much). There were even laws for what people were allowed to rescue from their homes if they caught on fire.

So once again, Jesus responded, reminding them of some of their own addenda to the Sabbath law. For instance, you weren't allowed to lift anything heavy on the Sabbath, but if your lamb fell into a ravine, it was okay to get it out. So Jesus applied this to people, saying that if they could be kind to an animal, why was it wrong to be kind to a human? And when he healed the man on the Sabbath, the Pharisees were enraged—they accused him of breaking the law.

Jesus's point was to show that God was more concerned with loving and helping people than with keeping the Pharisees' crazy rules and regulations. It was a point he made over and over again. Unfortunately, the most religious people rarely got it. They didn't even want to get it. They were too caught up in their own world.

But we can get caught up in our own world too. We can become so self-focused that we don't see where Jesus is trying to lead us. So before we find ourselves in a corner, let's open our eyes and our ears—tune in to him.

My Prayer

> Dear God,
>   Thanks for reminding me, again, that you care more about people and relationships than anything. Help me to keep my eyes on you.
>   Amen.

Final Word

> I am not trying to please people. I want to please God. Do you think I am trying to please people? If I were doing that, I would not be a servant of Christ.
>
> Galatians 1:10 CEV

Stone for the Journey ·

God's love in me results in acts of kindness toward others.

Day 3 • Real Power

Words from the Rock ·

But if I am casting out demons by the Spirit of God, then the Kingdom of God has arrived among you. For who is powerful enough to enter the house of a strong man like Satan and plunder his goods? Only someone even stronger—someone who could tie him up and then plunder his house.

Matthew 12:28–29 NLT

The Pharisees were at it again. This time they accused Jesus of being connected to Satan, saying, "How else could he do his magic tricks?" They honestly believed Jesus got his power from Satan! It might have been laughable except that it was so mean-spirited on their part. Naturally, Jesus came back with a great response, asking why he would cast out demons (Satan's little friends) if he was in partnership with Satan. Wouldn't that be slightly self-defeating?

But the Pharisees were searching for something—anything—to discredit Jesus's power and authority. And the more they tried, the sillier they looked. Still, it's cool to see how Jesus took advantage of their attacks. He used their accusations to teach bystanders, to make important points, and to gently but firmly expose the Pharisees' ignorant arrogance. And the whole while he had enough power to annihilate them all. But he didn't. That's real power—power under control, power that makes the most out of a tough situation.

God wants to do the same thing in your life today. What tough situation are you facing? What challenge feels insurmountable to you? Give it to God. Trust his power to transform pain or suffering into something good. Because God won't waste anything when you let him in.

My Prayer ·

Dear God,
   Thank you for being the most powerful force in the universe.

*And thank you for caring for me. Use your power to change my
world.*

    Amen.

Final Word ·

God's children cannot keep on being sinful. His life-giving
power lives in them and makes them his children, so that they
cannot keep on sinning.

1 John 3:9 CEV

Stone for the Journey ·

My hardships are transformed into strengths with God's power.

Day 4 · Cling to the Holy Spirit

Words from the Rock ·

I tell you that any sinful thing you do or say can be forgiven.
Even if you speak against the Son of Man, you can be forgiven.
But if you speak against the Holy Spirit, you can never be for-
given, either in this life or in the life to come.

Matthew 12:31–32 CEV

Because of this Scripture, some Christians worry that it's possible to lose
their salvation and be unforgivable. But that's certainly not Jesus's plan.
He's just warning us to be careful. He's saying, don't slam or slander God's
Holy Spirit. But what does that really mean? Is he suggesting that if we get
angry and say something stupid against the Holy Spirit that we will be struck
down with lightning and go to hell? Probably not. But he is strongly cautioning
us—he wants us to understand how serious our words are.

There are a series of steps—rather, missteps—that are possible for you to
take, and if you do, you could arrive at the place that's "unforgivable." For
starters, you could decide to disobey God, resulting in some form of sin in
your life. Jesus says that he's still there and ready to forgive you. But what if

you don't come to him? What if you refuse to confess your sin, and you refuse to be forgiven? And what if that makes you bitter, and, as a result, you get mad at Jesus? Well, Jesus says he can still forgive you for that—you just need to come to him and ask.

But what if you don't? What if you allow your heart to become so hard and bitter that you say bad things about the Holy Spirit? Remember, the Holy Spirit is the quiet God-voice inside you—the personal link who connects you to God. What happens when you tell the Holy Spirit to take a hike? It's possible that at that point you've reached a place where you've turned your back on God. You've shoved him out of your life and severed all ties. And that means you no longer have a relationship with him—period. Jesus says don't go there.

My Prayer

> *Dear God,*
> *Please help me to confess any and all sins to you ASAP. Help me to keep a clean slate and to never become bitter toward you. Amen.*

Final Word

> God has shown us how kind he is by coming to save all people. He taught us to give up our wicked ways and our worldly desires and to live decent and honest lives in this world.
>
> Titus 2:11–12 CEV

Stone for the Journey

> God won't turn his back on me unless I turn my back on him first.

Day 5 • The Power of Words

Words from the Rock

A good tree produces only good fruit, and a bad tree produces bad fruit. You can tell what a tree is like by the fruit it produces. . . . Your words show what is in your hearts. Good people bring good things out of their hearts, but evil people bring evil things out of their hearts. I promise you that on the day of judgment, everyone will have to account for every careless word they have spoken.

Matthew 12:33–36 CEV

If you saw a restaurant with golden arches, you'd assume it was McDonald's, and maybe you'd begin to salivate for fries. If you saw a shoe with a swoosh, you'd guess it was Nike, and maybe you'd have a sudden urge to run. Those are brands—little signals that tell you what you're getting into. Sort of like if you saw apples growing on a tree, you'd realize you were looking at an apple tree.

Jesus says that your words are kind of like that. They're like signals of what's going on inside you. If you go around spouting negativity, or you slam people, or you complain about everything, that's a symptom that not all is well inside you. By the same token, if you speak positively, or if your words are kind and encouraging, that probably means you're allowing God to change you. Or else you're really good at covering things up. And while some people attempt to fake others out with sugarcoated words, the truth comes through eventually.

But there's another reason Jesus warns about words. It's because he knows how powerful they are. He knows that words have the power to heal or to kill. He knows that someday we'll all have to explain what was going on with our words . . . and there might be some apologies due.

Think about it. Have you ever been hurt by someone's words? Is it possible that you've hurt others in that same way? So listen to yourself. Listen to the tone of your voice and the words coming out of your mouth. And think of those words like a brand—a signal of what's inside. If you don't like what you're hearing, ask God to help you change it.

My Prayer ·

> *Dear God,*
>
> *Help me to realize that my words are important—but not as important as the condition of my heart. Please help me to sound and look more like you.*
>
> *Amen.*

Final Word ·

> Remain in me, and I will remain in you. No branch can bear
> fruit by itself; it must remain in the vine. Neither can you bear
> fruit unless you remain in me.
>
> John 15:4 NIV

Stone for the Journey ·

> As God changes my heart, my words will follow.

Week 19

 ## Day 1 · Birdseed Faith

Words from the Rock ·

> A farmer went out to sow his seed. As he was scattering the
> seed, some fell along the path, and the birds came and ate it up.
>
> Matthew 13:3–4 NIV

Jesus told this parable to a crowd at the lake one day. Jesus often used parables, which are actually stories, to teach critical life lessons—probably because he knew we'd do better recalling a story than a boring twelve-part lecture. He also understood that most listeners wouldn't fully grasp the meaning of the story the first time they heard it, but perhaps over time (as it's told again and again), the truth would sink in.

The soil in this story represents our hearts. In other words, Jesus compares our hearts to dirt. (Before you get offended, remember that God formed humans from the earth.) The seed in this story represents the gospel—the Good News that Jesus was God's Son sent to earth to offer humankind a new and improved relationship with God. Unfortunately, not all who hear this Good News will take it seriously, and that explains this parable.

The reaction of some listeners is like a tough old road. The seed lands on the hard-packed dirt and then just sits there because it can't penetrate the hardened surface of a well-traveled road. It's as if the road rejects it. Kind of like people with hardened hearts or heads. They're unwilling to listen, simply rejecting the Good News as soon as it hits them. It almost seems that the seed is wasted. In fact, Jesus adds that the birds come and eat it—the precious Good News is nothing more than worthless birdseed to them.

Maybe we don't think we fall into this birdseed kind of faith category, but there are times when anyone can be a little hard-hearted—times when we might choose to disobey God or reject a truth he's shown us. Jesus doesn't want us to treat his words like birdseed. He wants hearts that are softened and ready to welcome his Good News, allow it to grow, and make strong roots.

My Prayer

Dear God,
   Please keep my heart plowed and tilled (with your Word and your truth) so that, unlike birdseed, my faith will root deeply into you.
   Amen.

Final Word

When anyone hears the message about the kingdom and does not understand it, the evil one comes and snatches away what was sown in his heart. This is the seed sown along the path.

Matthew 13:19 NIV

Stone for the Journey

I won't allow myself to become hard-hearted toward God.

Day 2 • Tumbleweed Faith

Words from the Rock ·

> Some [seed] fell on rocky places, where it did not have much soil. It sprang up quickly, because the soil was shallow. But when the sun came up, the plants were scorched, and they withered because they had no root.
>
> Matthew 13:5–6 NIV

Now Jesus is talking about another kind of farming challenge. This particular seed (still representing Jesus's Good News) fell onto rocky places—ground that hasn't been plowed, cultivated, or prepared for agriculture. It's probably rough, uneven, full of stones, and basically not the kind of soil to grow much of anything (besides tumbleweed, which can be here one day and gone the next).

This rocky ground represents those with a willingness to hear the Good News. They might even experience a positive reaction to it—initially—but that's about all. They haven't reached the place in life where they want to take God's words and promises seriously, so they adopt a kind of fair-weather faith. Maybe they say, "Yeah, I know Jesus is real and he cares about me, and that's cool," but they don't grasp the hugeness of a relationship with God. For them, faith is more like a fad—when temptations or tough times come, they let their faith slip away like last year's fashion trends.

These people are similar to a plant that grows up without a strong root system. Their seed gets wedged between a rock and a hard place with little real soil—following a gentle spring rain, the plant pops up and might even seem healthy for a while. But then a few hot, sunny days come along, and because the plant doesn't have real roots, it simply dries up and blows away, kind of like tumbleweed. Those people who make a showy commitment to Christ but don't really take it seriously can spiritually dry up and blow away too.

Jesus wants us to have healthy and established roots that go deeply into him to strengthen our faith. Then we can grow and flourish even during drought times.

My Prayer ·

> *Dear God,*
>> *Please help me to establish strong roots in you so I can withstand*
> *whatever storms or droughts life throws my way.*
>> *Amen.*

Final Word ·

> The one who received the seed that fell on rocky places is the
> man who hears the word and at once receives it with joy. But
> since he has no root, he lasts only a short time. When trouble or
> persecution comes because of the word, he quickly falls away.
>
> Matthew 13:20–21 NIV

Stone for the Journey ·

> I will root myself deeply into God.

 ## Day 3 · Weedy Faith

Words from the Rock ·

> Other seed fell among thorns, which grew up and choked the
> plants.
>
> Matthew 13:7 NIV

This third category in this seed parable is interesting. From what we can tell, this seed has fallen on some fairly good soil because it actually grows into a plant. The only problem is that there are weeds and thorns growing in this same patch of ground. The trouble with weeds and thorns is that they hog the water, the sun, and the nutrients in the soil, and they can eventually take over and choke out an otherwise healthy plant.

This weed-infested garden represents those who hear Jesus's Good News and willingly receive it. They happily plant the seed into their hearts, where the soil seems nicely plowed and ready for cultivation, and the seed develops roots and grows. Everything is cool, right? Except that the plant isn't the only thing growing there. Sure, those itty-bitty weeds may not look terribly threatening at first. Maybe they even resemble flowers. But weeds left to grow will get out of control and eventually ruin the garden.

Weeds and thorns are symbols for sin. Like weeds that take over a garden, sin can take over our hearts. We need to confess our sin to God and receive his forgiveness, but that's not all. Just like a farmer who diligently pulls weeds from the field, God wants to uproot sin from our lives. He knows that when we neglect those weeds and continue doing what we know is wrong, the weeds will take over and possibly choke out our faith completely.

My Prayer

Dear God,

Thank you for your forgiveness. I know that sin is as common as weeds, but please help me to deal with it on a daily basis.

Amen.

Final Word

The one who received the seed that fell among the thorns is the man who hears the word, but the worries of this life and the deceitfulness of wealth choke it, making it unfruitful.

Matthew 13:22 NIV

Stone for the Journey

I will not allow sin to crowd out my faith.

Day 4 • Amazing Faith!

Words from the Rock · · · · · · · · · · · · · · · ·

> Some [seed] fell on good earth, and produced a harvest beyond
> [the farmer's] wildest dreams. Are you listening to this? Really
> listening?
>
> Matthew 13:8–9 Message

At the end of Jesus's parable about the challenges of planting seeds, we finally get to hear about the seeds that not only survived but flourished and thrived. Jesus simply says, "Some fell on good earth." But what does that mean? What makes earth good?

Jesus begins this parable by saying that a farmer went out to sow some seed. Now if you ask an experienced farmer about the best way to plant a successful crop, he'll immediately give you the lowdown on field preparation. He'll suggest nutrients and explain the importance of plowing and turning the soil. And he'll definitely point out that timing is everything.

So what do our hearts have in common with dirt? For starters, we need to be plowed (another word for *plowing* is *breaking* the soil), and that can be painful. Sometimes it's when life knocks us around and beats us up that we become ready to hear and receive God's Good News. It's like the hard times have plowed through and softened our hearts.

There's also the matter of timing. Only a foolish farmer would try to plant seeds in hard, frozen earth, but a freezing-cold winter also helps to break up and prepare the soil for planting. Kind of like when we go through a season that feels like winter—it could be preparing our hearts. Then spring comes, and like soil that's warm and soft, our hearts are ready to receive a seed. The timing is right, seeds are planted, the soil is fertile, plants appear, and in due time—a harvest!

Jesus describes this harvest as beyond a farmer's wildest dreams. What Jesus means is that this is just the beginning, because when his seeds of faith grow strong and healthy in us, we can't help but produce more seeds that we share with others, and the crop of faith gets bigger and bigger.

At the end of this parable, Jesus urgently asks, "Are you listening? Can you hear what I'm telling you?" This message is vital, so he wants us to really get it.

My Prayer

Dear God,

I want my heart to be plowed and ready to receive your seed of faith. Help me to be patient if it feels painful or it feels like I'm stuck in winter. I trust your timing.

Amen.

Final Word

But the one who received the seed that fell on good soil is the man who hears the word and understands it. He produces a crop, yielding a hundred, sixty or thirty times what was sown.

Matthew 13:23 NIV

Stone for the Journey

I submit my heart to God's plow so I will be ready to receive his faith seeds.

Day 5 • Puzzle Pieces

Words from the Rock

I have explained the secrets about the kingdom of heaven to you, but not to others. Everyone who has something will be given more. But people who don't have anything will lose even what little they have. I use stories when I speak to them because when they look, they cannot see, and when they listen, they cannot hear or understand.

Matthew 13:11–13 CEV

Jesus is responding to his disciples' question about why he so often used stories to teach people. First he reminds them that he's disclosed to them almost everything regarding faith and God already. Jesus's reasoning is that these twelve men, chosen by him, are capable of grasping some deep spiritual truths. In fact, that's why he chose them. At the same time, he knows that others aren't quite so ready—not yet.

Jesus knew that most of his listeners wouldn't really get the depth of his messages. That's because he was introducing what was about to begin a major revolution in religion—it would change everything! So he used stories in order to give his listeners a little something to hold on to for later. He knew that people are good at remembering and retelling stories. Even if they didn't get the real spiritual meaning in the story right away, they would recall the story later, and eventually the truth would sink in.

That's why he says that those who have something will be given more. It's like we all receive some pieces of this faith puzzle, and even if they don't seem to work or fit at first, they will eventually make perfect sense. In other words, none of us gets the whole picture of what God is up to right from the start. It's a process of living, learning, and experiencing God as we continue to follow his will, and as he makes himself known to us more and more.

My Prayer

Dear God,

Help me to understand that I can't possibly grasp all spiritual meanings right from the start. Help me to be patient and persistent as I get to know you better each day.

Amen.

Final Word

Jesus used stories to tell all these things to the people; he always used stories to teach them. This is as the prophet said: "I will speak using stories; I will tell things that have been secret since the world was made."

Matthew 13:34–35 NCV

Stone for the Journey

I believe God will provide the spiritual truth I need for this day.

Week 20

Day 1 • Enemy Seeds

Words from the Rock ·

The kingdom of heaven is like what happened when a farmer scattered good seed in a field. But while everyone was sleeping, an enemy came and scattered weed seeds in the field and then left.

When the plants came up and began to ripen, the farmer's servants could see the weeds. The servants came and asked, "Sir, didn't you scatter good seed in your field? Where did these weeds come from?"

"An enemy did this," he replied.

Matthew 13:24–28 CEV

Jesus is using another agricultural metaphor—more seeds and planting and weeds. But this story takes a different twist. This time the seeds represent the lives of believers—believers who were carefully planted by Jesus in a field ready for cultivation. The field represents the world we live in—a world where anything can happen, a place where good and evil cohabitate and sometimes collide. The weeds represent those who try to destroy the faith of believers. And Jesus states clearly that the weeds are not planted by him; they are planted by the enemy.

Jesus understands the frustrations of trying to be a strong Christian while evil influences push in from all sides—kind of like those obnoxious weeds crowding in. He knows what we're up against. Whether it's sleazy things we see or hear or the way someone mistreats us, Jesus realizes that it's not easy being a Christian and that it can be a challenge to consistently make good choices. Although we have control over our own actions, we can't control what others do. We can't prevent weeds (evil) from cropping up next door.

Fortunately, Jesus has a strategy for dealing with the weeds all around us, and he has a plan to rescue us. Mostly we just need to sink our roots into him and trust his timing.

My Prayer

Dear God,

I see that, like weeds, evil is alive and well on planet earth. Help me to root myself deeply into you so you can protect me.

Amen.

Final Word

The one who sowed the good seed is the Son of Man. The field is the world, and the good seed stands for the sons of the kingdom. The weeds are the sons of the evil one, and the enemy who sows them is the devil. The harvest is the end of the age, and the harvesters are angels.

Matthew 13:37–39 NIV

Stone for the Journey

I trust that God will deal with the evil in this world.

 Day 2 · In Due Time

Words from the Rock

His servants then asked, "Do you want us to go out and pull up the weeds?"

"No!" he answered. "You might also pull up the wheat. Leave the weeds alone until harvest time. Then I'll tell my workers to gather the weeds and tie them up and burn them. But I'll have them store the wheat in my barn."

Matthew 13:28–30 CEV

The farmer's servants are asking if they should go out and weed the field. Knowing that weeds are generally bad news, we expect the farmer to say, "Yeah, get rid of those weeds, and hurry it up." But his answer is an emphatic *no!*

He explains that pulling up the weeds will harm the young wheat plants. This suggests that the infestation of weeds is extremely severe—that the weeds are so prolific and so entrenched into the soil that they might destroy the wheat if they're pulled up.

Now remember that the seeds (in this case seedling plants) represent believers and the weeds represent evil. So what Jesus is really saying is that there is so much evil, and it's such a big part of this world, that it's impossible to get rid of all of the evil without getting rid of everything. In other words, he's saying that we have to endure it—that evil is simply a part of living in this world.

Does that mean we give in and let the weeds (evil) take over our lives? Of course not. Jesus wants us to have strong roots and to grow up healthy and whole. He wants us to hang in there until it's time for him to finally remove the weeds (destroying evil once and for all), to rescue his believers, and to reward them with heaven—where no weeds are allowed!

My Prayer

Dear God,

I look forward to the day when I will be free from the influence of evil. In the meantime, teach me how to be strong and stand up against it.

Amen.

Final Word

The picture of thistles pulled up and burned is a scene from the final act. The Son of Man will send his angels, weed out the thistles from his kingdom, pitch them in the trash, and be done with them.

Matthew 13:40–41 Message

Stone for the Journey

I trust God's plan and timing to eradicate evil from this world.

Day 3 · Small Beginnings

Words from the Rock · · · · · · · · · · · · · · · · ·

> God's kingdom is like a pine nut that a farmer plants. It is quite small as seeds go, but in the course of years it grows into a huge pine tree, and eagles build nests in it.
>
> Matthew 13:31–32 Message

Most versions of the Bible call this the mustard seed faith parable. But the Message uses a pine nut to describe faith. If you've ever made pesto sauce, you know that a pine nut is pretty small (and tasty). Yet it's capable of growing into an enormous tree.

If you think about it—really consider the fact that the insignificant pine nut contains the "magical" ingredients to transform itself into a towering pine tree—it's nothing short of miraculous. That is exactly the way Jesus describes faith in God's kingdom. It starts out small, then grows into the biggest thing imaginable.

Think about your own life. Do you remember when you first put your trust in God? How big was your faith compared to the size of God's kingdom? Did it resemble an insignificant pine nut next to a majestic pine tree? Or maybe you haven't even taken that step yet. Maybe your faith seems impossibly small and you're fairly certain it could never grow into anything. But if you have just that tiny bit of faith, and if you plant that faith by asking Jesus to come into your life and to begin building his kingdom inside your heart, it will grow.

Most people come to God with all sorts of doubts and questions, and their faith feels puny and weak at first. But over time, and with God's help, faith grows, and eventually it's transformed into the most enormous thing in the universe—God's kingdom.

My Prayer ·

> *Dear God,*
>
> *Help me to recognize the huge potential that you've planted inside of me—my faith in you and your kingdom! Help my faith to grow and to strengthen.*
>
> *Amen.*

Final Word ·

Faith is the assurance of things hoped for, the conviction of things not seen.

Hebrews 11:1 NASB

Stone for the Journey ·

My faith in God's kingdom is growing daily.

 ## Day 4 • Major Minors

Words from the Rock ·

God's kingdom is like yeast that a woman works into the dough for dozens of loaves of barley bread—and waits while the dough rises.

Matthew 13:33 Message

Most people don't give something like yeast much thought. It seems like a pretty minor baking ingredient, and it comes in small packages. But again, this "insignificant" substance has the power to increase and transform something else.

It seems slightly ironic that Jesus used so many "minor" elements to teach major lessons. But consider Jesus's coming to earth. It was as if God wanted to make a point by using what seemed small and unimportant—in fact, a tiny, helpless baby—to do something so enormous that it changed the world forever. Yet for most people who lived then, it seemed like no big deal.

At the same time in history, many religions relied on flashy, splashy, huge, over-the-top kinds of gimmicks to persuade worshipers to follow them. Enormous golden idols and ornate buildings were the norm—anything to impress and draw attention. But those religions were all show and no go. The way Jesus got people's attention was simply through his presence. He spoke and they listened. He did miracles and they watched. He was only one man, and he had no ornate temple, no golden statues, no splashy clothes, no flashy musicians—he was so *not* Las Vegas. In fact, he probably seemed fairly minor when he started his ministry. Not only did people not give him much attention, many of them put him down as a nobody. They said nothing good could come from his hometown.

Early on, Jesus got about as much respect as a tiny seed or a flake of yeast, yet he was God's own Son, and his relatively short life on earth would transform the world. In the same way, he wants to have an impact on our lives. When Jesus begins a relationship with us, the changes in our lives might seem minor, but as we get to know him better, he transforms us into people who are able to do major things.

My Prayer

Dear God,

Help me to nurture what may seem like minor things in my life. Acts of kindness, truths quietly shared, unrewarded generosity . . . small things that transform lives.

Amen.

Final Word

The people were upset with Jesus. But Jesus said to them, "A prophet is honored everywhere except in his hometown and in his own home." So he did not do many miracles there because they had no faith.

Matthew 13:57–58 NCV

Stone for the Journey

Jesus at work in me can accomplish major things.

Day 5 • Secret Treasure

Words from the Rock

The kingdom of heaven is like what happens when someone finds a treasure hidden in a field and buries it again. A person like that is happy and goes and sells everything in order to buy that field.

Matthew 13:44 CEV

D id you ever dream of finding an ancient treasure map when you were a kid? Or maybe you dug a big hole at the beach hoping that you'd stumble across some pirate's hidden trunk of gold and jewels? Almost every kid has fantasized about things like that. In fact, millions of grown-ups buy lottery tickets every day just hoping to strike it rich.

When Jesus tells this parable, you can imagine how some of his listeners' eyes light up when he mentions a secret treasure hidden in a field. Maybe they even wonder if he actually knew of such a field. Of course, he isn't talking about a physical treasure—something that would be here today and gone tomorrow. He's talking about himself. He's like a treasure—an everlasting treasure that can do more to transform your life than billions of dollars.

Jesus is saying that it's worthwhile to devote all of your attention to getting this treasure. Just like the person who sells all he owns to buy the field that contains the treasure, you'll never be sorry if you invest all of yourself into knowing and following Jesus. The riches he brings to your life (love, forgiveness, hope, peace) will far outweigh any sacrifices you made.

Do you understand the value of what Jesus is offering you? Do you know its worth? How much have you invested so far? How much are you willing to invest?

My Prayer

Dear God,

Help me to understand the enormity of what you have for me. Show me ways I can invest more of myself into experiencing more of you in my life.

Amen.

Final Word

You cannot serve two masters: God and money. For you will hate one and love the other, or else the other way around.

Matthew 6:24 TLB

Stone for the Journey ·

I will invest my whole heart into knowing Jesus better.

Week 21

 ## Day 1 · What Cost?

Words from the Rock ·

Again, the kingdom of heaven is like a merchant looking for fine pearls. When he found one of great value, he went away and sold everything he had and bought it.

Matthew 13:45–46 NIV

Salvation is free, right? Or is it? We know that we can't write a check and purchase our faith. We know that anyone who tries to get us to open our wallets and pull out some money to purchase God's forgiveness is a fraud. Yet Jesus is telling another story about the cost of something. What does it mean?

In this parable a man is searching for valuable pearls. He finds a single one that's so exquisite, so valuable, he can hardly believe it. Unfortunately, he doesn't have enough money to buy such an incredible pearl. So he goes off and sells all he owns just so he can come back and purchase that perfect pearl.

Okay, we already know that the perfect pearl represents Jesus and God's kingdom. But the fact that Jesus is repeating parables like this (first the one about the treasure in the field, and now this one) suggests that this is extremely important. He wants us to get it.

Jesus is telling us to invest ourselves completely into our faith. No holding back. No cheapskates allowed. Maybe it's because he knows that we get what we pay for—in this case, spending all we have in order to receive all we need. And if we consider our "everything" (which isn't much) compared to God's "everything" (which is beyond what we can imagine) . . . well, he's only offering the best deal on the planet. So why hold anything back?

My Prayer

Dear God,
Help me to get this, to wrap my head around the fact that you
want me to give everything so you can give everything back.
Amen.

Final Word

For where your treasure is, there your heart will be also.

Matthew 6:21 NIV

Stone for the Journey

I am willing to pour out all I have to receive all God has for me.

 ## Day 2 • Finders Keepers

Words from the Rock

God's kingdom is like a fishnet cast into the sea, catching all kinds of fish. When it is full, it is hauled onto the beach. The good fish are picked out and put in a tub; those unfit to eat are thrown away. That's how it will be when the curtain comes down on history. The angels will come and cull the bad fish and throw them in the garbage. There will be a lot of desperate complaining, but it won't do any good.

Matthew 13:47–50 Message

Most people don't really want to think about the end times. The term sounds pretty ominous and, well, final. But the interesting thing about the end times is that it happens in *everyone's* lifetime—everyone's life will end eventually. It's inevitable. So make no mistake, you will see the end times—someday.

So maybe you're wondering what throwing out fish has to do with the end times. In some ways, this story seems similar to the one about the weeds growing in the grain field, where everything is harvested together but the weeds are thrown away. Likewise, in this metaphor, all the fish (representing people) are gathered up together. The net is cast into the sea, catching all kinds of fish—the good, the bad, and the ugly. Naturally, the fisherman hopes that all the fish caught in the net will be keepers. A good fisherman doesn't want to throw anything back. Neither does Jesus.

In fact, Jesus gives everyone the same invitation to believe and follow him. It's just that some reject that invitation. Again and again some will stubbornly refuse. Although Jesus never stops trying to get people to accept him, there comes a time (the end time) when the net is cast and the final decision is just that—final.

Of course, Jesus is the only one who knows which "fish" are keepers and which ones will get tossed—and there are sure to be a lot of surprises in heaven because, knowing Jesus, he'll probably give some of those stubborn fish one last chance to change their minds. Still, why would you want to wait until the last minute when you could be enjoying a relationship with Jesus for your entire life?

My Prayer

> *Dear God,*
> *I reaffirm my faith in you. I don't want to be like the fish that's tossed aside. Keep me safe in your net.*
> *Amen.*

Final Word

> If anyone loves God, this one is known by Him.
>
> 1 Corinthians 8:3 NKJV

Stone for the Journey

I will serve Jesus until the end of time.

Day 3 • Equipped and Ready

Words from the Rock · · · · · · · · · · · · · · · ·

> Every student of the Scriptures who becomes a disciple in the kingdom of heaven is like someone who brings out new and old treasures from the storeroom.
>
> Matthew 13:52 CEV

Jesus has just done a spot-check with his disciples by asking if they're really getting what he's been telling them mostly in parables. They assure him that they have a handle on it, which must be a relief to him because he has so much more to teach them, and a relatively short time to do it.

But he takes a moment to encourage them. He reminds them of the fact that they've been well trained in Judaism. These guys grew up attending synagogue, studying Jewish laws, and learning about the prophets. It was a good foundation for the new things Jesus was now teaching them. Their prior education was important because it wouldn't be long before these same men would be teaching others and building the first Christian church.

Jesus says that this kind of preparation—of having old teaching combined with new—is like being a wealthy homeowner or shopkeeper, a person with all kinds of materials available and ready. Whether he has a valuable antique he can trade or something modern and useful, this person will be well equipped and ready for anything.

That's what Jesus wants for us too. He wants us to understand his words and his teachings and to appreciate how they change our lives so that we too can be ready and equipped for whatever might come our way.

My Prayer · · · · · · · · · · · · · · · · · ·

Dear God,

Help me to commit to spending more time reading your Word, learning about you, and making your teaching a vital part of my life.

Amen.

Final Word · · · · · · · · · ·

If they listen and obey God, they will be blessed with prosperity throughout their lives. All their years will be pleasant.

Job 36:11 NLT

Stone for the Journey · · · · · · · · · · · · ·

I will take time to know God better.

 ## Day 4 · Miracle Meal

Words from the Rock · · · · · · · · · · · · · · ·

The disciples came to [Jesus] and said, ". . . Send the crowds away so they can go to the villages and buy food for themselves."

But Jesus said, "That isn't necessary—you feed them."

"But we have only five loaves of bread and two fish!" they answered.

"Bring them here," he said. Then he told the people to sit down on the grass. Jesus took the five loaves and two fish, looked up toward heaven, and blessed them. Then, breaking the loaves into pieces, he gave the bread to the disciples, who distributed it to the people. . . . About 5,000 men were fed that day, in addition to all the women and children!

Matthew 14:15–19, 21 NLT

Jesus has just heard the disturbing news that his cousin John the Baptist was brutally murdered. In need of some serious downtime, Jesus travels by boat to a remote place. But as it turns out, thousands of fans follow him to that out-of-the-way spot, and instead of spending time alone, Jesus spends the entire day helping and healing people. Suddenly everyone begins to get hungry, but because they're out in the sticks, there's no handy place to get food. No McDonald's, no convenience mart, not even a produce stand. Nothing.

So what does Jesus say when his disciples suggest that he send the crowds home so they can eat? He says that's not necessary, and he tells his disciples,

"You feed them." Can't you just see their confused expressions? How are they supposed to feed thousands when all they have are five small loaves of bread and two fish? It's barely enough to feed just a few people. What does Jesus expect them to do?

Jesus expects them to have faith. In fact, one of the reasons he does miracles like this is to increase their faith. So he takes the bit of food they have, holds it up, and asks God to bless it. Then he tells his disciples to hand it out to the thousands of people. Imagine how stunned they must have been when not only did they have enough to feed the thousands, but after everyone was thoroughly stuffed, there were twelve large baskets of leftovers!

How do you react when Jesus asks you to do what seems impossible? Maybe he wants you to be kind to someone you can't stand—so you ask for his help, and he empowers you to do it. Or perhaps it feels bigger, like needing God to provide you with college tuition money—and trusting he'll do it. The point is, he wants you to remember that he's the one who will actually perform the miracle. You only need to believe him and obey.

My Prayer

Dear God,
Thank you for reminding me that you're able to do miracles in my life. Help me to increase my faith by being obedient to your will. Amen.

Final Word

Those who know your name trust in you, for you, O LORD, do not abandon those who search for you.

Psalm 9:10 NLT

Stone for the Journey

I will believe that God can work a miracle in my life today.

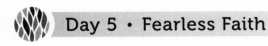

Day 5 • Fearless Faith

Words from the Rock · · · · · · · · · · · · · · · ·

> At once, Jesus said to them, "Don't worry! I am Jesus. Don't be afraid."
>
> Matthew 14:27 CEV

Jesus's disciples are freaking out when Jesus says these words to them. Ironically, this takes place shortly after Jesus's miracle of feeding the thousands. Jesus has sent the disciples out in a boat when a huge squall breaks out. If you've ever been on a small boat during a big storm, you might understand why they're so frightened—the wind is whipping tall waves right over their boat, and it doesn't look good. Perhaps the disciples wonder why Jesus sent them out in this kind of weather. Doesn't he care about them?

Then suddenly they spot someone walking toward them—on the water! At first they think it's a ghost, and they're even more terrified. Maybe they think it's the Grim Reaper coming for them. Then the man on the water calls out to them and tells them not to be afraid. It's Jesus! Peter yells back at him, "Lord, if it is really you, tell me to come to you on the water" (v. 28 CEV). Jesus tells Peter to come, and suddenly Peter is walking on the water too. But then he takes his eyes off Jesus and focuses on the wind and the waves. He starts to sink, crying out to Jesus for help. Jesus takes his hand, steadying him, and then tells Peter that he doesn't have much faith.

Peter had enough faith to climb out of that boat and walk on the water. He was really trusting Jesus in that moment. But when he took his eyes off Jesus and focused on what was going on around him (the wind, the waves, and *walking on water*), he got scared.

That can happen to you too. You might be in a tough spot, yet you believe that God is helping you and it's going to be okay. Then suddenly you take your eyes off God and stare at what's going on around you, and your faith fades and you begin to go down. God wants you to have fearless faith—the kind of faith where you keep your eyes on him and know he can get you through anything.

My Prayer ·

Dear God,

Help me to be faithful to keep my eyes on you and what you're doing in my life. Remind me that if I feel like I'm sinking, I can still call out to you for help and you'll answer.

Amen.

Final Word ·

I love everyone who loves me, and I will be found by all who honestly search.

Proverbs 8:17 CEV

Stone for the Journey ·

I will keep my eyes on God and believe he can get me through anything.

Week 22

Day 1 · Fake Faith

Words from the Rock ·

And why do you, by your traditions, violate the direct commandments of God? For instance, God says, "Honor your father and mother," and "Anyone who speaks disrespectfully of father or mother must be put to death." But you say it is all right for people to say to their parents, "Sorry, I can't help you. For I have vowed to give to God what I would have given to you." In this way, you

say they don't need to honor their parents. And so you cancel
the word of God for the sake of your own tradition.

Matthew 15:3–6 NLT

Jesus has just been challenged by some religious leaders whose goal is to
make him look bad by accusing him of ignoring their laws and traditions.
They're slamming him for not going through a somewhat ridiculous and very
tedious ceremonial hand-washing exercise before eating. But Jesus tosses the
question right back at them. His purpose is to point out their hypocrisy and
selfishness because he knows how they manipulate religious laws for their own
benefit. He is aware of how these supposed religious leaders get rich at the
expense of the very people they are supposed to be serving.

To further drive his point home, Jesus quotes from one of their own prophets,
Isaiah, by saying, "These people honor me with their lips, but their hearts are
far from me. Their worship is a farce, for they teach man-made ideas as commands from God" (vv. 8–9 NLT).

It seems that nothing aggravated Jesus more than religious hypocrisy. In
fact, the only times Jesus showed real anger was in regard to religious fakers.
Who could blame him? What is worse than someone pretending to be godly
so they can take advantage of others? It's like they think they can use God
for their own benefit, whether it's a TV evangelist who extorts money from
a poor, guilt-ridden viewer, or a teenage girl who fakes her Christian faith in
order to get the attention of a cool Christian guy. It all stinks.

Jesus wants you to avoid being a fake by keeping your faith authentic and
honest—straight from the heart. Really, why would you settle for anything less?

My Prayer

> *Dear God,*
>   *Help me to keep my faith real, even if it means admitting my
> faults to others. Teach me to guard my heart against hypocrisy.*
>   *Amen.*

Final Word

Give me understanding, that I may observe Your law and keep
it with all my heart.

Psalm 119:34 NASB

Stone for the Journey ·

I will keep my faith real.

Day 2 • Weight of Words

Words from the Rock ·

> Listen ... and try to understand. It's not what goes into your
> mouth that defiles you; you are defiled by the words that come
> out of your mouth.
>
> Matthew 15:10–11 NLT

Jesus makes a bold statement here. On the surface he seems to be address-ing the religious leaders' compulsive obsession about ceremonial hand washing before eating, but his true meaning is much deeper. Remember how the hypocritical religious leaders had criticized Jesus and his disciples, saying they were defiled and dirty because they had eaten their lunch with "unclean" hands? Jesus tells these men that even if they eat "dirty" food, it wouldn't hurt them—not like it would hurt them if they speak dirty words.

And wasn't this what the Pharisees were doing? Those phonies acted like they were so clean and pure—better than everyone else. But it was only on the surface. Underneath their fancy robes and "good" manners, and beneath their disguise of godliness, they were selfish and mean and hypocritical. While pretending to serve God, they were actually conniving to trip up God's own Son and the world's Savior. This was made obvious by the words that spilled from their mouths.

That was Jesus's point. It's not what goes *into* our mouths that messes us up; it's what comes *out* of them. Our words reflect what's inside of us. Even if we try to sugarcoat them to hide something corrupt, our true feelings can be revealed through a single slip of the tongue. It's better to clean up what's inside of us than to act like everything's cool on the exterior. To do that, we need God's help.

My Prayer

Dear God,

I realize I need your help to cleanse my heart. Please do your work in me so my words will show that I really do belong to you.
Amen.

Final Word

Don't just pretend to love others. Really love them. Hate what is wrong. Hold tightly to what is good.

Romans 12:9 NLT

Stone for the Journey

My words represent what God is doing inside me.

 Day 3 · Religious Traps

Words from the Rock

Every plant not planted by my heavenly Father will be uprooted, so ignore [the Pharisees]. They are blind guides leading the blind, and if one blind person guides another, they will both fall into a ditch.

Matthew 15:13–14 NLT

Jesus is describing religious hypocrites again, plainly stating that despite the Pharisees' "godly" claims, they do not truly represent God. Jesus knew that God would eventually take away their so-called authority by uprooting them. In the meantime, he warned his followers to ignore leaders like them. He understood that their form of religion was to bind people with ridiculous legalistic restrictions, to the point where they became too distracted to see God or to recognize his Son.

It's like those leaders were religious traps. They were set on ensnaring people and essentially preventing them from hearing or understanding the real truth—Jesus. Fortunately, Jesus was able to cut through their deceptive ways again and again. He did this openly and publicly so that his followers would remember these incidents when Jesus was no longer physically living among them.

Did you know there are still religious traps today? These traps come in many disguises, but most of them are rooted in legalism, not God. Legalism happens when we create or follow man-made rules in order to make ourselves "acceptable" to God. When we believe that it's our own actions that earn our way to God, we have fallen into a religious trap. Time and again Jesus says we come to God through him—via his grace, his forgiveness, his love. Thankfully, that's not something we can manufacture on our own.

My Prayer

Dear God,

Help me to remember that the only way to you is through your Son. Don't let me fall into any religious traps—whether of my own making or someone else's.

Amen.

Final Word

We say with confidence, "The Lord is my helper; I will not be afraid. What can man do to me?"

Hebrews 13:6 NIV

Stone for the Journey

I will not be led astray by legalism.

 ## Day 4 • Real Sign

Words from the Rock

If the sky is red in the evening, you say the weather will be good. But if the sky is red and gloomy in the morning, you say it is going to rain. You can tell what the weather will be like by looking at the sky. But you don't understand what is happening now. You want a sign because you are evil and won't believe! But the only sign you will be given is what happened to Jonah.

Matthew 16:2–4 CEV

Those religious leaders are trying to trip up Jesus again. Is it just that they have nothing better to do, or are they simply afraid that he's going to ruin their influence on the people? Whatever the case, they have just demanded that Jesus show them a "sign from heaven" to prove he was really sent from God. Naturally, Jesus declines their invitation, making it clear that it is God who calls the shots, not them. Then he points out that they are better at predicting the weather than they are at understanding God.

The arrogance of these supposed leaders is actually pretty mind-blowing. Do they honestly think they can force Jesus to send them a sign from heaven while they clearly refuse to accept that he is who he says he is? Isn't that kind of like challenging Michael Jordan to prove he's Michael Jordan by insisting he engage in a game of one-on-one with you?

Not only does Jesus deny these jokers' request, but he tells them that the only sign they'll get is "what happened to Jonah." And Jonah was swallowed by a whale after he refused to listen to God. Hint hint.

So how does this apply to you and your life today? Is it possible that Jesus doesn't want your faith to be the result of some supernatural sign sent down from heaven? Jesus wants you to believe in him because you've personally experienced his love and forgiveness. He wants you to be so rooted in him and to make him so much a part of your life that your faith is sort of organic—it has simply grown out of your relationship with him, almost like you can't help it. You are beginning to look and act like him—and that's a real sign from heaven!

My Prayer ·

Dear God,

I don't need you to send down flashy signs from heaven to prove yourself to me. Help me to remember the best sign you can give me is the quiet work you do inside my heart.

Amen.

Final Word ·

Finishing is better than starting! Patience is better than pride!

Ecclesiastes 7:8 TLB

Stone for the Journey ·

Jesus in me is the best sign of God's existence.

 # Day 5 • Who Is He?

Words from the Rock ·

Simon, son of Jonah, you are blessed! You didn't discover this
on your own. It was shown to you by my Father in heaven. So
I will call you Peter, which means "a rock." On this rock I will
build my church, and death itself will not have any power over
it. I will give you the keys to the kingdom of heaven, and God
in heaven will allow whatever you allow on earth. But he will
not allow anything that you don't allow.

Matthew 16:17–19 CEV

This is quite a promise that Jesus has just given to Simon Peter. It's in response
to a conversation Jesus just had with his disciples. He asked them what
people were saying about him, and they answered that some people thought
he was John the Baptist, others thought he was one of the old prophets such
as Elijah or Jeremiah. Then Jesus asked his disciples what they thought: "What
about you? . . . Who do you say I am?" (Matt. 16:15 NIV).

It was Peter's answer that blew Jesus away: "You are the Christ, the Son of
the living God" (v. 16 NIV). And that's when Jesus gives Peter that amazing
blessing. He also points out that Peter's answer is correct only because God
had revealed it to him. Jesus knows that because God had revealed these things,
Peter is truly the best choice to lead what would soon become the first church.

This must have been a happy day for Peter. His faith truly did seem rock solid.
For Jesus to commend him like that . . . well, Peter must have been just about
bursting with pride. Yet the day would come when Peter would deny Jesus—
not just once but three times. And still Jesus would build his church on Peter.

Jesus wants all his followers to know who he is. If he came to you today and asked you, "Who am I?" how would you answer? Do you understand that your answer matters? Would you call him your friend or just a casual acquaintance? Would you say he's a nice guy or the Son of God? Would you describe him as your Lord and Savior or just a godly man who once walked the earth? Who is he to you?

My Prayer

Dear God,

Please show me who you are in my life. Son of God, Lord, Savior, reveal to me who you are and help me to proclaim it.

Amen.

Final Word

We know that Jesus Christ the Son of God has come and has shown us the true God. And because of Jesus, we now belong to the true God who gives eternal life.

1 John 5:20 CEV

Stone for the Journey

When I know who Jesus is, I will know who I am.

Week 23

 Day 1 · Kingdom Keys

Words from the Rock

And that's not all. You will have complete and free access to God's kingdom, keys to open any and every door: no more barriers between heaven and earth, earth and heaven. A yes on earth is yes in heaven. A no on earth is no in heaven.

Matthew 16:19 Message

It's an awesome feeling when your parents hand you the keys to the car for the first time. But what Jesus gives to Peter (after hearing Peter's correct answer) is far better. Jesus is handing over the keys to God's kingdom, promising Peter that he can open all doors and that there will be nothing to separate him from heaven. His words on earth will have the same weight in heaven. What a deal! And all this just because Peter knows who Jesus is—because he understands that Jesus is God's Son, the one who has come to save the world. Peter's reward is the keys to the kingdom.

Guess what? The same reward is offered to anyone who acknowledges Jesus in the same way Peter did. We all have equal access to the kingdom keys, but some people get confused. They think if they have the keys to the kingdom, it'll be like having a magic wand that they can wave, and whatever they want will be theirs. Wrong.

The real key is *knowing* Jesus—and when we truly know Jesus, all we want to do is what he wants us to do. As a result, our "yes" on earth really does become a "yes" in heaven. When we ask for something, we receive it—because our goal is to do things according to God's perfect will, not our own.

Naturally, this doesn't happen overnight. It's a day-by-day, faith-walking process that is carried out one step at a time.

My Prayer

Dear God,
Help me to really know you so I can have access to your king-dom keys and live my life within your perfect will.
Amen.

Final Word

If any of you lacks wisdom, he should ask God, who gives generously to all without finding fault, and it will be given to him.

James 1:5 NIV

Stone for the Journey · · · · · · · · · · · · · · · · · · ·

The more I know God, the more I know his will.

 ## Day 2 · Followers

Words from the Rock ·

If anyone would come after me, he must deny himself and take up his cross and follow me.

Matthew 16:24 NIV

Jesus has just been talking to his disciples about his impending death, but they're in total shock and disbelief. Even Peter (remember, the faithful rock?) doubts Jesus's sensibilities here, and Jesus actually reprimands him for it.

Clearly, the context of this Scripture is death. Jesus is talking about dying literally. His words about taking up his cross are in direct reference to the cross he will be nailed to, the cross he will die on. His disciples are stunned. Furthermore, they wonder if Jesus is asking them to die alongside him. Maybe so. Time will tell.

This is not an easy message for anyone to hear, and not something to be taken lightly. But what does it mean for you? What Jesus implies in this verse is that if you truly want to follow him and honestly want to be his disciple, you must be willing to put your own plans to death. To be completely faithful to Jesus, you have to nail your own hopes and expectations to the cross. You do this in exchange for the guidance and direction he will give you, and then you are ready to be led.

It's kind of like getting out of the driver's seat and letting Jesus get in. So even if it looks like you're about to get in a big wreck, you sit there on the passenger side and trust Jesus's ability to drive. Even if you're nervous, you don't try to grab the steering wheel away from him. Although he might take a different road than you would have, or drive a little faster or a whole lot slower than you'd like, you know that he will get you to where you need to go. Once you settle in and really trust him, you will actually enjoy the trip, and you will be extremely thankful when you arrive at a place that exceeds all your original hopes, dreams, and expectations!

My Prayer ·

> *Dear God,*
>
> *Help me to trust you so implicitly that I allow you to lead in every aspect of my life. Teach me to follow you wherever you want to lead.*
>
> *Amen.*

Final Word ·

> If you love me, you will do what I have said, and my Father will love you. I will also love you and show you what I am like.
>
> John 14:21 CEV

Stone for the Journey ·

> Only as I set aside my will can I find God's.

 # Day 3 · Lost and Found

Words from the Rock ·

> For whoever wants to save his life will lose it, but whoever loses his life for me will find it.
>
> Matthew 16:25 NIV

Life, death, commitment—these are all pretty heavy topics. And Jesus doesn't sugarcoat his message one bit. He's telling his disciples that they're entering into an all-or-nothing sort of agreement. He's making a very somber prediction—that they will lose their lives for him someday. In fact, after Jesus's death and resurrection, ten of his disciples (and many other followers) will eventually be put to death for following him. Yet they will not waver in their faith. Not one of them will regret their commitment to him or the pain and suffering as a result of it.

But what do these words mean for you personally? Is Jesus literally asking you to be killed for believing in him? Probably not, since that's not happening much in the United States these days (although Christians are put to death for their faith in some countries). Even so, these words should pack a pretty stiff punch.

Jesus is saying that if you love your life more than you love him—if you cling to your own dreams more tightly than you cling to him—your life and your dreams will slip right through your fingers, and you will lose everything completely.

On the other hand, if you give up your life for Jesus (remember the steering wheel image?), if you surrender all control to him, he will give you back a life that's far beyond anything you could ever hope for. But you have to let go first. You have to trust him with everything. You have to believe that only God knows what you truly need—only Jesus in the driver's seat will get you where you really need to go.

My Prayer

Dear God,
I really don't want to lose my life. Show me how to let go, and help me to trust you completely. Thank you for getting me to where I need to go.
Amen.

Final Word

Because he has loved Me, therefore I will deliver him; I will set him securely on high, because he has known My name.

Psalm 91:14 NASB

Stone for the Journey

When I lose my life for God, I will find it.

Day 4 • How Much?

Words from the Rock ·

What will you gain, if you own the whole world but destroy
yourself? What would you give to get back your soul?

Matthew 16:26 CEV

Some people will do anything to get rich. Some will even lie, cheat, and steal
to get what they want. Others will simply work incredibly hard—shoving all
else aside to make "success" their number one goal. Now there's nothing wrong
with hard work or earning an honest living, but that's not Jesus's point in this
particular verse.

Jesus is giving us a warning. He understands how we think and what motivates us. He's aware of common human character flaws such as greed, pride,
and selfishness. He knows that we are all subject to these weaknesses. He also
knows that the *love* of money and material things will ultimately lead to our
destruction. He comprehends the way our hearts work and knows that if we
value anything above God, it will be our undoing.

It's not easy living in a materialistic world where merchandise and fads are
constantly thrust in our faces, where credit cards are pressed into the hands
of teenagers, and where millions of dollars are spent on marketing items that
promise happiness. But Jesus is saying not to fall for those lies. Don't be caught
up in "having it all." Don't be trapped into thinking that more is better, because
the end result is always the same—you lose. People who spend all their time
and energy accumulating this world's riches will end up spiritually bankrupt.
And by the time they figure it out, it will be too late. Jesus doesn't want you
to be one of them.

My Prayer ·

Dear God,
  *Please help me to remember that material things will not bring
me real or lasting happiness. Help me to value you above all else
and to keep you first in my life.*
  Amen.

Final Word ·

The love of money causes all kinds of trouble. Some people want money so much that they have given up their faith and caused themselves a lot of pain.

1 Timothy 6:10 CEV

Stone for the Journey · · · · · · · · · · · · · · · · · · ·

I will not trade my soul for earthly riches.

 ## Day 5 · Real Hunger

Words from the Rock ·

Truly, truly, I say to you, you seek Me, not because you saw signs, but because you ate of the loaves and were filled. Do not work for the food which perishes, but for the food which endures to eternal life, which the Son of Man will give to you, for on Him the Father, God, has set His seal.

John 6:26–27 NASB

Jesus knows that his time on earth is limited, yet he has this huge message to get across. Unfortunately, human minds have difficulty grasping spiritual meanings. Not to mention they are easily distracted by things as ordinary as hunger or boredom. Jesus's popularity is on the rise, but it may have more to do with people looking for food and entertainment than the realization that they are spiritually starving.

Yet Jesus understands people. Plus he is aware that times are hard, and he knows how his followers relate and respond to basic necessities like food and drink. So he uses these rather ordinary images to connect to the people. First Jesus candidly tells them that they're seeking him for food. He calls a spade a spade. Then he points out that it's not spiritual food they're looking for either. They simply want something to fill their bellies—perhaps some more of that delicious bread and fish with which he fed the thousands.

Jesus tells the people that he has another kind of nourishment to offer them—a kind of food that will feed their souls and change their lives, a kind of food that's been sent from his Father. It's the same thing he offers to you—a piece of himself. He wants you to be as hungry for him as you are for your favorite food. In fact, he wants you to be even hungrier for him. Food is here and gone just like that, and then you get hungry again. But what Jesus offers will satisfy that deep inner longing in a way that a pizza simply can't.

My Prayer

> *Dear God,*
> *I want to be hungry for you. Help me to see that my soul needs your nourishment even more than my stomach needs food.*
> *Amen.*

Final Word

> The eyes of the LORD range throughout the earth to strengthen those whose hearts are fully committed to him.
>
> 2 Chronicles 16:9 NIV

Stone for the Journey

> My spiritual hunger can only be satisfied by God.

Week 24

Day 1 • Job Description

Words from the Rock

> This is the only work God wants from you: Believe in the one he has sent.
>
> John 6:29 NLT

We live in a culture where jobs and work are taken fairly seriously. Most high schools put a lot of emphasis on planning for college, focusing on career options, offering work-study programs or internships, and generally preparing you for life as a responsible, self-supporting adult. That's all well and good, and your parents probably encourage these same ideals—since they don't want to support you forever—but Jesus plainly says that the only work God has for you is to believe in him.

So does that mean you won't need to get a job? Probably not. What it does mean is that there is nothing more important for you to invest your time and energy in than the maintenance of your faith. Your most important work is to believe in the one God has sent.

In other words, God wants you to take your faith even more seriously than you would a career. That means you must work at it. Some of the ways you can do that are by reading and studying God's Word, praying regularly, attending some form of fellowship, and sharing God's Good News with others. But mostly you need to work on the condition of your heart by keeping it right with God. That's your job—yours alone—and God says it's the most important thing you can do. And here's some more good news: the more diligently you work on maintaining your faith, the more God will direct you in other things like finding the perfect career. So really, it's a win-win situation.

My Prayer

Dear God,

Help me to remember that you want me to work at believing in you. Show me new ways to do this—and help me not to be a slacker. Amen.

Final Word

Trust in the LORD with all your heart and lean not on your own understanding; in all your ways acknowledge him, and he will make your paths straight.

Proverbs 3:5–6 NIV

Stone for the Journey

My most important job is to believe in God.

Day 2 • Soul Food

Words from the Rock ·

> I am the bread that gives life. Whoever comes to me will never be hungry again. Whoever believes in me will never be thirsty.
>
> John 6:35 NLT

This is a very bold statement, and one that many of Jesus's listeners could not quite wrap their heads around. Was Jesus suggesting that they were supposed to turn cannibal and actually eat him? Seriously, some people asked this very question. Yet this is only the beginning of what will be a long string of food metaphors in which Jesus doesn't simply compare himself to food; he actually says he is food.

Of course, you probably know by now (at least in your head) that Jesus is talking about spiritual food. The problem is that he's trying to get this message across to an audience who isn't very good at listening with spiritual ears. To them, food is food, drink is drink. They're confused.

Maybe you are too. Can you grasp the reality that Jesus wants you to be so connected to him that it's almost as if you had physically consumed him? He wants to be such an integral part of your life that it's as if he's asking you to take a great big bite of him and hold that within you. Maybe that creeps you out. If that's the case, it's because you're hearing his words with your physical ears instead of your spiritual ones.

Jesus wants to pour himself into you so much that you won't feel spiritually empty or famished. He wants to nurture that deep hunger inside of you until you're full. He wants to satisfy you with himself, his love, his forgiveness, his mercy, his joy, his grace—so many things he wants to fill you up with. But until you recognize that you're spiritually starving without him, he can't do it. He doesn't force himself on anyone.

My Prayer ·

Dear God,

I know that I'm spiritually hungry, but sometimes I forget to come to you. Please fill my empty spaces with all you have for me. Satisfy my longing with your presence.

Amen.

Final Word ·

As the deer pants for water, so I long for you, O God. I thirst for God, the living God. Where can I find him to come and stand before him?

Psalm 42:1–2 TLB

Stone for the Journey · · · · · · · · · · · · · · · · · ·

Only God can fill the emptiness inside of me.

 ## Day 3 · No Rejection

Words from the Rock · · · · · · · · · · · · · · · · · · ·

Those the Father has given me will come to me, and I will never reject them. For I have come down from heaven to do the will of God who sent me, not to do my own will. And this is the will of God, that I should not lose even one of all those he has given me, but that I should raise them up at the last day.

John 6:37–39 NLT

Everyone gets rejected by someone sometime. If it hasn't happened to you yet, just wait, it will. It's just the way life goes. But Jesus promises that he will *never* reject you. That's a promise you can count on. Jesus also wants his listeners to understand that not only will he never reject them, but that he has come to do God's will as well. He directly connects himself to God, but at the same time he makes it perfectly clear that God is the one calling the shots, not Jesus.

Jesus knows these people have a basic, although somewhat flawed, understanding of God. He hopes that their respect for and belief in God will somehow translate into how they relate to him as God's ambassador. Jesus also knows (thanks to those hypocritical Pharisees and other religious leaders) that the people he's addressing have a serious fear of God's rejection. Day in and day out it hangs over their heads like a black cloud—that all-consuming worry that if they don't live their lives "perfectly" (according to a bunch of impossibly crazy laws), God will reject them. What a heavy load to carry.

Somehow Jesus must convince them (and us) that not only will he never reject anyone, but he will also make a way for everyone to be reunited with God—permanently. That's an even greater promise—no rejection and a never-ending connection. Of course, at this point Jesus isn't finished with his work on earth. Consequently, his listeners still feel confused. But just hearing the sweet promise that Jesus would never reject them must have been a huge comfort. It's a promise you can cling to as well.

My Prayer

Dear God,
   Thank you for accepting me just as I am. Thank you that you will never reject me. Please help me to never reject you either!
   Amen.

Final Word

What can we ever say to such wonderful things as these? If God is on our side, who can ever be against us?

Romans 8:31 TLB

Stone for the Journey

God will never reject me.

 ## Day 4 • Big Promise

Words from the Rock

The Father is the One who sent me. No one can come to me unless the Father draws him to me, and I will raise that person up on the last day.... No one has seen the Father except the One who is from God; only he has seen the Father. I tell you the truth, whoever believes has eternal life.

John 6:44, 46–47 NCV

Jesus is drawing a tight connection between himself and God. It's imperative that people get this. If they don't understand that God is his Father and that Jesus and God are one, the plan for salvation will all unravel. Jesus knows this is a tough concept for people. They have questions and doubts. How can an earthly man also be God's Son? How is it possible that this Jesus dude, who looks normal and has no wings, has really come from heaven? It just does not compute. Not yet anyway.

They also question how Jesus is able to make such huge promises. How is he able to guarantee that *he* can give them eternal life? As much as they may want to believe this is possible, it's a struggle. Again, it's because Jesus's work on earth isn't done yet. In time it will begin to make more sense—missing pieces of the puzzle will appear and the full picture will be revealed.

Fortunately, we have those pieces now. We know the full story. Yet sometimes we're like Jesus's listeners who were still in the dark. We struggle with our own doubts and questions. Maybe we tell ourselves that it sounds too good to be true. Or we question how it's possible that Jesus can really make such an amazing offer. But Jesus just keeps it simple. He clearly states that if we believe in him, we will have eternal life. He's taken care of everything for us. Except for one thing—we have to choose to believe in him. That's up to us.

My Prayer

Dear God,

 I do believe in you. I believe you sent Jesus to show me the way to you. I believe that you have already given me eternal life. Help my faith to grow stronger.

 Amen.

Final Word

Anyone who believes in God's Son has eternal life. Anyone who doesn't obey the Son will never experience eternal life but remains under God's angry judgment.

John 3:36 NLT

Stone for the Journey

My belief in Jesus is my ticket to eternity.

Day 5 • Living Bread

Words from the Rock ·

> I am the bread of life. . . . I am the living bread that came down from heaven. If anyone eats of this bread, he will live forever. This bread is my flesh, which I will give for the life of the world.
>
> John 6:48, 51 NIV

Jesus doesn't simply compare himself to food—he plainly states that he *is* food. He is the Bread of Life. He has been sent from heaven. Anyone who eats of him will live forever.

These are hard words for his listeners to swallow. Again their minds leap to things like cannibalism, and they recall some of the strange heathen religions where people do creepy things like sacrificing humans. Surely that's not what Jesus is saying! Or is it?

Again Jesus puts emphasis on the fact that he came from heaven. He's not earthly bread. He's not trying to introduce a new cannibal religion. He just wants his listeners to open their spiritual ears and really hear what he means. He wants them to know that he longs to be as closely connected to them as that chunk of barley bread and olive oil they consumed for lunch, which gave them energy and nourishment. Jesus wants to be as immersed into their beings as the red wine with which they washed down the bread is immersed into their bloodstream. He doesn't want this to happen in the physical sense—you get that by now—but in the spiritual sense.

Jesus loves us so much that he wants to be a vital part of our lives. He wants to be tightly connected, to be united, to be one with us. He wants to flow through our lives, and he wants us to welcome his presence in the same way our bodies welcome wholesome food.

My Prayer ·

> *Dear God,*
>   *I invite you to fill me with all the goodness you have for me.*
> *Help me to ingest you into my being until I am full.*
>   *Amen.*

Final Word · · · · · · · · · · · · · · ·

He satisfies the thirsty and fills up the hungry.

Psalm 107:9 NCV

Stone for the Journey · · · · · · · · · · · · · ·

Jesus is the Bread that gives me life.

Week 25

 ## Day 1 · Life Blood

Words from the Rock · · · · · · · · · · · · · ·

I tell you the truth, unless you eat the flesh of the Son of Man and drink his blood, you cannot have eternal life within you.... For my flesh is true food, and my blood is true drink. Anyone who eats my flesh and drinks my blood remains in me, and I in him.

John 6:53, 55–56 NLT

Imagine the horrified gasps that might have been heard when Jesus made this startling statement. Again, was he really telling them to eat his flesh and drink his blood? Or maybe they didn't hear him right. Some listeners might have been so disgusted that they turned and hurried away. Others might have been so caught up in the sensation that they wanted more—similar to the way drivers slow down to gape at a nasty traffic accident. The reactions probably varied, but you can be sure Jesus got everyone's attention when he spoke these words.

It was one thing for Jesus to call himself the Bread of Life and invite them to eat that bread. Perhaps they were even starting to understand this on some level. Now suddenly he's telling them to eat his flesh and drink his blood. How can this be? What does it really mean?

Blood is a symbol of both life and death. And Jesus offers both life and death to everyone. He is inviting us to participate in his life by first participating in his death. He knows that his physical blood will soon be shed and that his earthly life will come to an end. He also knows that it's only through his death that the entire human race will finally be reunited with God the Father, and it's only through the spilling of his blood that he can offer them real life, eternal life.

Of course, his listeners can't grasp this. Even his loyal disciples don't get it. They don't want Jesus to die. And they certainly don't want to drink his blood. They're just as confused as anyone. Maybe you feel confused too. Maybe it's overwhelming to think about things like drinking Jesus's blood. But remember, Jesus is speaking in spiritual terms. He is simply offering himself and his death as your ticket to eternal life. Blood equals life. But again, in order to receive it, you must be willing to accept it.

My Prayer

Dear God,

Thank you for this amazing gift of life. I know that the cost was Jesus's death and his blood, and I am ready to embrace that. Thank you!

Amen.

Final Word

All mankind scratches for its daily bread, but your heavenly Father knows your needs.

Luke 12:30 TLB

Stone for the Journey

Jesus's blood equals eternal life for me.

Day 2 · Life Bread

Words from the Rock · · · · · · · · · · · · · · · · · · ·

> I live because of the living Father who sent me; in the same way, anyone who feeds on me will live because of me. I am the true bread that came down from heaven. Anyone who eats this bread will not die as your ancestors did (even though they ate the manna) but will live forever.
>
> John 6:57–58 NLT

Do you think Jesus repeated himself simply because he liked the sound of his own voice? No, of course not. It was only because he knew that his listeners weren't getting it. He had to make this whole thing as clear as possible, even if that meant pounding it into them. He was offering the words of life, and they needed to get a hold on them.

He drives home his point even more by reminding his listeners of their ancestors, because he knows that everyone there has heard the old story—how Moses led the children of Israel out of captivity in Egypt, how they got hungry out in the wilderness, and how God rained down bread from heaven to feed them. It was a happy, miraculous story that they'd heard repeated since childhood.

Then Jesus reminds them that those same ancestors, the ones who enjoyed that heavenly bread, still died in the end. Although the bread filled their bellies for a while, it didn't give them eternal life. Jesus wants you to understand that God created a deep-down hunger inside of you. If you try to fill that hunger with pizzas, cheeseburgers, or fries (which might add to your waistline), you'll still be spiritually starving. Until you get that Jesus is the only one who can satisfy that hunger, you'll try to fill the void with something else.

Jesus is the Bread of Heaven. When he's inside you, you're satisfied and full, and you have eternal life. Why would you want to settle for less?

My Prayer ·

> *Dear God,*
>
> *I realize that I'm spiritually hungry. I want Jesus, the Bread of Life, to fill that emptiness inside of me.*
>
> *Amen.*

Final Word ·

My God will meet all your needs according to his glorious riches in Christ Jesus.

Philippians 4:19 NIV

Stone for the Journey ·

Jesus satisfies my deepest hunger.

Day 3 • Wrong Expectations

Words from the Rock ·

Does this throw you completely? What would happen if you saw the Son of Man ascending to where he came from? The Spirit can make life. Sheer muscle and willpower don't make anything happen. Every word I've spoken to you is a Spirit-word, and so it is life-making. . . . This is why I told you earlier that no one is capable of coming to me on his own. You get to me only as a gift from the Father.

John 6:61–63, 65 Message

Jesus knows his words have really stretched his audience. He knows they're confused and doubtful and possibly on the verge of just giving up. Perhaps they wonder why he doesn't just tell them some more of those "nice" stories or do some healing miracles. Or maybe all his talk about bread has gotten their stomachs growling, and they're wishing he'd just pull out some loaves and fishes and feed everyone.

Instead he's pulling out the big guns. He's laying it on the line, spelling it out that he really is the Son of Man and that he's been sent from his Father. Everything he's telling them is spiritual, and he gives them words of life. Maybe you wonder why it's so hard for them to get it. Why does he have to keep pounding it into them?

For one thing, it's not yet time for them to fully grasp who he is or exactly why he came. Jesus is aware of this. He knows he's doing the groundwork. But the other reason, perhaps the bigger reason, is that the way God's will is going to play out is not what these people expect. This is not the way they thought God would work. Thanks to some of their faulty leaders and wrong assumptions, they just never expected God to send them salvation and life in this way. Now maybe if Jesus was clothed in shining white garments trimmed in gold, and perhaps if he rode in on a huge white horse, shooting fire from his fingertips . . . well, that might have been more like it.

But that's not how God is working. His plan is bigger and better and far beyond anything their human minds could imagine or dream. Yet they find it hard to budge from their old, worn-out, and wrong expectations. They had learned long ago to put God in a box, and it's very difficult for them to let him out. Yet Jesus is getting ready to break that box wide open.

My Prayer

> *Dear God,*
>
> *Help me never to put you in a box. Remind me of how big you are and how you work in my life in some unexpected but amazing ways.*
>
> *Amen.*

Final Word

> Because of Christ and our faith in him, we can now come boldly and confidently into God's presence.
>
> Ephesians 3:12 NLT

Stone for the Journey

> My God is full of surprises.

 ## Day 4 · Recognize Truth

Words from the Rock

> The things I teach are not my own, but they come from him who sent me. If people choose to do what God wants, they will know

that my teaching comes from God and not from me. Those who teach their own ideas are trying to get honor for themselves. But those who try to bring honor to the one who sent them speak the truth, and there is nothing false in them.

John 7:16–18 NCV

Jesus has just been teaching in the temple, and suddenly he's being questioned and challenged. While it's perfectly acceptable for "learned" men to teach casually in the temple, the Jews questioning Jesus don't believe he's had sufficient education. Perhaps they're threatened by him, or maybe his words have made them uncomfortable. And don't forget that these people are still stuck in their own wrong expectations. Their comfort zone is to keep God safely in a box.

Again Jesus cuts to the chase. He tells the Jews in no uncertain terms that he's not teaching his own ideas or personal opinions (unlike the Pharisees); he is simply teaching God's truth. He also tells them that if they were truly connected to God, they would know that Jesus really is God's spokesman (in fact, God's own Son). But these men are still in the dark. They are still caught up in their own misinformed beliefs. Sure, they might be hoping for the coming of the Christ (the Messiah), but they are certain that Jesus could not be the real deal.

This is, in fact, the question that every single person must face in their own lifetime—is Jesus really the Son of God, and if he is, what does that mean to them personally? When we remain caught up in our own false beliefs and wrong expectations, and when we refuse to accept that Jesus was sent from God, we are essentially rejecting God's love and forgiveness, since that's what Jesus came to earth to give us. But when we believe that Jesus is sent from God, when we embrace his truth and receive his love and forgiveness, then we are connected to God, not only here on earth but for eternity.

My Prayer ·

> *Dear God,*
> *Please teach me to separate fact from fiction. Show me how to know the difference between what is your truth and what isn't.*
> *Amen.*

Final Word · · · · · · · · · · · · · · · ·

> As for God, His way is perfect; the word of the LORD is proven;
> He is a shield to all who trust in Him.
>
> Psalm 18:30 NKJV

Stone for the Journey · · · · · · · · · · · · · ·

> God's truth is unchanging.

 ## Day 5 · Learn to Discern

Words from the Rock · · · · · · · · · · · ·

> I did one miraculous thing a few months ago, and you're still
> standing around getting all upset, wondering what I'm up to. . . .
> Don't be nitpickers; use your head—and heart!—to discern what
> is right, to test what is authentically right.
>
> John 7:21, 24 Message

Imagine that you're a doctor and you hear about a far-off island where all the people suffer from some horrible, deadly disease. Now imagine that you have the only cure, a vaccine you invented, and you decide to get it to them. It's going to cost you—you must sell your home and fancy car to afford enough of the vaccine, but you do it anyway. Then you travel to the island, and although the people are sick and dying, they refuse to believe that you're really a doctor or that your vaccination will save their lives. How frustrating!

In a small way, that might have been how Jesus felt. We probably have no idea how frustrated he must have been at times. He knew who he was, he knew who had sent him, he knew he had the words of life . . . and yet sometimes it seemed as if no one was getting it. Or else they were getting distracted and arguing over silly things—kind of just muddying up the waters.

Sometimes we do the exact same thing. We turn into religious nitpickers and get into ridiculous arguments over whether the Bible said this or that. Instead of remembering that the main message of the Bible is to love one another, we use the Bible to beat each other up. Jesus is saying to use our heads *and our hearts* so we can understand what's right (and what's wrong). In other words, he's saying we need to develop discernment—we need to be able to recognize when something is true or not, when something is good or not. But to learn how to do that, we need to go to him, because he's the one who gives discernment.

My Prayer

Dear God,

Help me to be discerning. Teach me to use both my heart and my head to think, and help me to avoid silly arguments.

Amen.

Final Word

Do not conform any longer to the pattern of this world, but be transformed by the renewing of your mind. Then you will be able to test and approve what God's will is—his good, pleasing and perfect will.

Romans 12:2 NIV

Stone for the Journey

God can teach me to use my head and my heart.

Week 26

Day 1 • The Connector

Words from the Rock

Yes, you know me, and you know where I am from. But I have not come by my own authority. I was sent by the One who is true, whom you don't know. But I know him, because I am from him, and he sent me.

John 7:28-29 NCV

Jesus has just been teaching in the temple, and suddenly it seems that the light is starting to click on in some people's minds. They actually begin to talk among themselves, speculating about whether or not Jesus really might be the Messiah. This is a real milestone for Jesus's ministry. They're starting to get it!

So he directs this statement to them. He tells them they are absolutely right, that they have recognized him, and that their suspicions about where he's come from (God) are on target. His words probably catch them by surprise since they'd been whispering among themselves. It would seem that he has their full attention. And that's when he points out that they don't really know God.

Although Jesus is simply being honest and direct, it probably feels like a slap in the face to these religious men. Especially since they're in the temple at the time, putting on a pretense of godliness. So these men, now angered and offended, attempt to have Jesus arrested. It's not time for that yet, so despite their efforts, Jesus just slips away.

But his point has been made. Jesus knows God because he is from God, and God is the one who sent him. Once again it's all about connection—Jesus is connected to God, and he wants to be the one to connect you to God. He knows that without that connection, you'll easily be misled and confused, and life will be empty and meaningless.

My Prayer

Dear God,
I do want to be connected to you. Thank you for all that you've done to be connected to me. Help me to remain connected always.
Amen.

Final Word

Therefore everyone who hears these words of mine and puts them into practice is like a wise man who built his house on the rock.

Matthew 7:24 NIV

Stone for the Journey ·

I know God, and he knows me.

Day 2 • Mountain Movers

Words from the Rock · · · · · · · · · · · · · · · · ·

What a generation! No sense of God! No focus to your lives! How many times do I have to go over these things? How much longer do I have to put up with this? . . . You're not yet taking God seriously. . . . The simple truth is that if you had a mere kernel of faith, a poppy seed, say, you would tell this mountain, "Move!" and it would move. There is nothing you wouldn't be able to tackle.

Matthew 17:17, 20 Message

Can't you just hear the frustration in Jesus's words? It's like he's standing there with his arms outstretched and holding out all the answers for them, yet the people won't take them. It's like their minds are stuck and they can't really believe him. They hesitate and balk and doubt and question him. They never quite get to that place where they really grasp what he's trying to give them. It must have been a challenge for him to remain patient.

In this portion of Scripture, Jesus's disciples have just asked him to help them heal an epileptic boy. He has made it clear that they already have what it takes to do these miraculous healings themselves because of their connection with him. But they hold up their hands helplessly and plead with him because it's not working. So Jesus steps in once again and heals the boy. Then he uses this opportunity to remind them that it takes only a tiny bit of faith on their part—a tiny mustard seed is all that's needed to do great things. If they took God seriously, they could do anything with his help.

The cool thing is that before long (after Jesus's death and resurrection), these same disciples are doing all kinds of amazing miracles. Things turn out just as Jesus said. Their seed-sized faith grows into something huge and powerful, something even greater than moving a mountain—their faith and works change the history of the entire world.

My Prayer

Dear God,

> *Sometimes my faith seems smaller than a mustard seed. Please remind me that you can do anything, and that all I need to do is believe in you and my faith will grow.*
> *Amen.*

Final Word

Don't fall for that nonsense. This is your Father you are dealing with, and he knows better than you what you need.

Matthew 6:8 Message

Stone for the Journey

I will plant my seed-sized faith in God.

Day 3 • Three-Part Plan

Words from the Rock

The Son of Man is going to be betrayed into the hands of men. They will kill him, and on the third day he will be raised to life.

Matthew 17:22–23 NIV

Although Jesus predicts his death and resurrection several times, it almost seems that his disciples aren't paying attention—or maybe they don't really believe it will happen. Especially when you see how rattled they become when Jesus is arrested and crucified—it's like they're blindsided. Or maybe they're simply in deep denial because they love him so much and don't want him to leave. Whatever the case, Jesus doesn't keep his impending death a secret. He lays it out there for his disciples to see.

To be fair, it would be pretty shocking to have a dear friend tell you that (1) he's going to be betrayed, (2) he's going to be killed, and (3) after three days he'll come back from the dead. That's a lot to wrap your head around.

You have to appreciate that Jesus doesn't keep this plan to himself. It's not like he's trying to surprise anyone (although the whole world would eventually be astounded). As always, Jesus is up-front with his disciples. He lays his cards on the table by telling them exactly what's coming. Even if they don't fully grasp that he'll be put to death and then come back to life, he still warns them ahead of time. Jesus knows they'll remember what he's told them eventually, when it begins to play out. In time, everything would make sense.

It's like that in your life too—you can't always see what's around the next corner. But Jesus can. He'll give you what you need to get where you're going, but not all at once. Sometimes it's like putting a puzzle together, one piece at a time—eventually the full picture is revealed. In the same way, God's complete plan would be shown only after Jesus's death and resurrection.

My Prayer

Dear God,

Thank you for sending Jesus to earth so I could have a relationship with you.

Amen.

Final Word

Listen! I am standing and knocking at your door. If you hear my voice and open the door, I will come in and we will eat together.

Revelation 3:20 CEV

Stone for the Journey

Jesus died and rose so I can live.

 # Day 4 • Taxes or Trust

Words from the Rock

The children get off free, right? But so we don't upset them needlessly, go down to the lake, cast a hook, and pull in the first fish that bites. Open its mouth and you'll find a coin. Take it and give it to the tax men. It will be enough for both of us.

Matthew 17:26-27 Message

Jesus has just been questioned about whether or not he and his disciples paid taxes. Ironically, taxes back then were just as much of a pain (maybe more so) as taxes nowadays. In fact, most of the tax collectors were crooks who took more money than was owed.

Jesus answers the question with a question. He reminds the tax collectors that in their country, only the foreigners were supposed to pay taxes, not the locals like Jesus and his disciples. While this was essentially true, it's not how things were being done. The locals were being taxed to the hilt, and there was no way to stop it.

After Jesus makes his point that these taxes were unfair, he then says he doesn't want to make trouble. So he tells a disciple to run down to the lake and catch a fish. Now that probably seems an odd response to paying taxes, but you can almost imagine the twinkle in Jesus's eye as he adds, "Open that fish's mouth and you'll find a coin inside, which will be enough to pay our taxes." Sure enough, that's what happens.

Jesus's point in this "transaction" seems threefold. First, he makes it clear that these taxes aren't fair. In fact, there are many things in life that aren't fair. Secondly, he says it's not worth it to get in a fight over taxes. It was no big deal. And why was that? That's the third point, where the fish comes in—Jesus knows that God will provide, and we should trust God to give us what we need more than we should worry about unfair taxes.

My Prayer ·

Dear God,
Teach me to trust in you for all things. Even when life's not fair, help me to believe you're watching out for me.
Amen.

Final Word ·

If they obey and serve him, they will spend the rest of their days in prosperity and their years in contentment.

Job 36:11 NIV

Stone for the Journey ·

Life's not fair, but God makes up for it.

Day 5 · Small Examples

Words from the Rock ·

I tell you the truth, unless you change and become like little children, you will never enter the kingdom of heaven. Therefore, whoever humbles himself like this child is the greatest in the kingdom of heaven.

Matthew 18:3–4 NIV

Who would have thought that a statement about little kids could be one of Jesus's most powerful and memorable teachings? Yet it is. Perhaps the impact comes from the fact that most people (both then and now) tend to think kids are rather insignificant and sometimes downright inconvenient. They can be noisy and obnoxious, yet they're easy to brush off, send to bed, push around. . . . After all, they're just kids.

But that's not how Jesus sees them. When he looks at little children, he sees *complete human beings*. Unlike their adult counterparts, these little people have yet to become jaded or cynical or apathetic or hopeless or prideful. Children are still young enough to be full of life and joy and faith and passion—the kinds of qualities Jesus wishes everyone could have.

Best of all, these children want to embrace Jesus. It's as if they instinctively know who he is and why he's so special. They can't wait to get close to him. In fact, that's why the disciples have been herding the kids away—so they won't "disturb" Jesus's teaching. But Jesus sees the little children as a great teaching tool for the grown-ups in the crowd. He tells his listeners to imitate them. He wants all of us to embrace his love and his gifts with eager, childlike enthusiasm.

My Prayer · · · · · · · · · · · · · · ·

Dear God,
    Please help me to have a childlike heart so I'm eager and passionate when it comes to loving you.
    Amen.

Final Word · · · · · · · · · · · · · · · · ·

Beware that you don't look down on any of these little ones. For I tell you that in heaven their angels are always in the presence of my heavenly Father.

Matthew 18:10 NLT

Stone for the Journey · · · · · · · · · · · · · · ·

I will stay childlike in my love for God.

Week 27

Day 1 · Defending the Defenseless

Words from the Rock · · · · · · · · · · · · ·

Anyone who welcomes a little child like this on my behalf is welcoming me. But if you cause one of these little ones who trusts in me to fall into sin, it would be better for you to have a large millstone tied around your neck and be drowned in the depths of the sea.

Matthew 18:5–6 NLT

Jesus wants us to really understand how important children are. In fact, he takes it a step further by saying the way you treat a child is the way you treat him. Those are powerful words. Especially when you consider the ever-increasing rates of child abuse, child neglect, and children's health and nutrition issues both in the United States and around the world. In a way, Jesus is putting a huge responsibility on all of us to take better care of the hurting children on the planet. Jesus is the ultimate defender of the defenseless.

To this end, Jesus delivers an extremely severe warning for anyone who causes a child "to fall into sin" by saying that a child abuser would be better off drowned in the ocean. One assumption is that Jesus is talking about someone who has sexually abused a child, and there are many who think that act should result in the death penalty. But Jesus could also be referring to those who physically or verbally abuse children. Any kind of abuse might cause a child to question life, to stop trusting God, and to make poor choices. It's no wonder Jesus condemned the abuser.

Fortunately, God is able to restore our broken spirits and can heal the wounds of a messed-up childhood, if we come to him with our pain and let him. But as for the ones inflicting the pain, Jesus put it plainly—they would be better off at the bottom of the ocean.

My Prayer

Dear God,

It grieves me to think of little children suffering. Please show me what I can do to help someone who is hurting. Let me be your caring hands.

Amen.

Final Word

Blessed is he who has regard for the weak; the LORD delivers him in times of trouble. The LORD will protect him and preserve his life; he will bless him in the land and not surrender him to the desire of his foes.

Psalm 41:1-2 NIV

Stone for the Journey

God can use me to help the helpless.

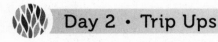 Day 2 · Trip Ups

Words from the Rock · · · · · · · · · · · · · · · · ·

> The world is in for trouble because of the way it causes people to sin. There will always be something to cause people to sin, but anyone who does this will be in for trouble.
>
> Matthew 18:7 CEV

Jesus gives everyone a stern warning here. He points out that the world in general is in trouble for the way it trips people up. However, this isn't anything new, and it's not all that surprising that Jesus is fed up. He's had run-ins with Satan from the very beginning. In fact, the reason Jesus has come to earth is to equip people to stand against the evil garbage Satan hurls at the planet on a daily basis. Even so, Jesus knows this kind of thing will continue after his earthly ministry ends. He also knows that Satan's attacks against Jesus's followers will only strengthen their commitment to God.

But Jesus's warning goes beyond saying that Satan will get his. This warning is similar to cautioning people not to harm children, but this time Jesus advises anyone who would purposely try to trip up someone else to watch out. Think about it—haven't we all done this a time or two?

In other words, Jesus is probably warning everyone. We all need to remember that sometimes a very small or seemingly insignificant thing we do could cause someone else to stumble. It could be a bad choice, refusing to listen, or being in the wrong place at the wrong time—and taking a friend along with you. Suddenly it all comes down, and you're in the hot seat with someone else pointing the finger at you. Jesus is saying not to go there. It's bad enough when you make a mistake that causes you to suffer. It's far worse when you drag someone else down with you.

My Prayer ·

Dear God,

Please help me never to trip someone else up. And if I do hurt someone, help me to quickly make things right and to learn from my mistake.

Amen.

Final Word ·

I've loved you the way my Father has loved me. Make yourselves
at home in my love. If you keep my commands, you'll remain
intimately at home in my love. That's what I've done—kept my
Father's commands and made myself at home in his love.

John 15:9–10 Message

Stone for the Journey ·

I will watch my step when it comes to my life and how I lead
others.

 ## Day 3 · Just Lose It

Words from the Rock ·

If your hand or your foot gets in the way of God, chop it off and
throw it away. You're better off maimed or lame and alive than
the proud owners of two hands and two feet, godless in a furnace
of eternal fire. And if your eye distracts you from God, pull it
out and throw it away. You're better off one-eyed and alive than
exercising your twenty-twenty vision from inside the fire of hell.

Matthew 18:8–9 Message

Jesus's warning about sin feels very extreme here. In fact, these words are
commonly misunderstood and questioned. Is Jesus really telling you to cut
off your hand or your foot? Does he really want you to gouge out your eye? If
Jesus loves you the way you thought he did, why would he want to make you
suffer like that?

Jesus is trying to make a point, and he wants to get our attention. Discuss-
ing the possibility of chopping off body parts tends to make a person sit up
and listen. But suppose that your foot really did have a mind of its own, and
it decided it was a good idea to go around kicking people. And suppose it
got really good at kicking people and started breaking old people's bones or
knocking small children in front of buses. (Sounds kind of like a Stephen King
novel.) Just suppose that really happened and you had absolutely no control

over this evil foot that could take out another person. Seriously, wouldn't it be better to have that foot amputated than to let it drag you first to prison, then to death row, and eventually to hell?

Jesus is saying that if something in your life is going to drag you into sin, get rid of it. In the long run, you'll be glad you did. Hopefully it's not a body part, but maybe it's something on the Internet that's messing with your mind, maybe it's a car you drive too fast, or maybe a boyfriend who pushes you too far. Just lose whatever it is, and in the end you will save yourself.

My Prayer

Dear God,
  Please help me to see if there's anything in my life that entices me to sin. Then give me the self-discipline to get rid of it.
  Amen.

Final Word

Obey my laws and live by my decrees. I am your GOD. Keep my decrees and laws: The person who obeys them lives by them. I am GOD.

Leviticus 18:4–5 Message

Stone for the Journey

I will not allow sin to take root in my life.

Day 4 · Persistent Love

Words from the Rock

If a man has a hundred sheep and one of them wanders away, what will he do? Won't he leave the ninety-nine others on the hills and go out to search for the one that is lost? And if he finds it, I tell you the truth, he will rejoice over it more than over the ninety-nine that didn't wander away! In the same way, it is not my heavenly Father's will that even one of these little ones should perish.

Matthew 18:12–14 NLT

It's not surprising that Jesus goes from talking about sin to telling a love story. This shepherd parable is about pure love—God's determined, persistent, and unconditional love. Unless you've ever been a shepherd, you probably don't really know what's entailed in caring for sheep, but let's just say it's not a glamorous job. In Jesus's day, shepherds were regarded almost like homeless people—losers who weren't good for anything more than watching dumb sheep. Quite likely, some probably earned the name.

But there were also some good shepherds who took their jobs seriously. They cared about the sheep and made sure they had good grass to eat and clean water to drink. They protected the sheep from predators and always kept head counts. Maybe they even knew the sheep by name. For sure, if a sheep went missing, a good shepherd would go out looking. He'd climb over rough terrain, and even if it took all night, he'd search and search. He'd know better than anyone that a lone sheep was in danger of becoming dinner for a hungry wolf. And when he found the lost sheep, he'd be over the moon with happiness because he truly cared about it.

As usual, Jesus's story has more than just one point. The example of the shepherd going the distance to find the lost sheep is for us too. Sometimes we get to be like that shepherd—we get to go the extra mile to rescue someone in distress. When we do this—not so we can get attention or a pat on the back, but because we truly love and care about that person in need—we imitate Jesus, and nothing could please him more.

My Prayer ·

Dear God,
    I want to be more like you. Show me ways that I can reach out to the lost. Give me a heart to love those in need.
    Amen.

Final Word ·

You are my hiding place! You protect me from trouble, and you put songs in my heart because you have saved me.

Psalm 32:7 CEV

Stone for the Journey ·

I can reach out to one lost person today.

 ## Day 5 · Work It Out

Words from the Rock ·

> If a fellow believer hurts you, go and tell him—work it out be-
> tween the two of you. If he listens, you've made a friend. If he
> won't listen, take one or two others along so that the presence
> of witnesses will keep things honest, and try again. If he still
> won't listen, tell the church. If he won't listen to the church, you'll
> have to start over from scratch, confront him with the need for
> repentance, and offer again God's forgiving love.
>
> Matthew 18:15–17 Message

Jesus knows that humans, by nature, don't really get along. Oh, things might go smoothly for a while, but eventually even the of best friends get into a dispute. Married couples have fights. Partners in business disagree. Even churches have been known to have their squabbles. So Jesus lays down some very important ground rules about relationships between Christians.

Unfortunately, many of us turn our backs on Jesus's words, tossing out these rules when it comes to settling differences. Sometimes we're more concerned about being right than making things right. So here are the rules. You might want to copy them down on an index card just in case you ever need them.

1. If a Christian does something that hurts you, go to that person and calmly tell him or her that you are hurting. Explain how his or her words or actions made you feel and why. Be honest yet kind.

2. If that person will listen, you can talk and work out your differences. That might mean taking responsibility for some of the blame. It might mean one or both of you need to forgive. But if you work things out, you have gained a true friend.

3. If that person won't listen to you, go to another Christian friend (or two) and explain the situation. But be honest and don't try to make the other person look like a jerk. There are always two sides.

4. The two or three of you should go to the other person—not to confront him or her but to speak honestly (with kindness and love) and see if you can resolve your differences. Usually this works.

5. If all that doesn't work (which is a rare case), and if you and the other person attend the same church, you can go to your church leadership and explain the situation. Then you simply start the whole process over again from step 1.

My Prayer ·

Dear God,
  Show me how to take good care of my relationships with others.
When I have a disagreement, help me to handle it correctly.
  Amen.

Final Word ·

Blessed are the peacemakers, for they will be called sons of God.

Matthew 5:9 NIV

Stone for the Journey · · · · · · · · · · · · ·

God can help me to love others even when it's not easy.

Week 28

 ## Day 1 · Power Promise

Words from the Rock · · · · · · · · · · · · · · ·

I promise you that God in heaven will allow whatever you allow on earth, but he will not allow anything you don't allow. I promise that when any two of you on earth agree about something you are praying for, my Father in heaven will do it for you. Whenever two or three of you come together in my name, I am there with you.

Matthew 18:18–20 CEV

Jesus makes a powerful promise to his disciples here. It's a promise for us too, but it only works when we're connected to Jesus. In other words, we can't do this on our own—the power comes directly from God, and Jesus is the transmitter. For us to imagine our words can make their way to heaven or that we can receive what we pray for—without being connected to Jesus—is like a table lamp bragging that it can illuminate a room without being plugged into an electrical outlet.

But when we remain connected to Jesus—praying to him, believing in him, experiencing his life in us—we will have this kind of power. We will be able to say and do things on earth that Jesus will stamp with his approval in heaven. We can get together with other believers and pray for God to do miraculous things, and we can be sure that God will do them. He's God and knows what's best, so he'll do what we ask in his time and in his way, but he will definitely move.

Perhaps the best part of this promise is that Jesus assures us that when we get together with other believers (even if it's only two or three) and our main purpose in being together is Jesus—if we're there to worship him, pray to him, learn more about him, or study his Word—then he will be right there with us. And when he is, we can be sure he'll be the one guiding our prayers and our words. We'll experience his answers to our prayers because of our connection to him.

My Prayer

Dear God,

Thank you for promising so much power to me. Remind me that the power comes from you and that I must be connected to Jesus to receive it.

Amen.

Final Word

If my people, who are called by my name, will humble themselves and pray and seek my face and turn from their wicked ways, then will I hear from heaven and will forgive their sin and will heal their land.

2 Chronicles 7:14 NIV

Stone for the Journey · · · · · · · · · · · · · · ·

Powerful miracles happen when I'm connected to God.

Day 2 • Forgive and Forgive

Words from the Rock · · · · · · · · · · · ·

No, not seven times ... but seventy times seven!

Matthew 18:22 NLT

You may have heard these numbers before. This is Jesus's response to Peter's question about how many times he should forgive a person. Maybe someone had offended Peter and he was getting tired of forgiving the same person again and again. So when Peter tossed out the number seven, he probably thought he was being generous. But Jesus comes back and multiplies seven by seventy, which really means you should always forgive—no limits.

To drive home his point, Jesus tells a parable about a rich man who had loaned out a lot of money and decided he wanted it back. One of the debts he wanted to collect was about a million dollars, but the guy who owed it was flat broke. So the rich man said he'd foreclose on all the deadbeat's properties (houses and livestock) and throw him in debtors prison. But the broke guy got on his knees and begged and pleaded, and the rich man actually had mercy, forgiving him his million-dollar debt!

Then this same man (who'd barely escaped foreclosure and prison) went to a guy who owed him about a hundred bucks and ordered this dude to pay up. And when the poor guy couldn't pay it all, the first guy (the one who'd just been forgiven a million-dollar debt) had him thrown in prison.

You can imagine how the rich man must have felt when he heard about this. How dare this man, who'd been forgiven a million-dollar debt, be so harsh and greedy as to throw someone into prison for something so small! Jesus tells

Peter that's how God feels when we refuse to forgive others after God has so generously forgiven us.

My Prayer

> Dear God,
>   Help me to remember how much you have forgiven me, and help me to be quick to forgive (again and again) anyone who offends me. Amen.

Final Word

> Put up with each other, and forgive anyone who does you wrong, just as Christ has forgiven you.
>
> Colossians 3:13 CEV

Stone for the Journey

> Because of God, there is no limit to forgiveness.

 ## Day 3 · Marriage Plan

Words from the Rock

> Haven't you read ... that at the beginning the Creator "made them male and female," and said, "For this reason a man will leave his father and mother and be united to his wife, and the two will become one flesh"? So they are no longer two, but one. Therefore what God has joined together, let man not separate.
>
> Matthew 19:4–6 NIV

The Pharisees have just questioned Jesus about divorce. As usual, they're trying to trap him up in their own mishmash of religious rules, probably hoping to publicly embarrass him. But, as usual, Jesus doesn't fall for their trickery. Instead he gives them a quick refresher course on God's best plan for marriage, quoting from an ancient Scripture that these "learned" men should recognize.

It's reassuring to hear Jesus remind everyone that God really did plan for marriage way back at the beginning of time. And the plan was really so simple. God made two genders—male and female—who would grow to an age at which they were old enough to support themselves separately from their parents. At that point the man and woman would marry and become "one flesh." They would join together not only physically and sexually but also emotionally, mentally, fiscally, and socially. "They are no longer two, but one." The focus is on joining two people, man and woman, to create something lasting.

But the real key is found in the last sentence: "What God has joined together, let man not separate." The key word is *God*. For a marriage to endure the test of time, God must become part of the equation (one man + one woman = marriage). If God is part of a courtship and marriage, and if the marriage relationship is built on God's rock-solid foundation (love, forgiveness, honesty, faithfulness), then no human will be able to blow the marriage apart.

Because God has such respect for marriage, he wants for you to respect him in the relationships you have *before* marriage. God knows that the way you handle your dating life (for better or for worse) will later impact your marriage, and he wants you to have the best marriage possible. So if you date, why not invite God to join you? After all, he's there with you anyway.

My Prayer

> *Dear God,*
> *I believe my life and future are in your hands. If that includes marriage, I trust that you'll lead me and show me what's best for me. Amen.*

Final Word

For the grace of God has been revealed, bringing salvation to all people. And we are instructed to turn from godless living and sinful pleasures. We should live in this evil world with wisdom, righteousness, and devotion to God.

Titus 2:11–12 NLT

Stone for the Journey

Only God can plan a marriage that will endure.

Day 4 · Hard Hearts

Words from the Rock ·

> Moses permitted you to divorce your wives because your hearts
> were hard. But it was not this way from the beginning. I tell you
> that anyone who divorces his wife, except for marital unfaithful-
> ness, and marries another woman commits adultery.
>
> Matthew 19:8–9 NIV

The Pharisees don't let Jesus off the hook after his refresher course on marriage. They come right back at him, demanding to know why Moses allowed legal divorces so many years ago, if marriage is designed by God. Their
plan is still to trip up Jesus, but he turns their plan against them to show what
they're really thinking.

Jesus is aware of the trend of religious leaders abusing the old divorce law
as an excuse to get rid of an unwanted wife. It's just another one of their nasty
little legal loopholes they use to get what they want (in this case, probably a
younger, prettier wife). Consequently, Jesus delivers his answer directly to the
Pharisees, saying the only reason they're permitted to divorce is because their
hearts are so hard, and that divorce only becomes an option if a spouse has been
unfaithful. And even in that case, he warns, a remarriage is considered adultery.

Naturally, this isn't what the Pharisees want to hear. They probably stomp
off mad. Jesus nailed it when he said their hearts were hard. It was, in fact,
the hardness of their hypocritical hearts that spoiled not only their marriages
but everything they touched. It made them bitterly jealous of Jesus, and sadly,
it blinded them to the fact that the God they supposedly served was doing
something amazing right in front of them.

Hearts sometimes get hardened when our plans don't match up with God's.
That's why he invites us to stay in relationship with him, so that our plans can
align with his and our hearts can remain soft.

My Prayer ·

> *Dear God,*
> *I know a hardened heart is like being blind and falling down*
> *flat on my face. Please let me never harden my heart toward you.*
> *Amen.*

Final Word ·

> When tempted, no one should say, "God is tempting me." For God cannot be tempted by evil, nor does he tempt anyone.
>
> James 1:13 NIV

Stone for the Journey · · · · · · · · · · · · · · · · ·

> I will trust God's perfect plan for my life.

 ## Day 5 • Single Hearts

Words from the Rock · · · · · · · · · · · · · · · · · ·

> Only those people who have been given the gift of staying single can accept this teaching. Some people are unable to marry because of birth defects or because of what someone has done to their bodies. Others stay single for the sake of the kingdom of heaven. Anyone who can accept this teaching should do so.
>
> Matthew 19:11–12 CEV

After Jesus answers the Pharisees about divorce, his disciples grow concerned and say, "If that's how it is between a man and a woman, it's better not to get married" (v. 10 CEV). You can almost hear the fear in their voices. It's no wonder, since the disciples (from varied homes and backgrounds) have suspected their lives would change as a result of following Jesus. Most are single, and some are married but away from their wives. Ones like Peter, in light of his call to ministry, might have been questioning the practicality of marriage in general.

Jesus gently but honestly answers them, saying that some people *do* have the gift of remaining single and that they would surely agree with what the disciples have just suggested. He also points out that some people don't marry because of the way they are, while some will stay single for reasons of faith. Obviously, based on his other teachings, Jesus believes many will find it best to marry.

Basically, Jesus is saying that everyone's situation, each one's path, will be different. We each have to figure out what God's best plan is for us. We shouldn't tell someone else how to live his or her life. Jesus obviously knew that the early church would begin after his death and resurrection, and he must have suspected marriage would be just one of the issues they would grapple with. Even so, Jesus doesn't lay down the law—that's not who he is. He simply speaks the truth, suggesting that each of us will have to figure out which is right for us—staying single or being married. It's between us and God.

My Prayer

> *Dear God,*
> *Whether you want me to remain single or get married someday, I want to do what you want me to. Please show me your perfect will for my life.*
> *Amen.*

Final Word

You followed my teaching, conduct, purpose, faith, patience, love, perseverance.

2 Timothy 3:10 NASB

Stone for the Journey

God will lead me down the path he has chosen for me.

Week 29

 ## Day 1 • Not Enough

Words from the Rock ·

> A man stopped Jesus and asked, "Teacher, what good thing must I do to get eternal life?"
>
> Jesus said, "Why do you question me about what's good? God is the One who is good. If you want to enter the life of God, just do what he tells you."
>
> The man asked, "What in particular?"
>
> Jesus said, "Don't murder, don't commit adultery, don't steal, don't lie, honor your father and mother, and love your neighbor as you do yourself."
>
> The young man said, "I've done all that. What's left?"
>
> "If you want to give it all you've got," Jesus replied, "go sell your possessions; give everything to the poor. All your wealth will then be in heaven. Then come follow me."
>
> That was the last thing the young man expected to hear. And so, crest-fallen, he walked away. He was holding on tight to a lot of things, and he couldn't bear to let go.
>
> Matthew 19:16–22 Message

This Scripture begins on a hopeful note. A young man approaches Jesus for advice on how to get eternal life. Yet this confident young man almost seems to have a hidden agenda—which, naturally, Jesus will see through and expose. In fact, right from the start Jesus counters with "Why not just go directly to God? He's good and will tell you what to do." But the young man wants specifics. So Jesus starts rattling off commandments, then waits for a response. The persistent young man announces that he's done all that and asks what else he must do.

Imagine Jesus in that moment. Does he pause hopefully, or does he already know the outcome? Whatever the case, he asks the man the big question—is he willing to give up everything? Can he sell all his belongings, give the money to the poor, and follow Jesus? Sadly, the answer is no. The reason? This young man is wealthy—he has many possessions, and he's not willing to part with them. Not even for Jesus.

If only he knew what he had given up . . . or maybe he does, and that's why he goes away sad. He rejects an eternal treasure that would only increase in value in order to hold on to his earthly "riches" that are worthless.

God wants us to realize and appreciate the difference between things this world values (like money, cars, clothes), and what he offers (like a fulfilled life, endless love, enduring peace). He wants us to choose what's most valuable and hold onto it.

My Prayer

> Dear God,
>   I don't ever want my attachment to things to keep me from serving you. Please remind me of what's really valuable and what's not.
>   Amen.

Final Word

Don't be greedy! Owning a lot of things won't make your life safe.

Luke 12:15 CEV

Stone for the Journey

The best I can do is to follow God.

 # Day 2 · Stumbling Block

Words from the Rock

I tell you the truth, it will be hard for a rich person to enter the kingdom of heaven. Yes, I tell you that it is easier for a camel to go through the eye of a needle than for a rich person to enter the kingdom of God.

Matthew 19:23–24 NCV

Most people just scratch their heads at the image of a camel going through the eye of a needle. It sounds crazy-impossible. But it could be that Jesus was really describing a particular entrance into the walled city of Jerusalem.

It seems that, due to security reasons, the only way to enter the city late at night was via an inconvenient entry that had been designed to prevent enemy invasions. The entrance was more like a large hole in the wall, big enough for people to pass through one by one. Perhaps a small, well-mannered, coordinated donkey—if it wasn't carrying a load—might be enticed to step through. But a camel—ridiculous.

Keep in mind that camels were usually the transportation of the very wealthy (like royalty or merchants), and they were usually loaded down with lots of valuable possessions. If it were even possible to get a large, awkward, and possibly ill-tempered camel to climb through this passageway (and that's assuming a lot), its rider would still have to unload all those expensive goods, setting them on the darkened street where bandits could be lurking. Then imagine as this frustrated rich man attempts to shove, push, or pull his camel through the tight hole. And what if the camel got stuck?

The point to all this? Jesus is saying that riches (money and material possessions) can be a stumbling block to anyone. What you love becomes your master. If you love material stuff more than Jesus, you will serve those things more than you serve Jesus. Which would you rather give your life to?

My Prayer

Dear God,

Help me to keep you as my number one priority. If material possessions ever distract me from loving you, please give me the strength to get rid of them.

Amen.

Final Word

Keep your lives free from the love of money and be content with what you have, because God has said, "Never will I leave you; never will I forsake you."

Hebrews 13:5 NIV

Stone for the Journey

I choose to love God more than anything else.

Day 3 · Impossible Possibilities

Words from the Rock ·

> With man this is impossible, but with God all things are possible.
>
> Matthew 19:26 NIV

This is a promise you can cling to—and maybe even memorize for the times you need an encouraging reminder—when you're faced with a challenge that seems impossible. And you'll have lots of impossible challenges if you're trying to live out your faith—that's just the way it goes. But if you're trying to live out your faith *without* God's help, it will be hopelessly impossible. Any attempt to live as a Christian without God isn't just futile, it's pathetic—not to mention foolish.

Imagine you're pretty good at basketball (maybe you are), and your big dream is to get really good. Yet for some reason you try to do this from your bedroom. Maybe you play basketball via a computer game or you have an old Nerf basketball with a hoop attached to your laundry basket. You stay in your room spending hours just shooting away, but your game's not getting better. Then imagine (okay, this takes some big imagination) that your last name is Jordan and your dad's name is Michael. He just happens to be a retired NBA star who's been waiting to play some one-on-one with you, but you're too busy "practicing" in your room to go downstairs to the big indoor gymnasium with real hoops and shoot with your dad. Get the picture?

That's kind of how silly it would be for you to try to do this Christian walk on your own without God's help. It is humanly impossible, but with God all things are possible. He's right there, always ready and waiting to help you with your game.

My Prayer ·

> *Dear God,*
>
> *Remind me not to get discouraged when something feels impossible, but to simply come to you and ask for help. All things are possible with you!*
>
> *Amen.*

Final Word

Let us hold tightly without wavering to the hope we affirm, for God can be trusted to keep his promise.

Hebrews 10:23 NLT

Stone for the Journey

I need God to accomplish the impossible.

 # Day 4 • Great Benefits

Words from the Rock

Yes, you have followed me. In the re-creation of the world, when the Son of Man will rule gloriously, you who have followed me will also rule. . . . And not only you, but anyone who sacrifices home, family, fields—whatever—because of me will get it all back a hundred times over, not to mention the considerable bonus of eternal life. This is the Great Reversal: many of the first ending up last, and the last first.

Matthew 19:28–30 Message

Jesus's disciples have pretty much given up everything to follow Jesus. They've left families, jobs, and homes just to be with Jesus, to learn from him, and to help with his ministry. At this stage, they might be wondering if it's really going to be worth what they've sacrificed. In fact, they have just asked Jesus that very thing—what will they get out of this?

This promise is Jesus's answer for his disciples. But it's also for all believers who will come later, who will love God enough to put him in that first-place position in their hearts—in essence, giving up everything to follow and serve him.

Jesus promises that whatever you give up for him will be returned to you a hundred times over—and that isn't even counting the promise of eternal life, which is returned about a million times over. In other words, he's saying you'll never be sorry that you chose to follow him. Sure, there will be times when life's hard or challenging, but holding fast to God will always be worth the effort. He promises to make it worth everything you give up and a lot more—not necessarily in your earthly life, although having God's presence in your daily life is better than anything. But Jesus promises that eternal life will be so incredible your earthly mind can't even begin to comprehend it.

My Prayer

Dear God,

Thank you for all that you have for me. Remind me that what I give up for you now is not only in my best interest, but it will be repaid again and again throughout eternity.

Amen.

Final Word

If you give to others, you will be given a full amount in return. It will be packed down, shaken together, and spilling over into your lap. The way you treat others is the way you will be treated.

Luke 6:38 CEV

Stone for the Journey

I cannot outgive God.

 ## Day 5 · First and Last

Words from the Rock

God's kingdom is like an estate manager who went out early in the morning to hire workers for his vineyard. They agreed on a [very generous] wage of a dollar a day, and went to work. Later, about nine o'clock, the manager saw some other men hanging around the town square unemployed. He told them to go to work in his vineyard and he would pay them a fair wage. They went. [The manager randomly hired workers like that into the afternoon, all for a dollar a day, and when the day ended and it was time to pay the workers, they all got the same pay, whether they'd worked all day or an hour. This made the ones who'd worked all day angry.]

[The manager] replied to the one speaking for the rest, "Friend, I haven't been unfair. We agreed on the wage of a dollar, didn't we? So take it and go. I decided to give to the one who came last the same as you. Can't I do what I want with my own money? Are you going to get stingy because I am generous?"

Matthew 20:1-5, 13-15 Message

This parable confuses and frustrates a lot of people, probably because it goes against almost everything our culture has taught us about work ethic. We believe in an honest wage for an honest day's work, but this parable is saying something altogether different. In a nutshell, some guys worked for an hour, while others worked for a full day, and they all got paid exactly the same.

So imagine you're desperate for a job. Times are hard, your children are starving, and you're about to lose your home. You're willing to do anything for a buck. You feel jealous when you see others working. Why can't that be you?

The day is almost done, your stomach is growling, and you know your kids will go to bed hungry again. Then, to your surprise, the field manager offers you work—and you'll receive a full day's wages! You can hardly believe it, and you jump in and work as hard as you can right up until sunset. You're so thankful that you wish you could have worked longer.

Jesus uses this story to show how people live their earthly lives. Some will spend a lifetime knowing, loving, and serving him. Others will spend most of their lives struggling to get along, making mistakes, and feeling spiritually lost. But as long as they all find their way into a relationship with God, whether early in life or at the very end of it, they will all get the same reward—eternal life! Why should anyone be resentful of that? Shouldn't we all be happy for everyone who receives eternal life?

My Prayer

Dear God,

I'm so thankful to have found you early in life. Help me to be gracious to anyone who takes longer.

Amen.

Final Word · · · · · · · · · ·

Here it is again, the Great Reversal: many of the first ending up last, and the last first.

Matthew 20:16 Message

Stone for the Journey · · · · · · · · · · · · · · · · · · ·

I will not question God's generosity toward me or others.

Week 30

Day 1 · Headed to the Cross

Words from the Rock · · · · · · · · · · · · · · · · · · ·

We are now on our way to Jerusalem, where the Son of Man will be handed over to the chief priests and the teachers of the Law of Moses. They will sentence him to death, and then they will hand him over to foreigners who will make fun of him. They will beat him and nail him to a cross. But on the third day he will rise from death.

Matthew 20:18–19 CEV

Again Jesus is predicting his death. Only this time he's much more specific about the details. Jesus and his disciples are on their way to Jerusalem when he makes this disclosure. He tells them privately because it's not time for anyone else to hear. Interestingly, we don't get to see or hear their reaction to this announcement. Maybe they were very quiet, trying to process what Jesus was saying. Or maybe they were in disbelief, wondering how all that could happen. Or perhaps they were simply in shock, hoping beyond hope that

Jesus was wrong about this. Whatever the case, no conversation is recorded to show their reaction.

What would your reaction be if you'd been there that day? How would it feel to hear Jesus saying these things? First he was going be handed over to those hypocritical religious leaders that no one really liked or respected? Who was going to hand him over? Then he would be sentenced to death? For doing what? And then he would be ridiculed by foreigners? How could that possibly happen?

But then it gets even grimmer—Jesus would be beaten and nailed to the cross? That was how criminals were put to death. Could you even bear to think of that? And finally, after three days, he would return to life? How was that even possible?

Maybe you would have been quiet too, just trying to wrap your head around all this dismal information and hoping it wasn't really going to happen. But how do you feel about it now, knowing that it did happen? It all went down just as Jesus had predicted. And it happened like that so God could extend his love and forgiveness to everyone, including you. How do you respond to that?

My Prayer ·

Dear God,

Thank you for sending Jesus to earth and for his willingness to die so I could have eternal life. I never want to take that gift for granted.

Amen.

Final Word ·

For God so loved the world that he gave his one and only Son, that whoever believes in him shall not perish but have eternal life.

John 3:16 NIV

Stone for the Journey ·

I'm thankful that Jesus went to the cross for me.

Day 2 · Who's on Top?

Words from the Rock · · · · · · · · · · · · · · · · ·

> You know that the rulers in this world lord it over their people, and officials flaunt their authority over those under them. But among you it will be different. Whoever wants to be a leader among you must be your servant, and whoever wants to be first among you must become your slave. For even the Son of Man came not to be served but to serve others and to give his life as a ransom for many.
>
> Matthew 20:25–28 NLT

Jesus says a lot of things that are hard to understand—at least at first. It often seems he's coming from a completely different direction. Or maybe he's just coming from heaven. But in this section he tells his disciples (and all who would follow him) that his way of measuring leadership is exactly the opposite of the way the world does it.

Think about it—if people want to be elected to positions of leadership, they make themselves known. Often they spend money to do this, campaigning for votes. They go hang with other "important" people. They get their picture in the news, and they hold fancy fund-raisers where only the rich get invited. It's pretty much in-your-face, and sometimes it's obnoxious.

Jesus says that if you really want to be a leader, you should act like a servant. A servant is someone who takes care of others, who cleans up other people's messes, who puts the needs of someone else over his or her own. It's not a glamorous job. Even less glamorous is the life of a slave. But Jesus says that if you really want to be on top, you need to be a slave. A slave can't even call his life his own. He's at the beck and call of someone else. The needs of his master and everyone else come before his own.

When you think about it, that's exactly what Jesus did. He left his kingdom in heaven to come to earth and take care of us, clean up our messes, put our needs above his own . . . and to eventually be put to death on the cross, which must have seemed like hitting rock bottom to some. But now he rules and reigns with God in heaven forever—from the bottom straight to the top. And he wants us to imitate him by humbling ourselves and being willing to serve like he did—that way he can be the one to lift us up.

My Prayer

Dear God,

Help me to see the value of being a servant. Show me ways I can put others' needs above my own. Make me more like you. Amen.

Final Word

Each one must do just as he has purposed in his heart, not grudgingly or under compulsion, for God loves a cheerful giver.

2 Corinthians 9:7 NASB

Stone for the Journey

Jesus can teach me how to be a servant.

Day 3 • Sealed Fates

Words from the Rock

I will be with you a little while longer. Then I will go back to the One who sent me. You will look for me, but you will not find me. And you cannot come where I am.

John 7:33–34 NCV

Jesus is in the temple when he makes this announcement. He says it loudly enough for all to hear, but he's directing it to the religious leaders who have just confronted him and are now attempting to have him arrested. Naturally, his words confuse these "educated" men. They can only assume that Jesus must be putting together some kind of devious plot to overthrow them. They even begin to fret that Jesus plans to take his teaching abroad, perhaps to the Jews who live in foreign lands. That is a huge concern to them. What if his ministry would expand? What if he would influence Jews to abandon their religion for his "heresy"?

Yet there are others in the temple who are growing increasingly interested in Jesus. They've seen some of his miracles and heard some of his teaching, and they're beginning to ask themselves if this man might truly be the Messiah. Of course, this only makes the religious leaders more fearful and jealous, and this drives them toward the final chapter of Jesus's earthly life.

It seems pretty obvious what Jesus is saying to these religious leaders. He's telling them that he's going back to the one who sent him—his Father. He already told them they don't know his Father. Now Jesus is saying they won't be able to find him once he's gone. Furthermore, they won't be able to go where he's going—simply because they have refused to believe that he is God's Son. They have rejected Jesus, and as a result, they have rejected the very same God they thought they'd been serving. They are sealing their own spiritual fate.

But Jesus has revealed himself to you. You know why he came to earth, what he did, and where he has gone. He wants you to believe in him so that one day you can join him in heaven. Where the unbelievers sealed their fate by dismissing Jesus, you seal your fate by believing in him.

My Prayer

Dear God,

I don't ever want to be like the Pharisees, rejecting you and the one who sent you. Thank you for sealing my fate with you so I can join you in heaven.

Amen.

Final Word

In this fellowship we enjoy the eternal life he promised us.

1 John 2:25 NLT

Stone for the Journey

I will be welcome in heaven because of my relationship with Jesus.

Day 4 • Thirst Quencher

Words from the Rock ·

> Anyone who is thirsty may come to me! Anyone who believes in me may come and drink! For the Scriptures declare, "Rivers of living water will flow from his heart."
>
> John 7:37–38 NLT

Jesus makes this declaration loudly, in the presence of the crowds of people who've come to Jerusalem to celebrate the Festival of Booths (a harvest celebration). His words capture the people's attention because he's quoting from one of the prophets who had predicted the coming of the Messiah. Suddenly some of the people seem to get it. They become excited, thinking Jesus is the real deal—he's the Messiah! Oh, how they have longed for the Messiah. They have thirsted for him like people lost in the desert. And they assume that Jesus will be the one to deliver them from their oppressors (primarily the Roman government occupying their country). They're ecstatic.

Others are wary. It's not that they wouldn't welcome the Messiah—and maybe they're a little bit thirsty. But among themselves they question Jesus's bold claim. They say doubtful things like, "How can Jesus be the Messiah if he's from Galilee?" and "Wasn't the Messiah supposed to be from the line of David?" and "The Messiah should have been born in Bethlehem, just like King David." Soon the people are arguing. Too bad they hadn't done their homework, or they would have known that Jesus was a descendant of King David and had been born in Bethlehem. Instead they rely on their own opinions and misinformation.

As the arguments grow louder, the religious leaders grow more agitated and concerned. They have absolutely no thirst for the truth or for Jesus. The only thing on their minds is, *How can we shut Jesus up for good?* They want him to be arrested and locked up, but it's not time for that yet. Although each day brings Jesus closer to his date with the cross, there's still work to be done. He knows that people are thirsty and growing thirstier each day, and he wants to give as much living water as possible in the time he has left for his ministry.

In the same way, he wants you to thirst for him. He wants you to know that only his love and truth can really quench your parched soul.

My Prayer

Dear God,

Sometimes there's a yearning deep inside me, but I don't realize it's a thirst for you. Remind me that you are the Living Water and when I come to you, I will be filled up.

Amen.

Final Word

I heard a loud shout from the throne, saying, "Look, God's home is now among his people! He will live with them, and they will be his people. God himself will be with them."

Revelation 21:3 NLT

Stone for the Journey

Only Jesus can quench my thirsting soul.

Day 5 · Throwing Stones

Words from the Rock

When they kept on questioning him, he straightened up and said to them, "If any one of you is without sin, let him be the first to throw a stone at her." Again he stooped down and wrote on the ground.

At this, those who heard began to go away one at a time, the older ones first, until only Jesus was left, with the woman still standing there. Jesus straightened up and asked her, "Woman, where are they? Has no one condemned you?"

"No one, sir," she said.

"Then neither do I condemn you," Jesus declared. "Go now and leave your life of sin."

John 8:7–11 NIV

The religious leaders are at it again, plotting and planning, and now they think they have Jesus between a rock and a hard place. They've caught a woman in the act of adultery. They drag her to where Jesus is teaching and throw her down in front of him and everyone else.

The Pharisees know Jewish law requires this woman to be put to death by the throwing of stones. They also know that Jesus teaches forgiveness. But how can he break Jewish law by forgiving an obviously guilty woman? To these men, it seems a cut-and-dried case, so they demand an answer from him: "What do you say?" (v. 5 NIV).

Jesus just stoops down and writes on the ground with his finger. They keep hammering at him, demanding that the woman be stoned. So he stands and says those unforgettable words: "If any one of you is without sin, let him be the first to throw a stone at her." Then he stoops down again, and one by one everyone slips away. No rocks are thrown. Because, after all, who hasn't sinned? And how gracious was Jesus? He didn't stare or point an accusing finger at the people. Yet he makes his point. Everyone has sinned.

So what gives one person the right to condemn another? Jesus didn't condemn anyone. He just told the woman to leave her life of sin behind. What a lesson that is for us—to be willing to admit that sin does exist, but without condemning a person for being a sinner. And if you think about it, when are you most eager to toss an accusation at someone else—could it be those times when you don't want someone else to accuse you?

My Prayer

Dear God,

Remind me that it's not my job to point the finger at someone else's mistakes. Let me imitate you in how you love and forgive others.

Amen.

Final Word

There is only one Lawgiver and Judge, the one who is able to save and destroy. But you—who are you to judge your neighbor?

James 4:12 NIV

Stone for the Journey ·

I will deal with my own faults instead of pointing out faults in others.

Week 31

 ## Day 1 · Life Light

Words from the Rock ·

I am the light of the world. The person who follows me will never live in darkness but will have the light that gives life.

John 8:12 NCV

People are naturally drawn to light. Whether it's sun seeking on a warm beach or star gazing on a dark night, gazing at a flickering candle in a dim room or staring into a crackling campfire, we are attracted to light. It offers warmth and comfort and illumination. Without light, this world would be a cold, dark place, and we would quickly cease to exist.

Jesus's light is not all that different. It too is a source of warmth, comfort, and illumination. Without Jesus's light, our hearts grow cold, our spirits grow uneasy, and we can't see where we're going, so we end up stumbling around. Despite all that, we still manage to shield ourselves from Jesus's light sometimes. Maybe it's in the form of spiritual sunglasses, which dim the brightness just enough so we don't have to see that certain sin area in our lives that needs attention. Or maybe it's a like a dimmer switch that somehow makes a dirty room appear more attractive. Everyone has ways of pushing Jesus's light away.

What happens when you live in a continually light-deprived condition? In your physical life, a number of things can occur as a result of the absence of sunlight—things like bone deterioration, invasion of germs and bacteria, or just plain old gloomy depression in the form of SAD (seasonal affective disorder). Your spiritual life is not so different. So if you want to be healthy and happy, soak in Jesus's light. If you don't want to stumble and fall down, let Jesus illuminate your path. Let the light shine in!

My Prayer

Dear God,

Please shine your light on me. I know I need it to find my way and to be healthy and happy. Teach me to welcome your light always. Amen.

Final Word

You are a chosen people. You are royal priests, a holy nation, God's very own possession. As a result, you can show others the goodness of God, for he called you out of the darkness into his wonderful light.

1 Peter 2:9 NLT

Stone for the Journey

God's light brings life.

Day 2 • Earthbound Minds

Words from the Rock

I know where I came from and where I am going, but you don't know this about me. You judge me by human standards, but I do not judge anyone. And if I did, my judgment would be correct in every respect because I am not alone. The Father who sent me is with me.

John 8:14–16 NLT

Although Jesus is talking to those thickheaded Pharisees, he could be talking to any of us since we're all a little dense at times, especially when it comes to grasping spiritual concepts. That's probably because we often try to understand spiritual things with our human, earthly minds, which is kind of like trying to use an old-fashioned television to receive HDTV. That old television's technology is too limited to receive the high-definition signals being transmitted. Without an adaptor, when it comes to catching anything from the airwaves, that old TV is pretty much useless.

That's how we are when we try to comprehend who Jesus is within the limitations of our earthly minds. It just doesn't work. And when we refuse to listen with our spiritual ears, we, like the Pharisees, are subject to doubt, skepticism, and cynicism. Think about it—isn't that how most nonbelievers react to Jesus? Spirituality does not compute within the confines of an earthbound mind.

But here's the good news: Jesus gets this, and he promises he won't judge us for being human (though he could if he wanted since he's connected to God, who's the highest and fairest judge in the universe). Jesus understands our human condition because he walked around the planet in human skin long enough to know how it feels. He won't judge us for being thickheaded at times.

By the same token, Jesus warns us not to judge him according to our human standards, because he knows that just won't work. Instead, he wants us to begin reasoning with our spiritual senses. And that involves faith. Don't forget that we don't need a huge amount of faith. Like Jesus said, even faith the size of a mustard seed can do miracles—as long as we plant our faith in him.

My Prayer

> *Dear God,*
>
> *I realize that I tend to use my earthbound brain more than I use my spiritual senses. Please help me to develop a stronger spiritual sense so that I will better understand in my heart who you are and what you're up to.*
>
> *Amen.*

Final Word

> No one can explain how a baby breathes before it is born. So how can anyone explain what God does? After all, he created everything.
>
> Ecclesiastes 11:5 CEV

Stone for the Journey · · · · · · · · · · · · · · · · · ·

My spiritual senses are limited only by my earthbound mind.

 ## Day 3 • Seeing Jesus

Words from the Rock · · · · · · · · · · · · · · · · · ·

You're looking right at me and you don't see me. How do you expect to see the Father? If you knew me, you would at the same time know the Father.

John 8:19 Message

Jesus has just informed the religious leaders that he speaks to them on behalf of his Father. He reminds these legalistic men that even in their own court, they require two testimonies as evidence, so he tells them that he and his Father are providing them with two testimonies. Naturally, this answer doesn't please them, so in another effort to trap him, they demand to know where his Father is. Once again, he doesn't answer according to their expectations. Remember, they're locked in their earthbound minds.

Jesus plainly tells them that even though they're looking directly at him, they still can't see him. Now they're probably thinking, *Are you nuts? Of course we can see you, you're standing right there.* But they can only see him with their earthly eyes. Their spiritual eyes are blind or shut because they clearly aren't seeing Jesus for who he is. They don't get that he's the Son of God. They don't know Jesus—who he really is—and that simply proves they don't know God.

So how does that relate to you? What's your reaction when you "see" Jesus? Keep in mind that there are many ways to see him. Sometimes you see him working in someone else, but perhaps it makes you uncomfortable. Sometimes you see him through something as basic as nature, like a beautiful sunset trying to remind you to praise God. Sometimes you see him when you're reading God's Word and a certain sentence really grabs you, or you're praying and you get a sense that God is telling you to take a certain action. When you see Jesus like this, do you always recognize him? Do you always respond?

My Prayer

Dear God,

   Please forgive me for the times I've "seen" you but then turned away. Help me to see what you want me to see and to respond in a way that pleases you.

   Amen.

Final Word

Be sure to fear the LORD and serve him faithfully with all your heart; consider what great things he has done for you.

1 Samuel 12:24 NIV

Stone for the Journey

My spiritual eyes hunger to see God.

Day 4 · Who's a Pharisee?

Words from the Rock

You people are from here below, but I am from above. You belong to this world, but I don't belong to this world. So I told you that you would die in your sins. Yes, you will die in your sins if you don't believe that I am he.

John 8:23-24 NCV

Do you ever wonder why so many of Jesus's words recorded in the Bible were directed to those stubborn, prideful, hardhearted, thickheaded Pharisees? Why did Jesus "waste" so much time on the men who not only refused to believe in him but eventually sought to have him killed? Why would Jesus do that?

Could it be that Pharisee–type people are somewhat universal? Is it possible that all of us have a bit of Pharisee trapped inside? If you don't agree, consider some of the common negative characteristics of the typical Pharisee in Jesus's time: (1) They thought they knew more than anyone else. (2) They believed playing by their own rules would ensure their success. (3) They were certain they were superior to everyone. (4) They questioned anyone who didn't agree with them. (5) They were selfish and greedy.

Now ask yourself, *Do any of those descriptions fit me?* Who doesn't think they know more than others at times? Who wouldn't like to play by their own rules? And so on. See, we all fall into the Pharisee category sometimes. It's likely Jesus knew that, and that's probably the reason so many of his words, though aimed at the Pharisees, can be applied to anyone. So Jesus keeps it simple. In this Scripture he bluntly tells the Pharisees (and all of us) that unless they believe in Jesus and believe that he's going to die for their sins, they will die.

My Prayer

Dear God,

I confess that I sometimes act like a Pharisee, like when I think I know more than anyone else. Help me to see myself for what I am, and then let me come to you to be changed.

Amen.

Final Word

The one who is the greatest among you must become like the youngest, and the leader like the servant.

Luke 22:26 NASB

Stone for the Journey

I will humble myself so that God can change me.

 ## Day 5 • Authorized by God

Words from the Rock

When you lift up the Son of Man, you will know that I am he. You will know that these things I do are not by my own authority but that I say only what the Father has taught me. The One who sent me is with me. I always do what is pleasing to him, so he has not left me alone.

John 8:28–29 NCV

Even though Jesus was the Messiah, the chosen one, and God's own Son—which means he's actually the same as God—he still understood that his life on earth was authorized by God. In other words, he knew that any power he had on earth came directly from God. He accepted that all he knew had been given to him by God, and he respected that all he did was a direct result of God's authorization. Jesus was totally aware of this amazing and powerful connection, and he never tried to function without God's authority. So why would anyone?

Yet we do. We live "unauthorized" lives when we try to get by without God. Maybe it's not intentional, but we do it just the same. There are times when we think we have enough strength or brains or resources or whatever, and we attempt to proceed through our lives without any assistance from God.

Even if we do manage to stumble through, we have to ask ourselves, how lame is that? Especially when we consider that God is just waiting for us to call on him, to connect ourselves to him, so that he can use his authority to direct us through life. Yet we continually come up with excuses to keep him at arm's length. Maybe we just have to learn the hard way.

We need to remember that Jesus, the Son of God, never tried to do anything on his own. He knew that he needed God's authority with him every minute of the day and every single step of the way. Jesus *never* took God's authority for granted. Why would we want to live life any differently?

My Prayer

Dear God,

I admit that I often leave you out of certain things. I'm not even sure why. Please remind me that I need you. Help me to remain connected to you and to notice what a difference your authority makes in my life.

Amen.

Final Word ·

> For God has not given us a spirit of timidity, but of power and love and discipline.
>
> 2 Timothy 1:7 NASB

Stone for the Journey ·

> To make my life really work, I must be authorized by God.

Week 32

Day 1 · Real Freedom

Words from the Rock ·

> If you continue in My word, then you are truly disciples of Mine; and you will know the truth, and the truth will make you free.
>
> John 8:31-32 NASB

Who doesn't long for freedom? There's a place inside of everyone that just wants to be free.

Sometimes you may get confused over what freedom really means. Maybe you think it's a day off from your normal routines and responsibilities. Or maybe you think it's getting something for nothing. Or maybe it's sliding through a situation where you should've been nailed—getting home free.

The freedom Jesus is talking about is a lot bigger and a lot more lasting than those things. It's a soul-deep sort of freedom that feels like a load's been lifted from your shoulders. It eases your conscience and helps you to sleep better. And it basically simplifies your life and lifts your spirits.

But this kind of freedom isn't really free—it comes with a cost. For starters, Jesus paid dearly for this freedom. The price was his death on the cross.

His resurrection became his ultimate freedom—and the reason this kind of freedom is offered to you. Yet there's still a cost for you. The price is simply everything. It's up to you to hand your entire life to God—to entrust all to him, believe in him, study his Word, and know his truth. When you pay that everything price, which is actually pretty small compared to what you receive in return, you will experience real freedom. Because you know God's truth, you are set free.

My Prayer

> *Dear God,*
> *I want your truth in my life. I'm willing to pay the price—to surrender all to you—so that I can have your real freedom.*
> *Amen.*

Final Word

> But when he, the Spirit of truth, comes, he will guide you into all truth. He will not speak on his own; he will speak only what he hears, and he will tell you what is yet to come.
>
> John 16:13 NIV

Stone for the Journey

> When I know God's truth, I become free.

Day 2 • A Slave to Sin

Words from the Rock

> I tell you most solemnly that anyone who chooses a life of sin is trapped in a dead-end life and is, in fact, a slave. A slave is a transient, who can't come and go at will. The Son, though, has an established position, the run of the house. So if the Son sets you free, you are free through and through.
>
> John 8:34-36 Message

A slave is someone who doesn't get to exercise their own will. The master calls the shots, and the slave must simply comply with the master's decisions. Now if the master is God, being a slave is a good thing, because God has only the slave's best interests at heart and would ask them to do only what would help them, not hurt them. But what if the slave's master is evil? What if the slave is being bossed around by sin?

That's what Jesus is talking about here. He's explaining how sin can become a master over you until it almost seems that you have no will of your own. You can be enslaved to deception—it might start with a small lie, but soon it becomes a habit, and before long you can't stop lying. You can be a slave to addictions, whether it's food or computer games or drugs or sex. You know you're a slave when your energy and resources are focused on a behavior that's hurting you, when you no longer control the activity but instead the activity controls you. While you're immersed in it, you are deceived into thinking you enjoy it. But later you are full of regrets, and it feels like you have no choice, like you're trapped. That's being a slave.

So how do you escape that kind of slavery? How can you get out of that trap? Only Jesus can set you free. And that won't begin until you accept the truth by being honest with yourself and openly admitting that you're enslaved to a particular sin. Then you need to ask God for help in surrendering all parts of your life, including that sin area. Maybe God will show you some practical steps to take, like joining a support group or a fitness club. But it's only God's truth (and your acceptance of it) that will set you free. And then you will be really free.

My Prayer

Dear God,

I don't want to be a slave to sin. Help me to be honest—really honest—and to welcome your truth into my life. Then show me the steps to take so I can be free.

Amen.

Final Word

You are tempted in the same way that everyone else is tempted. But God can be trusted not to let you be tempted too much, and he will show you how to escape from your temptations.

1 Corinthians 10:13 CEV

Stone for the Journey ·

God's truth will set me free from the slavery of sin.

 ## Day 3 · God at Work

Words from the Rock ·

It is not this man's sin or his parents' sin that made him blind. This man was born blind so that God's power could be shown in him. While it is daytime, we must continue doing the work of the One who sent me. Night is coming, when no one can work. While I am in the world, I am the light of the world.

John 9:3–5 NCV

Jesus's disciples have just asked why a man was born blind. They live in an era where physical disabilities or health problems are often associated with sin. So it's natural for them to assume that blindness was the result of sin, and if a person was born blind, perhaps that meant the parents' sin was the reason. But Jesus firmly tells them they are wrong, and then he says something remarkable—that the reason for the man's blindness was to reveal God's power.

That answer must have surprised his disciples. How was it possible that a person born with a handicap could make God look good? It seemed more likely that a person born with something like blindness would shake his fist at God for cursing him with that kind of hardship. In fact, that's the same attitude of some people today. They see someone suffering and ask why God would do that. They blame God for everything that seems to be wrong with the world.

Jesus says these problems and challenges are actually opportunities for God to show what he can do. He's saying that our weaknesses and defects are God's chance to strengthen us, to grow us up, or even to heal us. First we have to realize that we need God's help, and then we need to bring our hardships to him. After that, we need to step back and trust him to work, and once he does, we need to be willing to tell others about what he's done.

My Prayer

Dear God,

Help me to see my personal hardships and challenges as your opportunity to shine in my life. I want to trust you with everything. Amen.

Final Word

The mind of sinful man is death, but the mind controlled by the Spirit is life and peace.

Romans 8:6 NIV

Stone for the Journey

God can use my weakness to show his strength.

 # Day 4 • Blinding Pride

Words from the Rock

Jesus said, "For judgment I have come into this world, so that the blind will see and those who see will become blind."

Some Pharisees who were with him heard him say this and asked, "What? Are we blind too?"

Jesus said, "If you were blind, you would not be guilty of sin; but now that you claim you can see, your guilt remains."

John 9:39–41 NIV

Why would you pretend to be something you're not? Why would you deny an area of weakness in your life? Would it be because you wanted others to think you were better than you were? Would it be because of pride?

Pride kept the religious leaders and the hypocritical Pharisees from seeing who Jesus really was and that he'd come from God. In fact, pride blinded them. Would they admit they were blind? Of course not. They denied having a problem, insisting that everyone else, including Jesus, needed help. The

Pharisees were like, "We can see just fine, thank you very much." They were so sure of themselves that they probably thought their spiritual eyesight was 20/20. Yet they were totally blind. Jesus came to heal the sick and to make the blind see, but if people denied their blindness, like the Pharisees did, how could Jesus possibly heal them?

If we let pride rule us (like the Pharisees) and claim we're "just fine, thank you," Jesus can't help us. Our denial not only keeps us from being healed, it keeps us from God. It's only when we can admit our weaknesses, confess our blind spots (which we all have), and ask God to help us that we can be healed.

My Prayer

> *Dear God,*
> *I know I have blind spots and that pride can drive me into denial. Help me to confess my weaknesses and to come to you for healing.*
> *Amen.*

Final Word

> Doing wrong is fun for a fool, but living wisely brings pleasure to the sensible.
>
> Proverbs 10:23 NLT

Stone for the Journey

> I will not let pride separate me from the truth and from God's healing.

 Day 5 • Attention!

Words from the Rock

> I tell you the truth, anyone who sneaks over the wall . . . rather than going through the gate, must surely be a thief and a robber! But the one who enters through the gate is the shepherd of the sheep. The gatekeeper opens the gate for him, and the

sheep recognize his voice and come to him. He calls his own sheep by name and leads them out. After he has gathered his own flock, he walks ahead of them, and they follow him because they know his voice. They won't follow a stranger; they will run from him because they don't know his voice.

John 10:1–5 NLT

When Jesus told this parable, people were confused but interested. He'd definitely hooked them with a story that was suspenseful and intriguing. But what did it mean? Who were the thieves and robbers? And why were they sneaking over the wall and stealing the sheep? Really, it made no sense to the listeners. Yet Jesus had gotten their attention, and for a short while he just left them hanging there, wondering.

A lot of spiritual things come at us like that. Something hits us from out of the blue—usually in the form of an everyday incident. It could be something good like an unexpected award. Or it could be something tragic like the sudden death of a loved one. Something occurs that reaches into our lives, grabs us, and shakes us. It gets our attention, but we're not quite sure what it means. Often we don't know how to react. We don't realize that God wants to get our attention so he can show us something. Maybe we too are just left hanging there, wondering.

In this parable, which Jesus explains more fully in the next section of Scripture (which is in the next devotional), it's not hard to guess that Jesus is the shepherd, especially since he's used that metaphor before. But it's still not clear who the thieves and robbers are, or who the gatekeeper is. Mostly Jesus wants us to know that when we feel confused or even blindsided, we need to remember that he has the help and answers we need. When we understand who he is, we learn to rely on him. We look to him for direction and comfort, and we trust him to lead us to safety.

My Prayer •

> Dear God,
> I know that sometimes it takes something difficult to get my attention. Help me focus on you and trust you to get me where I need to go.
> Amen.

Final Word ·

I pray to you, LORD! You are my place of safety, and you are my choice in the land of the living. Please answer my prayer. I am completely helpless.

Psalm 142:5 CEV

Stone for the Journey · · · · · · · · · · · · · · · · · · ·

God needs to get my attention so he can lead me.

Week 33

 Day 1 · Our Entrance

Words from the Rock ·

I tell you the truth, I am the gate for the sheep. All who came before me were thieves and robbers. But the true sheep did not listen to them. Yes, I am the gate. Those who come in through me will be saved. They will come and go freely and will find good pastures. The thief's purpose is to steal and kill and destroy. My purpose is to give them a rich and satisfying life.

John 10:7–10 NLT

Now Jesus has the full attention of his listeners, and he begins to explain his parable about the sheep, the thieves, and the gate. First he says that the thieves and robbers came before him. It's easy to assume he means the religious leaders who never really cared for the people they were supposed to be serving. Instead of encouraging people to seek God, the Pharisees would trip them up with long lists of ridiculous rules, and then when people couldn't comply with the rules, the Pharisees would demand payment (sacrifices) from them. It was a lot like stealing.

But the new twist in this parable is that Jesus not only calls himself the shepherd, but he tells us he's the gate as well. Jesus is saying that he's our entrance—we must go through him to be saved and to reach God. So not only will he lead us where we need to go, he will also be the actual doorway, gate, portal, entrance, and so on, that will allow us passage from one side to the other. Once we accept him, we walk through that entrance and we're welcome to come and go freely. He will take care of our needs, and our relationship with him will be fulfilling and life changing.

Jesus paints a lot of word pictures for us, giving us image after image of what he's like so we will get it, so we will hold on to who he is and remember it. He calls himself the Bread of Life, the Living Water, the Light of the World, the Good Shepherd, and more. All are invitations to connect to him, to participate in the life he offers us. And when we accept his invitation to pass through him (as the gate), we are immediately transported to the best that life has to offer.

My Prayer

Dear God,

Thank you for inviting me to go through Jesus to reach you. I know the only reason you can give me this free ticket is because you willingly paid the price by laying down your life. I don't want to take that for granted.

Amen.

Final Word

I have told you all this so that you may have peace in me. Here on earth you will have many trials and sorrows. But take heart, because I have overcome the world.

John 16:33 NLT

Stone for the Journey

Jesus is my entrance to God's very best for me.

Day 2 · Good Shepherd

Words from the Rock

> I am the good shepherd. The good shepherd sacrifices his life
> for the sheep. A hired hand will run when he sees a wolf coming.
> He will abandon the sheep because they don't belong to him
> and he isn't their shepherd. And so the wolf attacks them and
> scatters the flock. The hired hand runs away because he's work-
> ing only for the money and doesn't really care about the sheep.
>
> John 10:11–13 NLT

Jesus continues to expound on his role as the Good Shepherd. He distin-
guishes himself from the sort of sheepherder who's not doing a good
job—aka the hired hand. This is a guy who took the job probably as a last
resort and couldn't care less about the sheep. The hired hand probably doesn't
count the sheep at night, he certainly doesn't know their names, and if there's
real danger (like a wolf), he will run off to protect himself and let the sheep
take care of themselves. He's only in it for the money.

Again, that was a description of many of the religious leaders of that day.
Unfortunately, there are still "shepherds" like that nowadays—people in church
leadership who don't really care about the congregations they're being paid
to serve. They're just in it for the money.

The good news is that Jesus is your Good Shepherd. Even if you should fall
victim to a bad shepherd at some point in time (and most people do eventually), that is in no way a reflection on Jesus. In fact, it can simply be a reminder
that there really is only one Good Shepherd, and that's Jesus. The more you
get to know your Good Shepherd, the more you'll learn to recognize Jesus's
voice, and the better you'll become at knowing what's true and what's not.
You won't be led astray by a bad shepherd.

My Prayer

Dear God,
Thank you for giving me my Good Shepherd. Help me to know
his voice and to respond quickly when I hear it.
Amen.

Final Word ·

> The LORD is good, a strong refuge when trouble comes. He is
> close to those who trust in him.
>
> Nahum 1:7 NLT

Stone for the Journey · · · · · · · · · · · · · · · · · ·

> I will tune my ears into the voice of my Good Shepherd.

 ## Day 3 • All for Us

Words from the Rock · · · · · · · · · · · · · · · · · · ·

> I am the Good Shepherd. I know my own sheep and my own
> sheep know me. In the same way, the Father knows me and I
> know the Father. I put the sheep before myself, sacrificing myself
> if necessary. . . . This is why the Father loves me: because I freely
> lay down my life. And so I am free to take it up again. No one
> takes it from me. I lay it down of my own free will. I have the
> right to lay it down; I also have the right to take it up again. I
> received this authority personally from my Father.
>
> John 10:14–15, 17–18 Message

What's the greatest gift anyone can give? Jesus tells us it's the ultimate sacrifice—to give up a life for someone else—and that's exactly what he's going to do. He will give all he has to give so we can have all he's promised us. It's no small thing. He surrenders his life so we can have eternal life. What a gift! Yet it's a gift that so many take for granted. Or worse, they reject it.

Maybe we take Jesus for granted because we really aren't so very different from sheep. Imagine a young man who has always wanted to be a shepherd. He practiced herding lambs as a child. He's honed his rock-pitching and spear-throwing skills (to scare away predators), and he's gotten into great shape so he can easily keep up with the sheep. He's even researched the best grassy slopes and cleanest streams. He finally gets his shepherding job and takes it very seriously. He always counts the sheep. He gives them names. He tends to their wounds. He even sings them to sleep at night.

But one dark night, a hungry lion decides to attack the herd. As the lion approaches the sleeping sheep, the shepherd throws rocks and spears at it, and finally, just in the nick of time, he tackles the lion. He manages to kill the beast with his knife, but in the midst of the battle the shepherd himself is killed. The sheep continue sleeping, unaware of what's just happened, with no idea of the price of their safety.

Jesus doesn't want you to be like a dozing sheep, oblivious to what it cost to protect you. Instead, he wants you to come to him, spend time with him, and be like the happy sheep, answering quickly when you hear your shepherd's voice.

My Prayer

Dear God,

I don't want to be like one of those sleeping sheep. I want to always appreciate the price you paid by allowing Jesus to die for me. Thank you for giving your all for me.

Amen.

Final Word

And I heard a loud voice from the throne saying, "Now the dwelling of God is with men, and he will live with them. They will be his people, and God himself will be with them and be their God."

Revelation 21:3 NIV

Stone for the Journey

Jesus gave his life so that I could have life.

 ## Day 4 • Safety Zone

Words from the Rock

I told you already, but you did not believe. The miracles I do in my Father's name show who I am. But you don't believe, because you are not my sheep. My sheep listen to my voice; I know them, and they follow me. I give them eternal life, and they will never die, and no one can steal them out of my hand. My Father gave my sheep to me. He is greater than all, and no person can steal my sheep out of my Father's hand. The Father and I are one.

John 10:25–30 NCV

Jesus is responding to some of the "educated" Jews who are questioning him for the umpteenth time. Jesus probably knows that they don't really want answers and that they're not actually seeking the truth. It's clear from the previous verses that they're more interested in slamming Jesus than anything. In fact, they've just accused him of being demonized or insane. Their goal is obvious—they want to put him down.

When people put others down, it's usually because they hope to make themselves look bigger or better. In this case, these guys probably want to appear scholarly and superior to the onlookers, some of whom actually believe Jesus and want to hear more of his teachings. Jesus, just like his Father, does not waste anything. He uses this as an opportunity to teach about who he really is.

He makes it clear that the guys hassling him are not his sheep (his followers). If they were, they wouldn't be saying such nasty things to him. They wouldn't be so cynical and mean. Jesus points out, once again, that his sheep listen to his voice because they know him and he knows them. He also makes it clear that his sheep will be protected. In essence, they're in a safety zone. No one is going to be able to come in and hurt them.

Jesus promises his sheep (and us) eternal life, and he assures us that as long as we remain in his safety zone, no one can steal us away—not even cruel people who would attempt to fill our heads with lies. We remain safe with Jesus because God is in control and because he and Jesus are one.

My Prayer ·

> *Dear God,*
>
> *I realize that when people put you down, it's because they don't know you. I'm so thankful I know you! And I'm thankful that you'll protect me from those who would try to steal my heart from you.*
>
> *Amen.*

Final Word ·

Though I am surrounded by troubles, you will protect me from the anger of my enemies. You reach out your hand, and the power of your right hand saves me.

Psalm 138:7 NLT

Stone for the Journey ·

I am safe because God knows me and I know him.

 ## Day 5 · Relationship Reflection

Words from the Rock ·

Do not believe me unless I do what my Father does. But if I do it, even though you do not believe me, believe the miracles, that you may know and understand that the Father is in me, and I in the Father.

John 10:37-38 NIV

It's really amazing how many chances Jesus gives the Pharisees and religious leaders to believe in him. Despite the fact that they are cruel and demeaning—even accusing him of blasphemy, which is the same as hating God—and despite the fact that they are plotting to kill him, Jesus continues to speak the truth to them. And here's the good news: a few of them actually got it. Oh, it didn't really sink in until after Jesus was killed and rose from the dead, but eventually a few of them figured it out, and you can bet they were sorry for how they'd treated him.

Jesus is telling the Pharisees that they *shouldn't* believe him—unless he does what the Father does and reflects a clear image of who God is. Of course, all Jesus does is represent God's love and mercy, and a lot of his followers already get that. But it's interesting that he says this to the Pharisees. It's almost like a challenge to them. Maybe it was reverse psychology.

Maybe Jesus is trying to remind us about our actions too. Could he be telling us that sometimes we don't act like we really believe him? And when we don't act like a believer, why should anyone think we belong to God? We should be able to see God at work in each other. If we don't, we might need to wonder why. Not that we should judge each other, but if a person claims to be a Christian and yet acts completely opposite of that, it could be that there's a connection problem.

A connected relationship with God miraculously changes who we are. That's because God transforms how we think and how we interact with others. Qualities like love and forgiveness begin to flow more naturally through us, and people around us begin to notice these changes. That's what Jesus is saying: "Look at my life and you'll see that the Father and I are one." He wants you to be able to say the same.

My Prayer

Dear God,
Help me to reflect who you are to those around me. I know I need to be tightly connected to you to become more like you. Help me to be who you want me to be so I can reach out to others. Amen.

Final Word

Don't forget to help others and to share your possessions with them. This too is like offering a sacrifice that pleases God.

Hebrews 13:16 CEV

Stone for the Journey

When I keep my eyes on God, his love reflects through me.

Week 34

 ## Day 1 · Confidence

Words from the Rock ·

> There are twelve hours of daylight every day. During the day people can walk safely. They can see because they have the light of this world. But at night there is danger of stumbling because they have no light.
>
> John 11:9–10 NLT

This seems like such an obvious statement. Of course it's easier to walk during the daylight hours, and yes, you might stumble around in the darkness of night. So?

When Jesus says this to his disciples, it's in response to their concern for his safety. He has just informed them that they'll be traveling to visit a sick friend. Their destination is the same place where the religious leaders recently attempted to get Jesus put to death by stoning. His disciples cannot believe Jesus is willing to return to that town. Isn't he concerned for his safety? Yet his answer to them is fairly nonchalant and seems almost irrelevant—he's talking about walking in the daytime versus walking at night. What is he saying? What does it really mean?

Jesus is simply saying it's not nighttime yet, but he's not talking about physical nighttime. He's talking about spiritual nighttime, a kind of darkness that's coming when it will seem like all the lights have gone out. He's talking about the time that's coming when he will be arrested, beaten, put to death, and in the tomb for three days. Those will be some very dark days for everyone. But Jesus knows it's not time for that yet, so he's not the least bit worried about his safety. His confidence is in God—and God's perfect timing. He knows that he's in his Father's hands. And he's comfortable with that. It's like walking somewhere on a warm, sunny day, when all is well.

It should be no different for us. When we remain in God's will, we can confidently walk in the light too. No fear. Sure, there might come dark times, just like there were for Jesus, but we'll always have that light to guide us. Even when we're surrounded by darkness and all we can see is that small light at the end of the tunnel, we know which direction to walk, and in time we'll make it to the other side.

My Prayer

> *Dear God,*
>
> *I want to remain in your will. Please show me how to be better at doing that. Then help me to walk confidently in your light. Amen.*

Final Word

> For I hold you by your right hand—I, the LORD your God. And I say to you, "Don't be afraid. I am here to help you."
>
> Isaiah 41:13 NLT

Stone for the Journey

> God's light reassures me that I'm walking in his will.

Day 2 • Sneak Preview

Words from the Rock

> I am the resurrection and the life. Those who believe in me will have life even if they die. And everyone who lives and believes in me will never die.
>
> John 11:25-26 NCV

Jesus says this to his friend Martha, but his words are for everyone. Martha is grieving the death of her brother, Lazarus, but Jesus is reassuring her that Lazarus will be fine. Her natural assumption is that Jesus means Lazarus will be fine in the afterlife, but that's not very comforting to her right now while her brother's death is so fresh in her mind. Several days ago, while Lazarus was still alive, she'd hoped Jesus would arrive in time to heal him.

But Jesus has something else in mind. Something far bigger than Martha or anyone else can imagine. After Lazarus has been dead and in his tomb for four days, Jesus miraculously raises him from the dead. This miracle is unlike anything Jesus has done up to this point, and people are stunned and amazed. As a result, many of them become true believers in Jesus! But a few doubters run off to tattle this news to the Pharisees.

What the people don't fully grasp is that this miracle is a like a sneak preview of what God is going to do with Jesus before long. Jesus will soon be killed and laid in a tomb, but three days later God will miraculously raise him from the dead. Jesus wants to prepare his followers for this by leaving this vivid memory of Lazarus in their minds. He wants them to get that he is the resurrection and the life, and whoever believes in him will have eternal life!

My Prayer

Dear God,

Sometimes it's hard to grasp that Jesus died and rose from the dead, but I do believe it, and because of that miracle, I believe I can live forever too. Thank you!

Amen.

Final Word

All of us who are still alive will be taken up into the clouds together with them to meet the Lord in the sky. From that time on we will all be with the Lord forever.

1 Thessalonians 4:17 CEV

Stone for the Journey

The gift of eternity is mine because of Jesus.

Day 3 • Total Trust

Words from the Rock •

> The time has come for the Son of Man to receive his glory. I tell you the truth, a grain of wheat must fall to the ground and die to make many seeds. But if it never dies, it remains only a single seed. Those who love their lives will lose them, but those who hate their lives in this world will keep true life forever.
>
> John 12:23–25 NCV

Jesus is predicting his death, and the day is getting closer. He uses the image of a grain of wheat. Now if you look at a grain of wheat, it doesn't look like much, but it has the potential to produce a whole lot more grain. In fact, over a period of years, one single grain could produce an entire crop—millions of grains. To do this, the grain must die. It has to go back into the earth, and the hard shell that protects the grain has to be broken and deteriorate so germination begins. After that the grain can actually grow into a plant.

Likewise, Jesus knows he has to die and come back to life so his followers can become firm in their faith and go out and tell others. He's like that one grain that falls to the ground and dies but then rises again to produce more grains (more believers), which over the course of time will number into the millions. Jesus trusts God his Father implicitly (to the point of laying down his life) in order to bring life to others.

Jesus takes this a step further by telling his disciples they need to have the same attitude about themselves—they need to trust God enough to be willing to give up their hold on their own lives and follow him. He tells them that if they love their lives, they will lose them. All except Judas take his words seriously because they trust Jesus and love him more than life. In fact, ten of them will be killed for their faith. But their deaths will inspire others to believe, and like the seed that dies, they will become part of the miracle of millions coming to faith. That is ultimate trust.

But Jesus's words aren't only for his disciples. He knows that if we love our own lives more than we love him, we'll ultimately lose our faith—and him. Because he doesn't want to lose us, he encourages us to love him with all we have, even unto death, and he knows that takes total trust.

My Prayer

Dear God,

I probably won't have to physically lay down my life for you, but help me to have the kind of total trust that allows me to love you with 100 percent of my being. I want to love you more than I love my own life.

Amen.

Final Word

Those who obey God's word truly show how completely they love him. That is how we know we are living in him.

1 John 2:5 NLT

Stone for the Journey

I trust God enough to love him more than anything in this life.

 ## Day 4 · Devoted Disciples

Words from the Rock

Anyone who wants to be my disciple must follow me, because my servants must be where I am. And the Father will honor anyone who serves me.

John 12:26 NLT

Again Jesus is talking to his disciples about total commitment here, telling them they must follow him and stay with him wherever he goes. He's aware that his death is just around the corner now, but he also knows that his disciples won't be killed with him—their time to die hasn't come yet. So what does he mean? It seems that he's trying to convey that, even after his death and resurrection, they can still have a relationship with him.

Naturally, the disciples don't get this. Not yet. But Jesus is trying to reassure them that they can continue to be with him and to serve him even though he'll be gone. And because he's Jesus and God's Son, he'll be able to deliver on that promise.

That promise isn't only for the disciples who were with him that day. He invites anyone to follow him and to become his disciple. So what is a disciple, and how do we become one? Disciples are ones who *discipline* themselves to become students and devoted imitators of a person they love and admire. Disciples conform themselves to their leader and are willing to change how they think and live in order to serve and be more like that person.

Jesus wants all of his followers to become his devoted disciples. He wants us to spend time with him, learn from him, and imitate him in how we love and forgive others. He wants us to obey him and be completely sold out to him. He promises that when that happens, the Father will honor us.

My Prayer

Dear God,

Teach me how to be your disciple. Show me ways that I can follow you and be with you. I want you to change me into someone like you.

Amen.

Final Word

Tune your ears to wisdom, and concentrate on understanding. Cry out for insight, and ask for understanding. . . . Then you will understand what it means to fear the LORD, and you will gain knowledge of God.

Proverbs 2:2–3, 5 NLT

Stone for the Journey

I commit myself to being a devoted disciple.

Day 5 · Children of Light

Words from the Rock · · · · · · · · · · · · · · · · ·

For a brief time still, the light is among you. Walk by the light you have so darkness doesn't destroy you. If you walk in darkness, you don't know where you're going. As you have the light, believe in the light. Then the light will be within you, and shining through your lives. You'll be children of light.

John 12:35–36 Message

Jesus has already made it known that he's the Light of the World. His disciples totally get this by now, not only in their heads but in their hearts as well. For more than three years, they've been experiencing Jesus's form of light up close and personal. Surely they remember what it was like before Jesus walked into their lives. Most likely their world was a dark and hopeless place. And thanks to the state of the Jewish religion at that time, they had probably given up on ever being united with God. They probably just went about their daily tasks, focusing only on what they needed to survive, to eke out a living—day in and day out, drearily trudging along.

When Jesus befriended them, it must have been the brightest day of their lives. And as they listened to his teachings and witnessed his miracles, it must have gotten even brighter. They were no longer hopeless. They had a purpose, and it all revolved around their relationship with Jesus.

But then he tells them that he's going to be killed and he'll no longer be with them on earth. Do you think they feel the darkness creeping back into their lives? Do they realize they're about to go through a brief period of darkness? That's what separation from Jesus feels like—cold, lonely, empty, heavy, depressing, confusing . . . darkness. Hope dies, the heart grows weary, life loses its color and its purpose, and we begin to stumble.

Fortunately for the disciples, that darkness would last only three days, but it must have felt like forever. Perhaps that time was a vivid reminder to them that they never wanted to live in the darkness again. Who would?

You don't have to live in the darkness either. Jesus promises that when you believe in him, his light will shine right through you. And what happens when Jesus's light is in you? You can see without stumbling. You can get where you're going without getting lost. And others can look at you and see God.

My Prayer

Dear God,

Please shine your light through me. I don't want to live in dark-ness—not ever! I need your light to show me where to go and how to live, and to bring warmth and color and life.

Amen.

Final Word

Never again will night appear, and no one who lives there will ever need a lamp or the sun. The Lord God will be their light, and they will rule forever.

Revelation 22:5 CEV

Stone for the Journey

Jesus's light gives me life.

Week 35

Day 1 • God's Light

Words from the Rock

Whoever believes in me is really believing in the One who sent me. Whoever sees me sees the One who sent me. I have come as light into the world so that whoever believes in me would not stay in darkness.

John 12:44–46 NCV

Jesus has a short amount of earthly time left, and he really wants to drive some things home. Yes, he's said things very similar to this before, but he knows his disciples (and everyone else) don't always get the real meaning the first time they hear it. In fact, that's why his disciples memorized his words, so they could keep them in their hearts and think on them later. Then they could share these life-giving words with others after Jesus was gone, and they could eventually write them down for future believers to hear and hopefully to memorize as well.

Again Jesus wants to make it crystal clear that when we believe in him, we believe in the Father. He and God are one. You can't have one without the other. You love Jesus, you love God. You serve Jesus, you serve God. They go hand in hand—there's no separating them. Jesus wants us to know that he's connected to the Father, and we are connected as well because of him. Nothing stands between us and God.

In Jesus's day, the religious leaders drove a wedge between people and God. They set up a legal barrier that made it difficult for people to know who he was. But Jesus tore down that barrier by saying, "You see me, you see God." No more middleman.

Once again Jesus announces that he is the Light of the World, a light sent down from heaven to help us. When we're linked with Jesus, we don't live in darkness anymore. As a result, we have no reason to be stumbling around. If we do stumble, it might simply be a reminder that we're not letting God's light shine down on us as much as he'd like—as much as we need it to.

My Prayer

> *Dear God,*
>
> *Thank you for sending Jesus so I can have a relationship with you that will last forever. Thank you for your light. I welcome it into my life.*
>
> *Amen.*

Final Word

> For I am convinced that neither death nor life, neither angels nor demons, neither the present nor the future, nor any powers, neither height nor depth, nor anything else in all creation, will be able to separate us from the love of God that is in Christ Jesus our Lord.

> Romans 8:38–39 NIV

Stone for the Journey ·

When I see Jesus, I see God.

 # Day 2 • Words of Life

Words from the Rock ·

> As for the person who hears my words but does not keep them,
> I do not judge him. For I did not come to judge the world, but to
> save it. There is a judge for the one who rejects me and does not
> accept my words; that very word which I spoke will condemn
> him at the last day. For I did not speak of my own accord, but the
> Father who sent me commanded me what to say and how to say
> it. I know that his command leads to eternal life. So whatever I
> say is just what the Father has told me to say.
>
> John 12:47–50 NIV

If a guy is starving and you offer him food, but he says "No thanks" and then dies of starvation, would you be to blame? By the same token, if a girl is dying of thirst and you offer her water, but she refuses to drink and then dies of dehydration, would you be to blame? Would their deaths be your fault? Could a judge convict you as a murderer? Of course not! You tried to help them, but they refused your help. They brought their deaths upon themselves.

It's not any different when Jesus offers us the words of life. If we reject his words, if we refuse to listen and believe, isn't it our own fault if we never receive eternal life? Jesus says he didn't come to judge the world. Just the opposite—he came to save the world. That means *everyone* in the world. His desire is that every single person who inhabits the planet will hear his words, and that every single person will receive them for what they are—words of life.

But he can't force anyone to do that, and he won't judge anyone for rejecting his words. That's not his job. Besides, he doesn't need to judge anyone, because those of us who reject his words of life seal our own fate. Just like the guy who refuses food or the girl who refuses water, each of us is responsible for the negative consequences of a bad decision—our own death. Jesus gives all of us lots of chances, right down to our last dying breath, to rethink that decision. He doesn't want anyone to miss out.

My Prayer

Dear God,

    Thank you for giving me your words of life. Please help me to always cling to them, believe in them, and share them with others. Amen.

Final Word

I have told you these things so that you will be filled with my joy. Yes, your joy will overflow!

John 15:11 NLT

Stone for the Journey

Jesus's words fill me with life.

Day 3 • Servant Heart

Words from the Rock

Do you understand what I was doing? You call me "Teacher" and "Lord," and you are right, because that's what I am. And since I, your Lord and Teacher, have washed your feet, you ought to wash each other's feet. I have given you an example to follow. Do as I have done to you. I tell you the truth, slaves are not greater than their master. Nor is the messenger more important than the one who sends the message. Now that you know these things, God will bless you for doing them.

John 13:12–17 NLT

Jesus is God—God come to earth—to be light and life and truth, and to show us the way to God's kingdom, where he rules and reigns forever. Yet Jesus gets down on his knees and washes his disciples' dirty feet.

In Jesus's day, it was customary to have guests' feet washed when they came to visit, but it was a job performed by the least of servants or slaves. The purpose of foot washing was twofold. First, it was good etiquette and a way to honor guests. Secondly, people wore sandals and walked on dusty roads, so their feet were dirty, and having them washed was simply good hygiene and a way to keep extra dirt out of the home. Even so, it wasn't the kind of task that servants were eager to do.

But Jesus tells his disciples, who are clearly uncomfortable seeing him down on his knees scrubbing their grubby toes, that he's doing this as an example. He's leaving them another vivid image—something to remember when he's gone—about how important it is for them to follow his example by being servants to each other.

Jesus was a slave to love—he came to serve. He put everyone's needs above his own, even to the point of dying on the cross. The reason he did this was simply because he loves us. He served out of a pure heart of love. And he wants us to imitate him by serving those around us. Maybe this means helping someone else to get ahead instead of pushing your way to the top. Or it could be listening to someone who needs a friend. If you ask, God can show you, and if you're willing, God can put you to work.

My Prayer

Dear God,

Thank you for loving me so much that you lowered yourself to serve me by going to the cross. Increase my love for you and others so I can imitate your servant's heart.

Amen.

Final Word

Always set a good example for others. Be sincere and serious when you teach. Use clean language that no one can criticize. Do this, and your enemies will be too ashamed to say anything against you.

Titus 2:7–8 CEV

Stone for the Journey

I learn to serve by imitating Jesus.

Day 4 • Full Disclosure

Words from the Rock · · · · · · · · · · · · · · · · · ·

> I am not saying these things to all of you; I know the ones I have chosen. But this fulfills the Scripture that says, "The one who eats my food has turned against me." I tell you this beforehand, so that when it happens you will believe that I Am the Messiah. I tell you the truth, anyone who welcomes my messenger is welcoming me, and anyone who welcomes me is welcoming the Father who sent me.
>
> John 13:18–20 NLT

Jesus previously implied that one of his disciples—one of the men he has loved and served—will betray him, causing him to be arrested and eventually put to death. In fact, that is about to happen. Judas Iscariot is planning to betray Jesus for thirty pieces of silver, yet he's sitting at the table eating with Jesus, listening to him talk, and acting like nothing is wrong.

Now Jesus, rather than calling Judas onto the carpet and pointing him out as a low-life, conniving jerk, simply makes a full disclosure to the other disciples by reminding them that long ago the prophets predicted all this would happen. He wants to make things perfectly clear so that when Judas does what he's about to do, the other disciples will remember Jesus's words and understand why it happened like that. Jesus doesn't want to leave them in the dark about these events, and he wants Judas's betrayal to be just one more thing that assures the disciples and everyone else that he really is who he says—the Messiah, God's Son, their salvation. No surprises. Full disclosure.

Jesus also wants his disciples to know that he doesn't categorize them with Judas. He knows who they are, and he trusts them with the message he's given to them. He knows they'll be faithful with his message even after he's gone, and he tells them that his Father will be so pleased with them that he'll welcome them into his kingdom.

In the same way, God will welcome you when you share his message with others. He'll also partner with you by showing you unique opportunities right there in your everyday life. It all starts with a willing heart.

My Prayer · · · · · · · · · · · · · · · · · · ·

Dear God,

Thank you for showing yourself to me. Please write your words on my heart and shine your light through me so those who see me will see you at work in me.

Amen.

Final Word ·

The world and its desires pass away, but the man who does the will of God lives forever.

1 John 2:17 NIV

Stone for the Journey · · · · · · · · · · · · · · ·

When I reveal who God is, I become his messenger.

 ## Day 5 • Love's Brand

Words from the Rock · · · · · · · · · · · · · · ·

I give you a new command: Love each other. You must love each other as I have loved you. All people will know that you are my followers if you love each other.

John 13:34–35 NCV

Jesus has already made many strong statements about love. He's told us to love our neighbors the same way we love ourselves. He's even told us to love our enemies. As simple as those commands might sound, they're not easy. Loving others as much as you love yourself doesn't come naturally. And loving your enemies—well, that's downright hard.

Now Jesus is giving a new commandment that really takes the idea of loving others up a few notches. He challenges his disciples (and all who would follow him) to love people the same way he loves people. Think about it—the way Jesus loved the world was to give up everything he had by leaving heaven and coming to earth. He became a servant to everyone by helping and healing and teaching. Then he showed the ultimate sacrifice of love by laying down his life so we could all be forgiven and received into his kingdom. Love just doesn't get any better than that. It's no small thing that he wants us to follow his example by loving others like he did.

How do we do that? First of all, we have to invite Jesus, the author of love, to lead us. That means we make sure that above all else, we're receiving his love and loving him in return, because it's out of our relationship with him that we can begin to love others. Then we need to remember the love basics that Jesus taught. "Love your neighbor as yourself" (Matt. 22:39 NIV) means loving others (including our enemies) in the same way we want to be loved—the same way Jesus loves us. That means our love is unconditional, kind, honest, energetic, selfless, genuine, humble, generous, thoughtful, and so on. And don't forget that love always goes hand in hand with forgiveness. Love without forgiveness isn't love.

When we live out this forgiving kind of love, it's like we're wearing a brand— a brand that shows we belong to God!

My Prayer

Dear God,

Thank you for loving me! I want to love others like that. Help me to learn from you so my love will remind people of your love. Amen.

Final Word

Love is kind and patient, never jealous, boastful, proud, or rude. Love isn't selfish or quick tempered. It doesn't keep a record of wrongs that others do. Love rejoices in the truth, but not in evil. Love is always supportive, loyal, hopeful, and trusting.

1 Corinthians 13:4–7 CEV

Stone for the Journey

When I love like Jesus, people see God at work.

Week 36

Day 1 • Second Chances

Words from the Rock ·

> Simon Peter asked Jesus, "Lord, where are you going?"
>
> Jesus answered, "Where I am going you cannot follow now, but you will follow later."
>
> Peter asked, "Lord, why can't I follow you now? I am ready to die for you!"
>
> Jesus answered, "Are you ready to die for me? I tell you the truth, before the rooster crows, you will say three times that you don't know me."
>
> John 13:36–38 NCV

Remember when Peter answered Jesus's question "Who do you say I am?" exactly right? Jesus was so pleased that he told Peter, "I'll build my church on you." Now Jesus is telling him that, before morning comes, Peter will deny him not once, but three times! Poor Peter. How do you think that made him feel? Or maybe he didn't believe it. After all, he loved Jesus with his whole heart. How was it possible he could deny him three times? Yet Jesus was right—Peter did deny him three times. Sure, it was out of fear that he too might be arrested and tortured, but the fact remains.

The real reason Peter denied Jesus was because he was operating on his own strength, and that was not enough, especially when times were beginning to get hard. But later on, after Jesus's death and resurrection, Jesus would return to give Peter and the rest of his followers a form of super strength (aka the Holy Spirit). After that, Peter would not only remain totally faithful to Jesus, he would also become that spiritual rock Jesus had described before—and an important part of the foundation of the early church.

Jesus gives second chances, and third chances, and as many chances as we need because he knows that, like Peter, we will blow it. We might even deny knowing Jesus when we're backed into a corner. But if we return to Jesus, like Peter did, and if we allow Jesus to empower us with his Spirit, our faith will grow stronger, and we'll learn from our mistakes. Then Jesus will be able to use us in ways we can't even begin to imagine.

My Prayer

Dear God,
    I don't ever want to deny you, but if I do, please remind me that you give second chances. Please strengthen my faith by the power of your Holy Spirit so I can serve you wholeheartedly.
    Amen.

Final Word

If we confess our sins, he is faithful and just and will forgive us our sins and purify us from all unrighteousness.

1 John 1:9 NIV

Stone for the Journey

When I need it, God gives a second chance.

 ## Day 2 · Home Sweet Home

Words from the Rock

Do not let your hearts be troubled. Trust in God; trust also in me. In my Father's house are many rooms; if it were not so, I would have told you. I am going there to prepare a place for you. And if I go and prepare a place for you, I will come back and take you to be with me that you also may be where I am. You know the way to the place where I am going.

John 14:1–4 NIV

These have to be some of the most reassuring words ever spoken. Jesus gives a priceless promise that can carry us through the tough times. He gives us his word that we'll be with him in heaven someday. But first he tells us not to let our hearts be troubled, which basically means don't be afraid and don't worry. Jesus knows we'll all face some hard times, times when it will be easy to be consumed with fear and worry. But he tells us to trust God and to trust him, and then he tells us a little about the place he's getting ready for us.

Jesus doesn't go into much detail about what heaven will be like. But consider the vast creativity of God and how beautifully he's made the earth, and consider some of our favorite places on this planet (like amazing mountains, gorgeous beaches, mystical rainforests, or tropical paradises). If we multiply those natural wonders many times over (because heaven will totally outshine earth), we might begin to have a tiny speck of an idea of how incredible our next home will be.

And the promise doesn't end there. No, Jesus wants us to know that he will personally escort us to this place. How or when this will happen is still a mystery, but it's reassuring to know that Jesus isn't going to leave us dangling between this life and the next. All we need to do is to love, trust, and serve him until that time comes.

My Prayer

Dear God,
 Thank you that you have a place waiting for me in your house. I admit that I can't even imagine how great that will be, but I trust you and know I won't be disappointed.
 Amen.

Final Word

Our bodies are like tents that we live in here on earth. But when these tents are destroyed, we know that God will give each of us a place to live. These homes will not be buildings that someone has made, but they are in heaven and will last forever.

2 Corinthians 5:1 CEV

Stone for the Journey

I will trust God for this life and the one that's yet to come.

Day 3 · Way, Truth, Life

Words from the Rock ·

I am the way, and the truth, and the life. The only way to the Father is through me. If you really knew me, you would know my Father, too. But now you do know him, and you have seen him.

John 14:6–7 NCV

Three rather ordinary-sounding words—*way*, *truth*, *life*. Yet when you connect these three little words to Jesus, they become everything. Really, what more do we need?

Jesus is the way. He's going to get us where we need to go. Once we believe in him, it's like we've climbed aboard this incredible ship that will transport us to God. Sure, there could be some rough seas, and it might not always look like he's taking us where we want to go, but he will get us to the right destination. And it'll be a voyage we'll never forget.

Jesus is the truth. We live in a world filled with tricksters. Deception and lies come at us on a regular basis, and sometimes it's hard to know just who's really telling you the truth. Perhaps it's enticing but false claims made by marketing gurus trying to sell their "latest greatest," an enemy posing as a friend, or someone trying to scam us on the Internet. But Jesus is the truth. His love and forgiveness are authentic. We can take him at his word and never be disappointed. He is the real deal.

Jesus is the life. Without Jesus, we're not really living. Oh, we might be breathing and eating and walking, but we won't be truly alive. Jesus is like an incredible life transfusion that restores us and invigorates us to a place where we really engage, where we become passionate, and where we truly experience the fullness of life God planned for us from the beginning. That's really living!

My Prayer ·

Dear God,

Thank you for being all that I need—the perfect formula. You're the way to get me there, the truth I can count on, and the life that energizes me into action.

Amen.

Final Word · · · · · · · · · · · · · · · · · ·

What you hope for is kept safe for you in heaven. You first heard about this hope when you believed the true message, which is the good news.

Colossians 1:5 CEV

Stone for the Journey ·

Jesus gives me all I need—the way, the truth, and the life.

 # Day 4 • Promising Promise

Words from the Rock · · · · · · · · · · · · · · · · · ·

Believe me when I say that I am in the Father and the Father is in me. Or believe because of the miracles I have done. I tell you the truth, whoever believes in me will do the same things that I do. Those who believe will do even greater things than these, because I am going to the Father. And if you ask for anything in my name, I will do it for you so that the Father's glory will be shown through the Son. If you ask me for anything in my name, I will do it.

John 14:11–14 NCV

Can you believe that you could do the kinds of things Jesus did during his earthly lifetime? Or even things that are greater? Do you think you could make a blind person see, make a wheelchair-bound person walk, or feed everyone in your school's cafeteria with your brown-bag lunch? It seems unlikely, doesn't it? Yet, as impossible as that sounds, Jesus says it could happen—if you believe in him.

Incredibly, it did happen for Jesus's disciples. After his death and resurrection, he returned to give the disciples his Holy Spirit, and suddenly miracles were happening left and right. Everyone who witnessed these things, including the disciples, was totally blown away. Thousands of people came to faith. It must have been fun.

Still, you have to wonder, can that possibly happen now? Is this promise really meant for everyone? You have to put it in perspective. Jesus says many times that his promises aren't limited to his disciples or followers more than two thousand years ago; they're for everyone throughout the ages.

So the conclusion has to be that miracles *could* happen. In fact, there are many modern-day miracles. Some of the most amazing ones happen in struggling third-world countries, where people are more desperate and therefore their faith might be stronger. Even so, we need to remember and cling to this promise: Jesus says that whatever we ask in his name, he will do. The key here is to ask in his name—ask according to who he is, according to his will. That means we have to be tightly connected with him, letting his life be lived out in us. That's when anything can happen!

My Prayer

> Dear God,
>   *I want my faith to grow, and I believe you can do great things through me. That means I need to stick close to you, and I need you to live your life in me.*
>   *Amen.*

Final Word

> Surely your goodness and unfailing love will pursue me all the days of my life, and I will live in the house of the Lord forever.
>
> Psalm 23:6 NLT

Stone for the Journey

> With God's help, I can do anything.

Day 5 • The Only Way

Words from the Rock · · · · · · · · · · · · · · · · · ·

I am the way, and the truth, and the life. The only way to the Father is through me. If you really knew me, you would know my Father, too. But now you do know him, and you have seen him.

John 14:6–7 NCV

Sometimes it's hard to grasp how tightly connected Jesus and God are—so intricately intertwined that they are inseparable; they are one. Maybe you're wondering, if they are one, why do we need both? Basically it's because God wanted to get our attention and we weren't listening. In fact, the human race had kind of tuned God out.

To understand this better, imagine you're a beekeeper. Okay, it's a stretch, but just go with it. Now imagine you own the only beehive in the world, but you know that all your bees are going to be wiped out by a rare disease. Your bees make great honey, and you really love them and don't want them to die. If only they would listen to you, they could change some of their bee habits and survive. So you stand over their hive telling them over and over what they must do to prevent their doom, but they don't understand you. Or maybe they're not listening, or maybe they're as busy as bees and totally oblivious to any danger. How do you communicate to them? How do you keep them from perishing?

What if you became one of them? What if you had the power to transform yourself into a bee? Then you could go inside the hive and talk directly to the bees. Speaking Bee-glish, you could make them understand your concerns.

Now, as silly as this bee metaphor sounds, it's a bit like God's decision to send Jesus to earth. Jesus was part of God, and God knew that if he became one of us, he could get our attention. Jesus became God's ambassador, the way to connect us to God. So how connected do you feel? How much more connected would you like to be?

My Prayer ·

Dear God,

Help me to grasp that you and Jesus are one, and that you poured yourself into Jesus so you could pour yourself into me.

Amen.

Final Word · · · · · · · · · · · · · · · ·

For God so loved the world that he gave his one and only Son, that whoever believes in him shall not perish but have eternal life.

John 3:16 NIV

Stone for the Journey ·

God and Jesus are one, and they want to be one with me.

Week 37

Day 1 · One and the Same

Words from the Rock · · · · · · · · · · · · · ·

Anyone who has seen me has seen the Father! So why are you asking me to show him to you? Don't you believe that I am in the Father and the Father is in me? The words I speak are not my own, but my Father who lives in me does his work through me. Just believe that I am in the Father and the Father is in me. Or at least believe because of the work you have seen me do.

John 14:9–11 NLT

What do you think you'd do if you had only a week to live? Maybe your first response would be to do something crazy and reckless, like skydiving or bungee jumping or drag racing. Or maybe you'd go on some wild spending spree and live large. Or you might take some time to be alone to contemplate. But before long, you'd probably want to focus on people and relationships. You might need to tell someone you love them or that you're sorry, or you might need to forgive someone. You'd probably want to really talk to the ones you love the most—to speak openly and from the heart.

If you knew your days were numbered, you'd probably want to connect on a much deeper level with anyone who meant anything to you, especially with the people you truly love. You'd want to make sure that your friends and loved ones understood who you were and what mattered to you, and in the same way, you'd want to understand them. Most likely, you would want to leave this world knowing that your relationships were in super good shape.

The verses above are words Jesus speaks just days before his death. You can hear the urgency in his message. More than anything, he wants to be sure his loved ones really know him. He wants them to understand how tightly connected he is to God so that when he's gone, his followers will realize that their connection to God is because of Jesus. He wants them to know that it's a connection that cannot be broken.

Those words are spoken to you too. Jesus invites you—in the same way he invited his disciples—to become partners with him and his Father.

My Prayer

Dear God,

It's easy to take relationships for granted. Please remind me of the importance of having a good one with you, and how it impacts my relationships with others.

Amen.

Final Word

A body is made up of many parts, and each of them has its own use. That's how it is with us. There are many of us, but we each are part of the body of Christ, as well as part of one another.

Romans 12:4–5 CEV

Stone for the Journey

I'm made strong by my relationship with Jesus.

Day 2 • Humble Entrances

Words from the Rock ·

Go over to the village across from you. You'll find a donkey tethered there, her colt with her. Untie her and bring them to me. If anyone asks what you're doing, say, "The Master needs them!" He will send them with you.

Matthew 21:2–3 Message

Not long before Jesus dies, he makes a historical ride into the city of Jerusalem. Now, remember that Jesus is the Son of God (the same God who created and rules the universe), and no mightier king has ever walked the earth. So how would a king of this magnitude enter the religious capital of the world? Nowadays an important ruler might arrive in a long motorcade of shiny limousines, escorted by security and motorcycle police. In Jesus's time, a powerful king might arrive on a majestic white stallion, surrounded by his army, with trumpets and flags and fanfare.

Yet what does Jesus tell his disciples to bring for his ride into Jerusalem? A donkey. And not even a grown donkey, but the colt of a donkey. Now keep in mind that, according to some historians, Jesus was taller than average, which means his legs were probably rather long. Can you picture a tall man riding on the back of a juvenile donkey, with his feet literally dragging on the ground? Does that sound like the way royalty usually travels? But long ago, prophets had predicted this very thing—that their king would arrive on a donkey's colt, and the people would recognize and welcome him. And they did.

Ironically, Jesus first entered the world as a helpless baby, born in a barn. Now he enters the city as a king riding on a baby donkey. Jesus arrives with an unexpected humility, yet he is the Son of God. For some reason this gets people's attention—a man with the power of the universe at his disposal who doesn't force his way.

Think about the quiet ways Jesus enters your life. Consider how you respond to his entrance. Do you welcome him?

My Prayer ·

Dear God,
    Thank you for the way you humbly enter my life, and for the way you quietly change my heart when I welcome you in.
    Amen.

Final Word ·

He is the image of the invisible God, the firstborn over all creation.

Colossians 1:15 NIV

Stone for the Journey ·

Jesus makes a humble entrance with powerful results.

Day 3 • Earth-Shaking Faith

Words from the Rock ·

I tell you the truth, if you have faith and don't doubt, you can do things like this and much more. You can even say to this mountain, "May you be lifted up and thrown into the sea," and it will happen. You can pray for anything, and if you have faith, you will receive it.

Matthew 21:21–22 NLT

Short of a volcanic eruption unlike anything man has ever seen, or a nuclear explosion that would most likely end life as we know it, it's pretty hard to imagine how a mountain could be lifted and thrown into the sea. Furthermore, why would anyone want that to happen? If those mountain-moving events really did occur, the results would probably include some major global warming, not to mention a total meltdown of the polar icecaps. Really, why would anyone want to move a mountain? Unless that mountain was in the way.

In Jesus's time, most travel was done on foot. If there was a mountain between point A and point B, travelers would have to go around it. A mountain was an obstacle, an obstruction, a hindrance to commuting. It slowed people down. For that reason, there might have been times when a weary traveler would have liked to toss the mountain into the sea. Of course, that wasn't possible.

Maybe that's why Jesus uses the mountain-moving metaphor—because it sounds so impossible. Maybe Jesus wants us to grasp that when we have faith in him, we are able to do the impossible.

What is the mountain in your life? What is it that gets in your way, slows you down, and comes between where you are and where you want to be? Is it a tough relationship? An addiction? An inability to forgive someone? Those kinds of things are like mountains—they obstruct your way. Have you asked Jesus to give you the faith to move that mountain?

My Prayer

Dear God,

Please help me to recognize the mountains that need to be removed from my life. Give me the kind of earth-shaking faith to move them.

Amen.

Final Word

What then shall we say to these things? If God is for us, who is against us?

Romans 8:31 NASB

Stone for the Journey

With Jesus, I can remove mountains from my life.

Day 4 • Miracle Key

Words from the Rock ·

> I tell you the truth, anyone who has faith in me will do what
> I have been doing. He will do even greater things than these,
> because I am going to the Father. And I will do whatever you
> ask in my name, so that the Son may bring glory to the Father.
> You may ask me for anything in my name, and I will do it.
>
> John 14:12–14 NIV

It's hard to imagine doing the kinds of amazing things Jesus did while he was on earth. For starters, Jesus performed miracles like feeding thousands of hungry people with a few loaves of bread. He restored vision to blind people, healed lame people, and cast out real live demons. He was able to walk on the water in the middle of the sea. He could stop a hurricane with the sound of his voice. He even raised the dead. Seriously, those are some pretty big sandals to try to fill. Yet Jesus tells us we can do even greater things. How is that even possible?

Perhaps we should start with our measuring tools. How do you gauge what's greater or better or more amazing when it comes to miracles? Don't you think the blind man (who received his vision) would have argued with the hungry person (who ate the loaves and fishes) that his eyesight miracle was superior? And what about the time Jesus helped Peter to walk on the water instead of drown? Wouldn't Peter think that was a pretty great miracle?

Maybe miracles are relative. Maybe it's the miracles each of us needs the most that are the greatest. For instance, what if you really want to tell a friend about how cool it is to have a relationship with God, but you get so nervous that you're always tongue-tied when you want to bring it up? But let's say you prayed and asked God to help you, and the next thing you know, you're sitting there telling your friend all about God. Wouldn't that seem like a pretty huge miracle?

Jesus is the key that opens the door to a miracle. Why not start asking for him to help you with some miracles in your life? Remember, with God anything is possible.

My Prayer ·

Dear God,

I want to believe that you can do some amazing miracles in my life. Show me some of the things you want to do, and remind me to ask for your help.

Amen.

Final Word ·

God began doing a good work in you, and I am sure he will continue it until it is finished when Jesus Christ comes again.

Philippians 1:6 NCV

Stone for the Journey ·

With Jesus I can do some miraculous things.

 ## Day 5 · On Second Thought

Words from the Rock ·

What do you think? There was a man who had two sons. He went to the first and said, "Son, go and work today in the vineyard."

"I will not," he answered, but later he changed his mind and went.

Then the father went to the other son and said the same thing. He answered, "I will, sir," but he did not go.

Which of the two did what his father wanted?

Matthew 21:28–31 NIV

Sometimes it seems easier to say yes and agree to something you really don't want to do simply to avoid conflict or to impress someone. Imagine that a youth group leader is asking for volunteers at the soup kitchen next weekend. Jenny Doe doesn't want to appear to be the selfish kind of person who'd rather sleep in on Saturday, so she smiles and politely raises her hand.

That way she looks good. But even as her hand is up, she's planning a way to conveniently forget all about this commitment, or maybe she'll neglect to set her alarm clock, or maybe she'll fabricate some other believable excuse like a case of the twenty-four-hour flu. The point is, she wants to look good.

There's a word for someone like that—*hypocrite*, or, as many were called in Jesus's day, *religious leaders*. Unfortunately, a lot of the most seemingly religious people were big fat hypocrites. When Jesus told this story, he was trying to make his listeners understand that the religious hypocrites were the ones pretending to serve God and others, but when no one was looking, they were serving only themselves. Like the son who says, "Yes, Dad," but fully intends to break that promise, the hypocrites could not be trusted.

What about the son who says, "No way, Dad," but later changes his mind and does what he's been asked? He represents the person who has rebelled against God—someone who's broken the rules—but later realizes his mistake and wants to change. Those are the kinds of people Jesus is looking for. People who recognize they're sinners but want to turn their lives around. Jesus can work with people like that.

So are you a yes person who secretly means no? Or are you a no person who, after a change of heart, wants to say yes to God?

My Prayer

Dear God,

I know I've made mistakes and I've broken some promises. I'm sorry, and I want to live my life the way you want me to. Please help me to do that.

Amen.

Final Word

You were rescued by the precious blood of Christ, that spotless and innocent lamb.

1 Peter 1:19 CEV

Stone for the Journey

With Jesus's help, I will keep my promises to God.

Week 38

Day 1 · Our Helper

Words from the Rock · · · · · · · · · · · · · · · · · · ·

> If you love me, you will do as I command. Then I will ask the Father to send you the Holy Spirit who will help you and always be with you. The Spirit will show you what is true. The people of this world cannot accept the Spirit, because they don't see or know him. But you know the Spirit, who is with you and will keep on living in you.
>
> John 14:15–17 CEV

What if you were suddenly transplanted into a completely different country—someplace where everything was totally foreign to you? What if you couldn't speak the language and your money was no good? Plus your clothes were all wrong, you were completely lost, you didn't know a single soul, and there was no American embassy. What would you do? Forget any hopes of enjoying your stay there, but can you think of anything that might make your visit a little less miserable?

How about a guide? What if a friendly local, someone who knew the area and language and could speak English, stepped up and offered you a helping hand? Wouldn't that be a huge relief?

Jesus knew that our spiritual journey wasn't going to be easy. In some ways, it would be like traveling through a foreign country. Jesus understood we would need some help to navigate our way. That's why he sent an invisible piece of himself to live inside of us. Whether we call this the Holy Spirit, our helper, our counselor, or even our personal guide, it is Jesus's Spirit living inside of us—and it's available to everyone who loves Jesus and believes in him.

But this Spirit can help us only when we let him. Remember the guide in the foreign country? What if he warned you not to go into a treacherous neighborhood or eat a lethal food, but you refused to listen? The outcome could be fatal. Similarly, Jesus gives you his Spirit to whisper truth to your heart, to gently guide you away from danger—but if you don't listen, you will get hurt.

My Prayer

Dear God,

I want your Spirit to live inside me. Help me to tune in to his quiet voice, heed his advice, and obey.

Amen.

Final Word

If the Spirit of him who raised Jesus from the dead is living in you, he who raised Christ from the dead will also give life to your mortal bodies through his Spirit, who lives in you.

Romans 8:11 NIV

Stone for the Journey

Jesus's Spirit can guide me through anything.

 ## Day 2 • Messes Welcome

Words from the Rock

I tell you the truth, the tax collectors and the prostitutes are entering the kingdom of God ahead of you. For John came to you to show you the way of righteousness, and you did not believe him, but the tax collectors and the prostitutes did. And even after you saw this, you did not repent and believe him.

Matthew 21:31–32 NIV

Can you picture the expressions on the faces of the religious leaders when Jesus targeted them with these strong words? Keep in mind that the religious leaders did everything possible to *look* good—they went out of their way to keep up the appearance of being holy and pure and spiritually superior to everyone else. Now Jesus was telling them that the lowlifes—the ones they considered to be the bottom-feeders of society—were going to make it into heaven ahead of them! They must have been seriously annoyed.

In that culture, no one was considered more messed up than prostitutes and tax collectors—prostitutes for obvious reasons, and tax collectors because they were considered "legalized" thieves. Jesus was declaring that messed-up people like that were actually going to heaven? How was that possible? Yet Jesus made it clear why messy lives would be welcome in heaven—it was because they welcomed the message that both John the Baptist and Jesus had shared with them. They admitted that they'd been caught in a corrupt lifestyle and wanted to change. They received Jesus's forgiveness and became believers. Of course they would be welcome in heaven.

In the meantime, most of the religious leaders refused to admit to their own shortcomings. They were trapped by their own pride and arrogance, and their biggest concern was to keep up the facade that they were better than everyone else.

Hiding our messes beneath a cloak of religion or fake goodness is always a mistake—it's like living a lie. Jesus encourages us to own up to our faults, to admit to our failures. And just as we welcome his forgiveness, he welcomes us into heaven!

My Prayer

Dear God,
Thank you for showing me that my life is messy. Give me strength to confess my problems to you so that you can forgive me and help me to get past them.
Amen.

Final Word

If we confess our sins, he is faithful and just and will forgive us our sins and purify us from all unrighteousness.

1 John 1:9 NIV

Stone for the Journey

When I confess to my mess, Jesus can clean me up.

Day 3 • Never Alone

Words from the Rock ·

No, I will not abandon you as orphans—I will come to you. Soon the world will no longer see me, but you will see me. Since I live, you also will live. When I am raised to life again, you will know that I am in my Father, and you are in me, and I am in you.

John 14:18–20 NLT

One of the greatest fears of small children is to lose their parents. Whether it be through death, abandonment, kidnapping, or whatever, young children do not want to be left parentless. Of course, this changes as kids grow older, and some teenagers might even act like they'd be perfectly fine without any parental influence. Although they probably know deep down that they still need a safe place to live and someone to watch out for them.

But what if the stakes are much higher for children than simply being sure that they'll have a roof over their heads, food on the table, and clothes to wear? What if the stakes are life and death . . . heaven and hell? That's what Jesus is talking about. He knows that his earthly life is about to end and that his disciples will feel like lost children when he's taken from them. Sure, they may be grown men and able to care for themselves when it comes to their earthly needs, but what about their spiritual needs? By now they know and respect Jesus as the Son of God. They understand that he is living water to their thirsty souls, the bread of life for their deepest hunger, and the key to the kingdom of heaven. What will they do without him?

Jesus assures his disciples that even though it might appear he's gone, he's not. He promises to show himself to them—and to us. He promises that he'll always be a part of us and we'll always be a part of him. We will never be spiritual orphans; we will never be abandoned. He will always be there, ready to provide for our spiritual necessities. That's his promise, and we can hold on to it until the end of time.

My Prayer

Dear God,

Thank you for the promise that you will never leave or abandon me. Please remind me of that when I feel lonely—remind me that you're still with me.

Amen.

Final Word

Christ gives meaning to your life, and when he appears, you will also appear with him in glory.

Colossians 3:4 CEV

Stone for the Journey

Jesus will never abandon me.

 ## Day 4 • Mismanagement

Words from the Rock

There was a landowner who planted a vineyard.... He rented the vineyard to some farmers and went away on a journey. When the harvest time approached, he sent his servants to the tenants to collect his fruit.

The tenants seized his servants; they beat one, killed another, and stoned a third. Then he sent other servants to them . . . and the tenants treated them the same way. Last of all, he sent his son to them. "They will respect my son," he said.

But when the tenants saw the son, they . . . threw him out of the vineyard and killed him.

Matthew 21:33–39 NIV

One of the most aggravating stories to make the news—and unfortunately it seems to happen too much—is when some mega-corporation, high-up executive swindles millions of dollars from his company. Maybe he even does it in a "legalized" manner, but just the same he's stealing from employees, shareholders, customers . . . and getting away with it. Workers might lose their jobs, pensions, and homes; shareholders might lose their savings; and sometimes innocent bystanders (taxpayers) get stuck with the bill. All because the exec, who got paid the really big bucks, was supposedly "managing" a corporation but secretly lining his own pockets at the expense of everyone else. It's maddening!

That's probably a little how Jesus felt when he was speaking to the religious leaders of his day, because these guys were a lot like that corrupt executive. Except that their job was to manage God's business. They were supposed to be caring for the spiritual needs of their people. Instead they were burying people in crazy religious rules, as well as extracting money and goods—essentially giving God a bad name. No wonder Jesus was so aggravated at them!

The story Jesus tells about the landowner and the vineyard is really about the religious leaders and how they've taken advantage of God's generosity, how they've mismanaged his people, and how they'll eventually kill God's Son. It's not a happy story, but it's one that needs to be told. And the message we can take away is that God gives everyone something of value to manage, and when we handle it his way, our story will have a happy ending.

My Prayer

Dear God,

Thank you for entrusting me with things like life, talents, family, and friends. Please help me to take good care of all you have given me.

Amen.

Final Word

Be strong in the Lord and in his mighty power.

Ephesians 6:10 NIV

Stone for the Journey

With God's help, I can manage what he puts in my life.

Day 5 · Love Driven

Words from the Rock ·

> Whoever has my commands and obeys them, he is the one who loves me. He who loves me will be loved by my Father, and I too will love him and show myself to him.
>
> John 14:21 NIV

Love is a mysterious thing, and there are many different kinds of love. Certainly, you can love a great pair of shoes, but not in the same way you love your mom or dad. You can love your grandmother's lasagna, but hopefully not as much as you love your grandmother. You can love playing soccer, but not as much as you love your best friend. Loving a pet might be intense, but it's not anything like how you'll feel when you fall in love.

Love is one of those complicated words with a whole lot of different meanings. But there is something that all the various forms of love have in common—motivation to act differently. Loving a great pair of shoes might motivate you to save up your money to purchase them. Loving your grandmother's lasagna might motivate you to pop on over to her house for Sunday dinner. Loving your best friend might motivate you to go out of your way to make him or her happy. Because you love someone or something, you're not concerned about the effort it takes or what it might cost—it's like you don't even think about it. That's because your love is driving you—your love is what motivates you into action.

That's how Jesus wants you to feel about him. He wants you to love him so much that you're motivated to do what he asks you to. He's the reason you obey his commands—why you can love others. This is because he loves you! He will ask you to do only the things that are good for you. Even if something feels hard, it will get easier if love motivates you—and in the end, it will be for your best.

My Prayer ·

> *Dear God,*
>
> *Thank you for loving me! Please help my love for you to grow, and let that love motivate me to do what you ask me to.*
>
> *Amen.*

Final Word ·

This I pray, that your love may abound still more and more in real knowledge and all discernment, so that you may approve the things that are excellent, in order to be sincere and blameless until the day of Christ.

Philippians 1:9–10 NASB

Stone for the Journey ·

Because I love Jesus, I will obey him.

Week 39

Day 1 · The Cornerstone

Words from the Rock ·

The stone the masons threw out is now the cornerstone. This is God's work; we rub our eyes, we can hardly believe it! This is the way it is with you. God's kingdom will be taken back from you and handed over to a people who will live out a kingdom life. Whoever stumbles on this Stone gets shattered; whoever the Stone falls on gets smashed.

Matthew 21:42–44 Message

If you look at the Empire State Building, you will see more than 1,450 feet of astounding height. A truly stunning building, it towers over New York City with an art deco style and a metropolitan majesty that is impossible to miss. But what is it that you don't see? Most people probably never think about the fifty-five-foot foundation that lurks underneath this amazing building. They can't even see it, but even if they could, it's not much to look at—just an enormous solid mass buried beneath the ground. Yet it's this very foundation that anchors that huge building to the earth. Unseen but essential.

As important as that foundation is, it's the cornerstone that really holds things together. The cornerstone, an integral part of the foundation, is the piece that ensures the building is straight and level and square. Without a true cornerstone, the Empire State Building would tip, the structure would fall, and all that would be left is a heap of rubble.

Jesus is like that cornerstone. He is the true foundational piece that God built his church on. Yet the religious leaders of Jesus's day rejected him and his truth. Is it any wonder that their world fell apart after they tossed him aside?

Jesus wants to be your cornerstone as well. He wants to be that solid rock, straight and true, that you build your life on. When you are securely anchored to him, you will be strong enough to withstand the worst earthquake.

My Prayer

> Dear God,
>   Thank you for being my rock-solid cornerstone. Help me to build my life on your foundation.
>   Amen.

Final Word

> Come to Jesus Christ. He is the living stone that people have rejected, but which God has chosen and highly honored.
>
> 1 Peter 2:4 CEV

Stone for the Journey

> Jesus is foundational to my life.

Day 2 • Teachable

Words from the Rock ·

> If people love me, they will obey my teaching. My Father will love them, and we will come to them and make our home with them. Those who do not love me do not obey my teaching. This teaching that you hear is not really mine; it is from my Father, who sent me.
>
> John 14:23-24 NCV

You've probably heard of the school of hard knocks (SHK). Maybe you've heard that it's the people with the hardest heads that attend that school. Some SHK students eventually figure things out, graduate, and move on. But some just keep repeating first grade over and over again. Why do you think some people insist on learning things the hard way? Is it because they're stubborn and thickheaded, and that's the only way to get through to them?

It could be they're slow learners or resistant to learning something new. Or maybe they're snoozing in class or drawing cartoons when they should be listening. Whatever their reasons, some people set themselves up to be unteachable. They think they already know it all, and no one can teach them anything. Unfortunately, that's the kind of attitude that sets a person up to be stupid.

Jesus wants you to embrace learning and to be teachable. He longs for you to love him so much, to trust him so completely, that you're eager to learn from him. He wants you to train your ears to recognize his quiet voice—the one that comes from his Spirit inside of you—so you can know when he's directing you and you can avoid learning things the hard way. Sometimes that quiet voice will tell you to wait on something because Jesus knows the timing isn't right. Sometimes that voice will tell you to speak up about something because Jesus knows the timing is perfect. But if you're not teachable, if you don't listen, you will miss out.

How teachable are you?

My Prayer ·

> *Dear God,*
>   *I want to be teachable. I want you to live in me and direct me, and I want to be quick to listen and learn. Please help me do that.*
>   *Amen.*

Final Word ·

Whatever you have learned or received or heard from me, or seen in me—put it into practice. And the God of peace will be with you.

Philippians 4:9 NIV

Stone for the Journey · · · · · · · · · · · · · · · · · ·

When I am teachable, I can learn.

 ## Day 3 · Priorities

Words from the Rock ·

"Let me see one of the coins used for paying taxes." They brought him a silver coin, and he asked, "Whose picture and name are on it?"

"The Emperor's," they answered.

Then Jesus told them, "Give the Emperor what belongs to him and give God what belongs to God."

Matthew 22:19–21 CEV

The religious leaders are at it again. Hoping to trap Jesus in a tricky question about taxes, which has always been a controversial subject, they ask him whether it's fair to pay taxes or not. In those days, taxation was more corrupt than ever. Most of the tax collectors were a slippery bunch of private contractors who went around demanding taxes from their own countrymen in a random and unfair way—adjusting the rates to whatever suited them at the moment. Then they would pocket much of what they collected and give the Roman government the rest. In most people's eyes, tax collectors were no better than thieves, and maybe even worse.

The religious leaders figure that if Jesus says it's fine to tax, it might seem he's condoning thievery. If he says it's wrong to tax, it's like suggesting they can break the law. Either answer can land Jesus in hot water. Or so the religious leaders hope. But instead of falling into their trap, Jesus asks them to show him a Roman coin (the kind used to pay taxes) and then asks them whose picture is on the coin. Of course, they say it's the emperor's image.

That's when Jesus turns the tables. He takes what they'd meant for trickery and uses it to make a crucial statement. He tells them to give the emperor what belongs to him and to give God what belongs to him. Jesus's answer shocks them so much that they just shake their heads and walk away.

What a point Jesus has made—it's as if he said, "Hey, taxes are just money, here today and gone tomorrow. But your soul was created by God, and it's meant to last for all eternity. Which is more important?" As usual, Jesus cuts through the crud and brings the topic back to what really matters. Who do you serve—God or man?

My Prayer

Dear God,

> *Thank you for reminding me of what matters most. Help me to keep my priorities in order and always put you at the top of my list. Amen.*

Final Word

We are like clay jars in which this treasure is stored. The real power comes from God and not from us.

2 Corinthians 4:7 CEV

Stone for the Journey

God gave me my life. I give it back.

 ## Day 4 • Gentle Reminders

Words from the Rock

These things I have spoken to you while abiding with you. But the Helper, the Holy Spirit, whom the Father will send in My name, He will teach you all things, and bring to your remembrance all that I said to you.

John 14:25–26 NASB

Some people use Post-it notes to remind themselves of things to do, errands to run, or someone to call. But sometimes Post-its are small and get overlooked. Or if you have too many, they become a sea of bright-colored squares with no meaning. Also, they can lose their stickiness and fall off and get lost. So they might not be the most reliable reminders. And sometimes you need a good reminder.

Let's say you have to get up early in the morning to take the SAT test. Maybe you set your alarm clock or rely on your computer's alarm to wake you . . . but what if there's a power outage? So you set your cell phone to go off, but what if the battery runs down? Finally, it might occur to you that the safest plan would be to have a person wake you up—like dear old Mom or Dad. They probably paid for the SAT test, so they wouldn't let you down.

Jesus knew that you'd need spiritual reminders too. That's just one more reason he decided to send his Spirit to live inside of you. Better than an alarm clock or a cell phone or even your parents, God's Spirit can nudge you when you need it. He can quietly warn you to take a different route, or jog your memory about a promise you made to God, or remind you of how much Jesus loves you, or teach you something completely new. The question is, are you tuned in and listening?

My Prayer

Dear God,

Thank you for sending your Spirit to keep me on track and teach me new things about you. Help me to tune in so I can hear the direction you give me.

Amen.

Final Word

Letting your sinful nature control your mind leads to death. But letting the Spirit control your mind leads to life and peace.

Romans 8:6 NLT

Stone for the Journey ·

Through his Spirit, God reminds me of his love.

 ## Day 5 • Priceless Peace

Words from the Rock ·

I am leaving you with a gift—peace of mind and heart. And the peace I give is a gift the world cannot give. So don't be troubled or afraid.

John 14:27 NLT

Some people spend their whole lives looking for something they cannot see, touch, hear, smell, or taste. Yet they long for this intangible thing like a starving man longs for food. Some people spend fortunes and purchase expensive homes, cars, boats—material possessions that they dream will deliver this elusive entity—and even when their money is gone, they remain unsatisfied. Some travel the globe, climb mountains, sit at the feet of gurus, and even withdraw in solitude in pursuit of this hard-to-find thing. A few go so far as to practice forms of self-torture and deprivation in the hopes that they will secure this obscure thing, yet it evades them. They cannot get their hands on it.

What is it they so diligently seek? What is it their souls crave? *Peace*. Peace of mind and peace of heart—a deep inner peace that the world doesn't offer, a peace that cannot be earned or bought. Jesus says that kind of peace is a priceless gift that only he can give. And he gives it to you for free. A priceless gift . . . *for free*.

In an era when prescription drugs, sleeping aids, and other pseudo substitutes for peace are more popular than ever, Jesus's peace is unique—one of a kind. It's the kind of inner calm that can keep you from losing it when everything around you is falling apart—a peace and assurance that can exist in the midst of chaos. Why wouldn't everyone be lining up to receive this kind of peace from Jesus? Why would you look anywhere else for it?

If people understood the depth and power of this peace, they wouldn't settle for anything less. Would you?

My Prayer

Dear God,

Thank you that your peace is a free gift. Remind me to come to you daily to receive this gift. Show me how to share this peace with others.

Amen.

Final Word

Therefore, since we have been made right in God's sight by faith, we have peace with God because of what Jesus Christ our Lord has done for us.

Romans 5:1 NLT

Stone for the Journey

Jesus's peace can keep me from falling apart.

Week 40

 ## Day 1 · Simple Laws

Words from the Rock

"Love the Lord your God with all your heart and with all your soul and with all your mind." This is the first and greatest commandment. And the second is like it: "Love your neighbor as yourself."

Matthew 22:37–39 NIV

The law was a big deal when Jesus walked the earth. Pages upon pages were written, and books were created—all to contain the thousands of religious laws that the leaders concocted on a regular basis. There were laws for everything imaginable. For instance, on the Sabbath (the day when no one was supposed to work) there were laws for how much you could salvage if your home was on fire. Never mind that you'd have to make dozens of trips since you were allowed to carry only one tiny handful at a time, but if you "broke the law," you'd be penalized later. Sure, your house might have burned to the ground, but you'd still have to relinquish something of value to the priests.

The purpose of these exhaustive and meticulous laws was to keep God's people in line—or so the scribes and legal minds of the day claimed. Then Jesus came along, and just like that, he condensed and streamlined those bulky, ridiculous laws into two straightforward and simple rules. He said to love God with all you have and to love your neighbor as you love yourself. Ironically, if you follow these two rules, you will automatically fulfill the original law (the Ten Commandments that God gave Moses thousands of years ago).

But as it turns out, these two rules, while simple, aren't exactly easy. Jesus understood that. He knew that you'd need his help to love God with every fiber of your being. He knew you'd have to go to him in order to learn how to love other people the way you love yourself. That's how he wanted it to be. He simplified the law so you'd be able to grasp it, but at the same time, he made it so all-encompassing that you'd need him to help you with it every single day of your life.

My Prayer

Dear God,

I choose to love you with all my heart, soul, and mind, and I choose to love others as I love myself. I need your help to keep this commitment. Thank you.

Amen.

Final Word

This is love for God: to obey his commands. And his commands are not burdensome.

1 John 5:3 NIV

Stone for the Journey ·

Jesus shows me how to love God and others.

 ## Day 2 · Love's Example

Words from the Rock ·

You heard me say, "I am going away and I am coming back to you." If you loved me, you would be glad that I am going to the Father, for the Father is greater than I. I have told you now before it happens, so that when it does happen you will believe. I will not speak with you much longer, for the prince of this world is coming. He has no hold on me, but the world must learn that I love the Father and that I do exactly what my Father has commanded me.

John 14:28–31 NIV

When Jesus tells us, "Love the Lord your God with all your heart and with all your soul and with all your mind," he is not trying to wax poetic. These words are a living by-product of his life. They are straight from his heart. Loving and obeying God is how Jesus lived on earth and why he died. His number one goal and purpose on earth was to be one with the Father and do his Father's will. Jesus proved that he loved his Father with his entire being—heart and soul and mind—by the way he obeyed God. Jesus gave everything; he held back nothing.

So when Jesus tells his disciples that he is going to the Father, he wants them to be happy for him. He wants them to understand how much he loves his Father and how nothing could be better than joining him. But it's not for his own sake that he wants his disciples to grasp this concept. It's because this kind of love is exactly what he hopes *all* his followers will one day experience. Jesus's desire is that we'll love his Father as much as he does. He wants us to follow his example.

Jesus knows that the more you love God, the more you will do what he wants you to. The more you do what God wants you to, the happier you will be. Love motivates you to live differently, and Jesus wants that motivation to draw you closer to his Father. Jesus knows that being one with his Father will satisfy you like nothing else can.

My Prayer

> *Dear God,*
>
> *Teach me to love you the way Jesus loves you. Show me ways I can spend time with you and honor you. Make me more like Jesus. Amen.*

Final Word

> God showed his love for us when he sent his only Son into the world to give us life.
>
> 1 John 4:9 CEV

Stone for the Journey

> My love for God changes who I am.

Day 3 • The Hypocrite Trap

Words from the Rock

> The teachers of the law and the Pharisees . . . make strict rules and try to force people to obey them, but they are unwilling to help those who struggle under the weight of their rules.
>
> They do good things so that other people will see them. They . . . love to have the most important seats at feasts and in the synagogues. They love people to greet them with respect in the marketplaces, and they love to have people call them "Teacher."
>
> Matthew 23:2, 4–7 NCV

Is it a coincidence that so many Scriptures containing Jesus's words are directed toward the religious community? Do you think Jesus's warnings about religion apply only to the leaders of his day? Or is there something we can all learn from Jesus's confrontations with religious hypocrites? As unfortunate as it is, sometimes the Christian community experiences some of the same problems as the scribes and Pharisees. Perhaps Jesus wants to remind all of us to beware of the hypocrite trap.

How do you feel about Christians who judge and criticize people with different beliefs? How do you react to Christians who seem to think they're better than nonbelievers? What do you think about Christians who act like they belong to an exclusive club—like their church is for members only? More importantly, what does Jesus think? Is it possible that Jesus regards some Christians as no different from the religious leaders of his day?

Jesus speaks out against those who make rules for the purpose of hurting and excluding others. He takes a stand against those who appear good on the outside but who are selfish and corrupt underneath. He has no patience with those who, under the guise of religion, elevate themselves above everyone else.

Now imagine how Jesus must feel when someone wearing the label of "Christian" does any of those things. How would he react to people who claim to know him but act just like the religious leaders that he took to task on a regular basis? Jesus wants you to guard your heart against religious superiority and hypocrisy. He wants you to love and serve and practice humility—in other words, to imitate him.

My Prayer

Dear God,
Please help me to be on the alert for hypocrisy in my life. Teach me to practice inclusive love. Make me more like you.
Amen.

Final Word

When you pray, do not be like the hypocrites, for they love to pray standing in the synagogues and on the street corners to be seen by men. I tell you the truth, they have received their reward in full.

Matthew 6:5 NIV

Stone for the Journey

Jesus can keep me authentic and free from hypocrisy.

Day 4 • Good Hurts

Words from the Rock ·

> I am the Real Vine and my Father is the Farmer. He cuts off every branch of me that doesn't bear grapes. And every branch that is grape-bearing he prunes back so it will bear even more. You are already pruned back by the message I have spoken.
>
> John 15:1–3 Message

Unless you live in a vineyard or near an agricultural community, some of Jesus's stories about farming might be lost on you. But back when Jesus told these stories, most of his listeners got the meaning—at least on a surface level. It might have taken a while for the real spiritual message to sink in.

To understand the metaphor that Jesus is using, you need to know a little about growing grapes and pruning. First of all, for the grapevine to flourish, the dead branches need to be cut off. And when a branch is healthy, it will produce big clumps of grapes, but the weight of the grapes can stress, weaken, or even break the branch. A good farmer knows this, and during the dormant season when grapes aren't growing, he'll cut back (prune) the healthy branches so they're not long, stringy, and weak. After they're cut back, they'll be sturdier and more capable of supporting heavy grapes.

Imagine you're a branch connected to the vine (Jesus), and suddenly the farmer (God) is taking a knife to you. After you recover from the fright, you should realize that (1) you're not a dead branch, so he's not permanently removing you, and (2) if he's pruning you back, it's for your own good so you can be stronger and healthier. Even if it hurts for a while, you need to remember that it would hurt a lot more if he didn't prune you and the weight of the grapes just broke you off.

Sometimes life is like that too. You experience something painful, something you can't even figure out, but later on you realize that was the very thing that made you strong.

My Prayer · · · · · · · · · · · · · · · ·

> *Dear God,*
>
> *Help me to remember that sometimes my injuries will make me grow. Sometimes the pain is to make me stronger and more capable to handle life's challenges.*
>
> *Amen.*

Final Word · · · · · · · · · · · · · · · · ·

> Consider it pure joy, my brothers, whenever you face trials of many kinds, because you know that the testing of your faith develops perseverance.
>
> James 1:2–3 NIV

Stone for the Journey · · · · · · · · · · · · ·

> My wounds draw me closer to Jesus.

 ## Day 5 · Spiritual Family

Words from the Rock · · · · · · · · · · · · ·

> All of you are equal as brothers and sisters. . . . Only God in heaven is your spiritual Father. . . . You have only one teacher, the Messiah. The greatest among you must be a servant. But those who exalt themselves will be humbled, and those who humble themselves will be exalted.
>
> Matthew 23:8–12 NLT

Jesus evens the playing field when he says believers are all equals—brothers and sisters. Upon first hearing, it sounds good and sweet, and you can almost hear the birds singing in the trees. But then when you think about it more, you realize that brothers and sisters can start up some rather feisty family feuds. Jesus knew that from personal experience—he had some half brothers. So maybe that's why he adds a bit more to this equalizing concept, pushing us beyond a family of squabbling siblings.

Jesus also points out that his followers must become like servants. What does that mean? And how do you do it? First of all, lose the notion that a servant is an uneducated, dull, unmotivated person—some poor loser who just goes around mopping the floors and saying, "Yes, sir." In Jesus's day, a good servant was smart, trustworthy, thoughtful, skillful, loyal, clever, and a real asset to his employer. In other words, he was a lot like a very devoted friend. In fact, a really good servant might be the best friend an employer ever had—maybe even closer than a sibling.

Jesus gave the example of being a servant like that. He always put the needs of others above his own. And he did practical things like healing the sick and feeding the hungry.

Now Jesus takes his teaching one step further by saying that when you refuse to be a servant and when you decide to put yourself above others, you will be knocked down and humiliated. Maybe not in this life, but eventually. On the other hand, if you put others above yourself and if you strive to be a good servant, you will eventually be lifted up and honored.

My Prayer · · · · · · · · · · · · · · · · · · ·

> *Dear God,*
>
> *Thank you for making your followers equals. Please teach me to be a good servant—smart and loyal and thoughtful. Let me follow your example.*
>
> *Amen.*

Final Word · · · · · · · · · · · · · · · · · ·

> Love each other as brothers and sisters and honor others more than you do yourself.
>
> Romans 12:10 CEV

Stone for the Journey · · · · · · · · · · · ·

> Jesus can teach me to serve others.

Week 41

 ## Day 1 • Fruit Connection

Words from the Rock · · · · · · · · · · · · · · · ·

> Remain in me, and I will remain in you. A branch cannot produce fruit alone but must remain in the vine. In the same way, you cannot produce fruit alone but must remain in me.
>
> John 15:4 NCV

Jesus wants his connection and relationship with you to be vital and life giving. You need to cling to Jesus like a healthy branch would cling to the main trunk of a plant—like you are one with it. What's the benefit of this connection? First of all, like a branch growing out of a tree, which receives the nutrients and water that come through the roots and the trunk, you will receive what you need from Jesus to grow and be healthy. That tight connection guarantees that his life (love, forgiveness, teaching) will flow into you. And Jesus's life keeps you vital and hardy and makes you grow. The result of growing healthy and strong is that you'll eventually bear fruit when the season is right.

Keep in mind that the quality of the fruit is dependent on the vitality of the branch. A wimpy, sickly branch can only produce wimpy, sickly fruit, but a healthy branch will yield top-notch fruit.

Now all this talk about fruit is fine if you're a farmer or you're planning to concoct a fruit salad. But what does it mean to you personally? Why do you need fruit in your life?

Fruit is a metaphor for good things. Who doesn't want more good things in their life? Maybe you'd like to be happier—what if you had more joy? Or maybe you'd like more friends—what if you became more patient and kind? Perhaps you'd like to avoid fighting with your parents or a sibling—what if you had more self-control? Those characteristics, and more, are considered the fruit of the Spirit. They are the results of hanging tight with Jesus. Fortunately, these kinds of fruits are more substantial than grapes or apples—with a much longer shelf life too. So stay connected to Jesus, and when the season is right, you'll be surprised and pleased to see what starts cropping up in your life. And so will the people around you.

My Prayer

Dear God,

Please help me to stay tightly connected to Jesus so that his fruit will become a normal part of my life.

Amen.

Final Word

The fruit of the Spirit is love, joy, peace, patience, kindness, goodness, faithfulness, gentleness and self-control.

Galatians 5:22–23 NIV

Stone for the Journey

My relationship with Jesus brings good things into my life.

 # Day 2 • False Religion's Reward

Words from the Rock

You Pharisees and teachers are in for trouble! You're nothing but show-offs. You're like tombs that have been whitewashed. On the outside they are beautiful, but inside they are full of bones and filth. That's what you are like. Outside you look good, but inside you are evil and only pretend to be good.

Matthew 23:27–28 CEV

You're already aware that Jesus is fed up with the religious leaders of his day. Now, knowing that his earthly hours are limited, he really lays into them in this portion of Scripture. In fact, the twenty-third chapter of Matthew has *thirty-six* verses of scathing condemnation where Jesus holds nothing back. He lays it all out for everyone to see, describing their shameful behavior in great detail and identifying them as liars, cheats, show-offs, hypocrites, tricksters, filth, snakes, and murderers. Finally, he warns them that they're headed for serious trouble. You have to believe that when Jesus, the Son of God who knows the ins and outs of the entire universe, says someone's in serious trouble, it's going to be bad.

Besides being arrogant, pompous, misleading, self-centered jerks, the religious leaders make themselves even more despicable to Jesus because of their constant attempts to appear good. He describes them as lovely white boxes that are probably ornately carved and attractive to look at—but inside the boxes are the rotting, stinking, putrid remains of cadavers. Not a pretty picture. As disgusting as that image is, it's how Jesus views religious hypocrisy. He cannot stand it.

Jesus wants you to be authentic—willing to admit to your failures and shortcomings. He wants you to live a transparent life in front of your family and friends, not put on false fronts or try to cover up your mistakes. It's through your honesty—and your willingness to have Jesus change you—that others are impacted. When others realize that you're the real deal and that you give God the credit for any goodness in your life, they want to know more.

My Prayer

> *Dear God,*
>
> *Please help me to never try to appear better than I am. Keep me away from false religion and hypocrisy. Let me be the real deal so you can shine in me.*
>
> *Amen.*

Final Word

> Do everything without complaining or arguing, so that you may become blameless and pure, children of God without fault in a crooked and depraved generation, in which you shine like stars in the universe.
>
> Philippians 2:14–15 NIV

Stone for the Journey

> My transparency allows Jesus's light to shine.

Day 3 • Hang Tight

Words from the Rock ·············

> I am the vine, you are the branches; he who abides in Me and I in him, he bears much fruit, for apart from Me you can do nothing. If anyone does not abide in Me, he is thrown away as a branch and dries up; and they gather them, and cast them into the fire and they are burned.
>
> John 15:5–6 NASB

Remember the grapevine metaphor? Jesus explained the need to prune branches so they'd be strong enough to support the weight of the grapes. But there's another reason to prune the branches. The act of cutting back a branch causes it to regenerate in a way that connects it even more tightly to the main vine or trunk of the plant. The more secure the branch is to the main trunk, the healthier it will be. The trunk literally gives life to the branch. A bad connection—due to things like lack of pruning, infestation, or even a bad storm—will weaken the branch. That's when a farmer might step in and prune it, use something to deal with the bugs, or bind the branch more tightly to the trunk.

The farmer understands that if the branch breaks away from the trunk and dries up, it's all over. Dead branches aren't good for much more than firewood. However, if there's still a little life left in the branch, the farmer can rescue it by grafting it back onto the trunk (or vine). However, the trunk must be wounded to do this so the sap will flow out and into the branch, revive it, and restore the connection—like how Jesus was wounded on the cross so his life could flow into us.

So while God has the work of being the farmer (mending, pruning, grafting), and Jesus has the work of being the main trunk (getting nutrients and water from the soil to the branches), your job (as a branch) is to hang tight to Jesus. Then you'll grow and be healthy and even bear fruit.

My Prayer ·············

Dear God,

Help me to remember that nothing is more important than for me to hang tight to Jesus. Thank you for all you do to keep me connected.

Amen.

Final Word ·

> Who will separate us from the love of Christ? Will tribulation, or distress, or persecution, or famine, or nakedness, or peril, or sword?
>
> Romans 8:35 NASB

Stone for the Journey ·

> Being connected to Jesus brings life.

 ## Day 4 · Wrong Expectations

Words from the Rock ·

> O Jerusalem, Jerusalem, the city that kills the prophets and stones God's messengers! How often I have wanted to gather your children together as a hen protects her chicks beneath her wings, but you wouldn't let me. And now, look, your house is abandoned and desolate. For I tell you this, you will never see me again until you say, "Blessings on the one who comes in the name of the Lord!"
>
> Matthew 23:37-39 NLT

Can you hear the anguish in Jesus's voice as he says these words? He's entering the city of Jerusalem, riding on the back of a baby donkey, yet being heralded as the King! People are shouting praises, waving palm branches, and throwing their coats down on the street for this parade. It's an amazing day—feverish excitement and hope charge the air. Everyone can feel it—something amazing is about to take place. So why is Jesus so disturbed? Why is he so saddened?

Since Jesus is God, he knows everything, and he knows that the same people shouting his praises will soon turn against him. It won't be long until they're yelling, "Crucify him!" The reason their hearts change so quickly has to do with their wrong expectations. These people are hungry for a leader. They've been waiting for a powerful king to deliver them from their oppressors (the Roman government). They're even ready to take up arms and fight for their deliverance—if only Jesus would lead them. But Jesus didn't come to fight an earthly battle; he came to win the greatest spiritual war of the ages. Yet the people didn't get this. They had wrong expectations.

It's easy to have wrong expectations about Jesus. Some people come to him expecting him to solve all their problems, but they're reluctant to do his will. Some think Jesus should give them what they want, but they don't realize that Jesus understands their needs better than they do.

Jesus doesn't want you to bring your agenda to him; he wants you to bring your heart. He doesn't want you to tell him what to do; he wants you to listen.

My Prayer

Dear God,

Thank you for loving me so much that you won't let me run the show. I want your will in my life. Help me to set my wrong expectations aside and trust you.

Amen.

Final Word

Don't get tired of helping others. You will be rewarded when the time is right, if you don't give up.

Galatians 6:9 CEV

Stone for the Journey

I will set my expectations aside and wait on God.

 ## Day 5 • In Sync

Words from the Rock

If you remain in me and my words remain in you, you may ask for anything you want, and it will be granted! When you produce much fruit, you are my true disciples. This brings great glory to my Father.

John 15:7–8 NLT

Some people hear Jesus's promise like this: "You may ask for anything you want, and it will be granted!" And they get all excited like they just won the lottery, or like Jesus is their personal Santa Claus. They ask for anything and it's theirs—who wouldn't jump on board? So they start making their wish lists. But they overlook the previous line of the verse: "If you remain in me and my words remain in you." What those people don't realize is that there's a prerequisite.

Jesus has already gone to great lengths for you to understand the magnitude of staying connected to him—nothing is more important than that. Now he's saying you're in him and his words are in you. That's a very intimate connection. It means your mind, heart, and soul are planted firmly in Jesus, and his words are buried deep inside of you. It's not simply being connected to Jesus; it's being completely enmeshed with him until he's such a part of you that you think, live, love, and act like him. It's a position that every believer should aspire to, but it will take a lot of surrendering on your part. If you reach that place of connectedness, you will be able to ask for anything you want and get it—because you will be asking for what Jesus wants too. You and Jesus will be in perfect sync.

But it's a process, and just like the vine must stay attached to the trunk so that in the right season and time it will bear fruit, you too must remain connected to Jesus. When you are one with Jesus, you can ask for anything—and you will get it.

My Prayer

Dear God,
> Please help me to remain in you, and let your words and your will remain in me so that together we can do amazing things!
> Amen.

Final Word

If you're serious about living this new resurrection life with Christ, act like it. Pursue the things over which Christ presides.

Colossians 3:1 Message

Stone for the Journey

When I am in sync with Jesus, I can ask for anything and he will do it.

Week 42

Day 1 • Stay in Love

Words from the Rock ·

As the Father has loved me, so have I loved you. Now remain in my love.

John 15:9 NIV

Human beings have some basic needs, including air, food, water . . . and love. It's true, love is as necessary as the air we breathe. As sad as it is, there's actual medical testimony about orphaned infants who've declined physically and even died for lack of love from their caregivers. Love is essential to life. But not only human love. We are created with a natural longing for another kind of love too. Our souls are designed to crave a deeper sort of love—a life-giving, spiritual love that comes only from God.

Jesus is the conduit of that love. God's love pours through Jesus to us. The only condition is that we stay linked to Jesus. He asks us to remain in his love. The word *remain* means "to stay put," "to linger," "to wait," "to hang about," "to stick around." It's something we automatically want to do when we love someone—we want to be with them.

What if someone gave you the latest, greatest video game console and every game and accessory that came with it? You get all set up and ready to play when you realize there's no power cord, so you have absolutely no way to connect this console to electricity. No other power cord will work, and consequently, the console won't work and you can't play a single game. Talk about frustration.

That missing power cord is kind of like Jesus. Without him, there's no connection to God. God's love (like power to the console) is transmitted when you are plugged into Jesus—when you remain in his love. So how's your connection? Are you plugged in?

My Prayer

Dear God,

I want to stay linked to Jesus so that your love will pour through him into me. Please show me everyday ways to keep myself plugged in.

Amen.

Final Word

If we believe that Jesus is truly Christ, we are God's children. Everyone who loves the Father will also love his children.

1 John 5:1 CEV

Stone for the Journey

Jesus is the conduit of God's love to me.

 Day 2 · What's Next?

Words from the Rock

See to it that no one misleads you. For many will come in My name, saying, "I am the Christ," and will mislead many. You will be hearing of wars and rumors of wars. See that you are not frightened, for those things must take place, but that is not yet the end. For nation will rise against nation, and kingdom against kingdom, and in various places there will be famines and earthquakes. But all these things are merely the beginning of birth pangs.

Matthew 24:4–8 NASB

For more than two thousand years, generations after generations of believers have been expecting and predicting the end of the world. Many of them expected it to end within their own generation—for good reason too. The atrocities that happened during some people's lifetimes were enough to make anyone long for life as they knew it to come to a screeching halt. Religious persecution, torturous deaths, bloody religious wars, plagues and pestilences, droughts and floods, earthquakes and hurricanes . . . all seemed to indicate that the end of the earth was near.

So predictions continued, and sometimes churches created doctrines based on their predictions. Sometimes they picked dates for when the earth would end. Some still pick dates today.

What is Jesus's response to all this? He says that all these things will happen—wars, famines, earthquakes—and that they're just "the beginning of birth pangs." What does that mean? The moment of childbirth is unpredictable. Some women experience only a few birth pains and then give birth. Some experience hours and even days of birth pains—which feel like an eternity—and finally the baby is born. In other words, it could be a short time or a long time. Only God knows.

Guess what? The end *is* near. In fact, it will be within your lifetime. Yet you don't even know how long your lifetime will be, so how can you know the end is near? Because everyone's earthly life will end. It always does. So whether your end will be a death of natural means or a result of the predicted "end of the world" is kind of irrelevant. It will happen. The question is, will you be ready?

My Prayer

Dear God,

Only you know when the end of the earth will be. Please help me to focus on staying connected to you instead of worrying about things I cannot control.

Amen.

Final Word

This one who is life itself was revealed to us, and we have seen him. And now we testify and proclaim to you that he is the one who is eternal life. He was with the Father, and then he was revealed to us.

1 John 1:2 NLT

Stone for the Journey

Jesus holds my future in his hands.

Day 3 · Real Joy

Words from the Rock · · · · · · · · · · · · · · · · · ·

If you keep My commandments, you will abide in My love; just as I have kept My Father's commandments and abide in His love. These things I have spoken to you so that My joy may be in you, and that your joy may be made full.

John 15:10–11 NASB

Joy—real joy—can be almost as elusive as peace. It is one of those things people constantly seek out but is extremely hard to find. Sometimes people think they've found it when they experience a rush or a thrill or a pleasant surprise. The problem is that kind of joy doesn't usually stick around for long. Now you see it, now you don't. Unfortunately, that small jolt of joy can sometimes set people up to attempt to find it again.

Most of the time, joy seekers look in all the wrong places. They might try extreme adventures, alcohol abuse, sexual experimentation, illegal drugs, or other dangerous activities in the hopes of finding a real thrill. But even when they experience a counterfeit sort of joy, it never lasts. Consequently, they might get trapped into an addictive behavior—chasing after that elusive rush they imagine exists.

The joy that Jesus offers is real and lasting. This joy comes as the result of participating in a committed, loving relationship with him. When you love Jesus so much that you're willing to live your life the way he wants you to, you will experience a fulfilling sense of joy. Sure, it might not be a giddy, crazy, roller-coaster sort of joy, but it will be authentic. It will be a joy that you can feel deep inside of you—a joy that will stay with you, bolstering your spirit during hard times. As your commitment to God grows stronger, it will be a joy that others will notice when they look at you.

Don't be tricked into seeking a counterfeit joy. Go to God for the real deal.

My Prayer ·

Dear God,

Please help me not to fall into the trap of looking for earthly joy. Remind me that when I love and obey you, your joy will become part of my life.

Amen.

Final Word · · · · · · · · · · · · · · ·

> Do not throw away your confidence; it will be richly rewarded.
>
> Hebrews 10:35 NIV

Stone for the Journey · · · · · · · · · · · · · ·

> God's joy comes when I obey him out of love.

Day 4 • Grim Warnings

Words from the Rock · · · · · · · · · · · · · · ·

> They are going to throw you to the wolves and kill you, everyone hating you because you carry my name. And then, going from bad to worse, it will be dog-eat-dog, everyone at each other's throat, everyone hating each other.
>
> In the confusion, lying preachers will come forward and deceive a lot of people. For many others, the overwhelming spread of evil will do them in—nothing left of their love but a mound of ashes.
>
> Matthew 24:9-12 Message

Jesus spoke some frightening words to his disciples here. As sensational and grim as this forecast sounded, all that he predicted eventually happened during his disciples' lifetimes. Because Jesus loved them, he wanted them to know the truth and to be forewarned.

There's something comforting about knowing what's around the next corner—even when it's something bad. For instance, an army that's about to be attacked would find it helpful to know some of the enemy's strategies and plans in advance. It would allow them to prepare themselves, plan a better line of defense, and hopefully suffer fewer casualties.

Following Jesus will not always be a walk in the park. It's not supposed to be easy-breezy. Hard times will definitely come your way—in fact, they'll make you grow stronger. If you let him, Jesus will stand by your side through those times; he will help you. Even though you probably won't suffer the same way his disciples did (some were burned, beaten, crucified, boiled in oil . . .

313

and almost all died gruesome deaths), you will experience some suffering and persecution simply because of your relationship with Jesus. When someone does attack you for your faith, you can be thankful—it shows you really do belong to God.

My Prayer

Dear God,
    I know that following you is supposed to come with some challenges. Remind me to ask you for help when they come my way.
    Amen.

Final Word

We live by faith, not by sight.

        2 Corinthians 5:7 NIV

Stone for the Journey

My relationship with God will bring some opposition.

Day 5 • Sacrificial Love

Words from the Rock

Now I tell you to love each other, as I have loved you. The greatest way to show love for friends is to die for them.

        John 15:12–13 CEV

Do you think you'd jump in front of a freight train to save your best friend's life if it meant you got killed in the process? Tough question, isn't it? You probably wish you could say yes, of course—you love your friend so much you'd willingly relinquish your life for him or her. But what would actually happen when the rubber met the road (or the steel wheels met the tracks)? Would you really give up your last breath for someone else? The truth is you might not be as brave or selfless as you'd like to think. Not many people are.

When Jesus told his friends this, he knew that he would soon be giving up everything, including his earthly life, for them. The reason he could make this sacrifice—and make it willingly—was because he loved them so much. Jesus knew that by surrendering his life, he was securing eternity for all who believed in him. His death was the greatest expression of his love. And he tells us to love each other with that same kind of commitment and intensity. But what does it mean? Seriously, how often does a person have to leap in front of a train to rescue a friend?

While it's somewhat unlikely that you'll physically give up your life for a friend, there are other ways to imitate Jesus's example of love. Every time you put someone else's interests above your own, set aside your own selfishness for them, or inconvenience yourself to help them, you are in essence dying to yourself. When you make personal sacrifices for the benefit of others, you practice the kind of selfless love that Jesus described.

My Prayer

Dear God,

Help me to put other people's needs above my own. Please remind me when I'm being selfish, and show me how to grow up in the way I love others.

Amen.

Final Word

Anyone who claims to live in God's light and hates a brother or sister is still in the dark. It's the person who loves brother and sister who dwells in God's light and doesn't block the light from others.

1 John 2:9-10 Message

Stone for the Journey

With God's help, I can love others selflessly.

Week 43

Day 1 • Everyone's Chance

Words from the Rock · · · · · · · · · · · · · · ·

> Because of the increase of wickedness, the love of most will grow cold, but he who stands firm to the end will be saved. And this gospel of the kingdom will be preached in the whole world as a testimony to all nations, and then the end will come.
>
> Matthew 24:12–14 NIV

Again Jesus is talking about what some people call the "last days." Remember, no matter what era believers live in (whether it's AD 12 or 2012), everyone experiences their own "last day." Everyone's earthly life will eventually end—it's inevitable. Yet here Jesus is warning that during your lifetime there might come some really hard challenges (like the death of a loved one, a broken heart, or a major disappointment). There might be times when it feels like your love for Jesus cools off, but he promises that if you hold on—if your faith doesn't crumble—you will be safe in the end.

Then Jesus gives us a clue as to when the end of the world actually will come. He says that after every single person on the planet has heard about him, including people from the most remote regions of upper Mongolia or sub-Saharan Africa or the Amazon rain forest—when they hear about Jesus's love for them and that he offers them forgiveness and a relationship with him—that's when the world as we know it will come to an end. That's when a new world will begin.

How will you participate in this monumental plan? What can you do right there in your own part of the world to help others come to know Jesus? How can you show his love and mercy to someone in your life? When you do this— when you share the gospel message by living the kind of life God wants you to—you help to change history!

My Prayer

Dear God,

I want you to use me to show others your love and grace. Live through me so they can see you.

Amen.

Final Word

Jesus lived the truth of this commandment, and you also are living it. For the darkness is disappearing, and the true light is already shining.

1 John 2:8 NLT

Stone for the Journey

God can use me to send a message of love to others.

Day 2 • True Friends

Words from the Rock

You are My friends if you do what I command you. No longer do I call you slaves, for the slave does not know what his master is doing; but I have called you friends, for all things that I have heard from My Father I have made known to you.

John 15:14–15 NASB

Do you realize the enormity of being called God's friends? Before Jesus came to earth to show us God's love, people felt distanced from God. The idea of being intimate with God, actually being considered his friend, was more far-fetched than expecting the president of the United States to invite you to dinner with the first family. It was like there was an insurmountable wall between people and God.

In fact, there was a huge curtain that hung in the temple where people gathered to worship God. These multiple layers of draperies were thick and heavy (like a wall) and were designed to separate God from his worshipers. This curtain symbolized a division—God on one side and the people on the other. After Jesus died on the cross, this thick curtain was miraculously split open from top to bottom to show that the wall dividing God from man was gone.

Jesus doesn't want anything to come between you and God. He wants to be your closest friend. Think about the kind of relationship that best friends have. Don't they usually tell each other everything? Don't they share secrets and confessions? In the same way, Jesus promises that as your intimate friend, he will tell you everything God has told him. No secrets. Full disclosure. Naturally, he expects you to be open and honest like that with him, because that's what friends do.

My Prayer

> Dear God,
> Thank you for being my friend. Help me to be a better friend to you and not hold anything back, because I know I can trust you with all my secrets.
> Amen.

Final Word

> You are God's chosen and special people. You are a group of royal priests and a holy nation. God has brought you out of darkness into his marvelous light. Now you must tell all the wonderful things that he has done.
>
> 1 Peter 2:9 CEV

Stone for the Journey

> When I'm God's friend, he shows me what I need to know.

Day 3 • Troubling Times

Words from the Rock ·

> This is going to be trouble on a scale beyond what the world
> has ever seen, or will see again. If these days of trouble were
> left to run their course, nobody would make it. But on account
> of God's chosen people, the trouble will be cut short.
>
> Matthew 24:21-22 Message

If you've ever run a marathon, you know that the last couple of miles are the worst. Your body is spent, each step feels harder than the last, and your lungs are aching. Some runners feel like they're about to die during the final grueling minutes of a race like that. Some even quit.

What if you're running a marathon and feeling so exhausted that you don't really think you can make the final two miles? You think, *Maybe next year.* . . . Then, out of the blue, the finish line is right in front of you—either your mileage estimation was wrong or someone shortened the distance of the marathon. Whatever the case, you'd be very glad to see that finish line.

In a small way, that's like what Jesus is describing. He's saying that troubles will come and that times will get hard. Remember how he promised to keep us informed because we're his friends? He doesn't trick us into believing that our lives will be all sweet and easy. He makes no secret that some challenges lie ahead. But he also promises that when we belong to him, he will cut the hard times short. In other words, he won't let us go through anything that's too much to bear.

God knows what we're made of and how much we can take. Because he loves us, he won't bury us in trouble—but he does expect us to call on him for help. At the same time, he knows that trying ordeals really do make us stronger—and like a marathon runner, the stronger we get, the longer we can run.

My Prayer ·

> *Dear God,*
> *I know that my life isn't supposed to be easy. Remind me to ask you for help and to remember that you don't give me more than I can take.*
> *Amen.*

Final Word ·

Join with me in suffering for the gospel, by the power of God, who has saved us and called us to a holy life—not because of anything we have done but because of his own purpose and grace.

2 Timothy 1:8–9 NIV

Stone for the Journey · · · · · · · · · · · · · · · · · · ·

When I depend on God, he sees me through.

 ## Day 4 · Chosen

Words from the Rock · · · · · · · · · · · · · · · · · · ·

You didn't choose me. I chose you. I appointed you to go and produce lasting fruit, so that the Father will give you whatever you ask for, using my name. This is my command: Love each other.

John 15:16–17 NLT

Do you know how it feels to be lined up and waiting to be chosen for a team? Like when team captains take turns picking the best athletes or their best friends to be on their team. Along with everyone else who's waiting, you don't want to be the last one standing there. You don't want to feel humiliated when you see disappointment wash over the face of the team captain who gets stuck with you.

You will never have to experience that kind of uncertainty and insecurity with Jesus. He points directly at you and says, "I want you. You belong with me. I need you on my team. Come on, let's go!" Jesus makes it clear right from the start that he chose you even before you knew him—he picked you to join him on a great adventure. He wants you with him.

Jesus also invites you to participate in his plan—his plan to reach out to others. The way he expects you to do that is actually fairly simple, and it's something that should sound familiar by now. Jesus reminds you of his commandment to love each other—repeating it often because he knows you need to hear it again and again. In the same way he chose you, the same way he made you his friend, the same way he loves you . . . he wants you to choose others, befriend others, and love others. That's how you show you're on Jesus's team.

My Prayer

Dear God,

Thank you for choosing me! Teach me to spot people who need to be included, and help me to reach out to them. Please show me new ways to love others.

Amen.

Final Word

Love means doing what God has commanded us, and he has commanded us to love one another, just as you heard from the beginning.

2 John 6 NLT

Stone for the Journey

God chose me to show his love to others.

 # Day 5 • Don't Be Tricked

Words from the Rock

If anyone tells you, "There [Jesus] is, out in the desert," do not go out; or, "Here he is, in the inner rooms," do not believe it. For as lightning that comes from the east is visible even in the west, so will be the coming of the Son of Man.

Matthew 24:26–27 NIV

Jesus is well aware that scam artists and charlatans have been around since the beginning of time, and he knows there are more to come. He also understands that many frauds will get involved in religion. So he warns you not to be deceived if someone tells you they can take you to see Jesus. You don't need to join a special group or go to a special place to be with Jesus. Those are the lines of a trickster.

There are several reasons people set up religious scams. Some frauds just want to get rich, and they know how to pick out people vulnerable to scams—people who are spiritually lost and desperate enough to believe they can buy their salvation. Other tricksters are so full of themselves and their false ideals that they hope to gather a following.

Some people have been tricked and don't realize it. Jesus doesn't want you to be deceived. He wants you to beware if someone suggests that giving money or services will secure your spot in heaven. He wants you to be skeptical if someone offers to "take you somewhere" to find Jesus. Don't forget that you have Jesus's Spirit to guide you—and that quiet discernment will help you to suspect when something's not quite right.

Jesus promises that when he comes, you will know it. In the same way you can hear a boom of thunder and see a flash of lightning in the sky, you will know without a doubt when Jesus shows up. It'll be a big deal! Anyone who tries to tell you differently is probably trying to trick you. Don't fall for it.

My Prayer ·

> *Dear God,*
> *Teach me how to be wise and not fall for anyone's tricks. I know I can trust you and that you make yourself known in ways that are indisputable.*
> *Amen.*

Final Word ·

> Things that are seen don't last forever, but things that are not seen are eternal. That's why we keep our minds on the things that cannot be seen.
>
> 2 Corinthians 4:18 CEV

Stone for the Journey · · · · · · · · · · · · · · · · · ·

> When my eyes are on Jesus, I cannot be tricked.

Week 44

Day 1 • Citizens of Heaven

Words from the Rock ·

> If the people of this world hate you, just remember that they hated me first. If you belonged to the world, its people would love you. But you don't belong to the world. I have chosen you to leave the world behind, and that is why its people hate you.
>
> John 15:18–19 CEV

When visiting foreign lands, you carry a passport with you. The obvious reason is that most countries won't let you in without one. But it's also a useful source of ID. If you plan to stay for an extended time in a foreign country, you'll need a visa as well. Visas and passports are the way that government officials identify what nation you belong to and where you have your citizenship. It's how the world at large works, and life goes a lot more smoothly when you know the laws of the land.

In some ways, the spiritual world is not that much different. Once you belong to God, your citizenship is in heaven. Sure, you're here on earth for the time being, but Jesus is like your passport—you are identified as his, and it's because of him that your allegiance is with heaven. As a result, you might sometimes be treated like a foreigner in this world, and sometimes foreigners aren't made to feel very welcome. In fact, Jesus says that if people hate him (and some do), they will likewise hate you. So you shouldn't be surprised when they do.

It might be a little easier to accept this kind of negative reaction when you realize that hatred and prejudice are products of ignorance. Some people, like those in other countries or cultures, might automatically dismiss or judge what they don't know or understand. So people who don't know Jesus might dislike him. That's when it's helpful to remember that Jesus wants you to be his ambassador and to love others. Hopefully then they will begin to see Jesus for who he really is—and they might become interested in gaining citizenship in his kingdom too!

My Prayer ·

Dear God,

Thank you for reminding me that my real home is in heaven with you. Please help me to reach out to others while I'm here on earth. Amen.

Final Word ·

Now we know that if the earthly tent we live in is destroyed, we have a building from God, an eternal house in heaven, not built by human hands.

2 Corinthians 5:1 NIV

Stone for the Journey · · · · · · · · · · · · · · · · · · ·

Jesus is my passport while I live on earth.

 ## Day 2 · Earth's Final Day

Words from the Rock ·

Then at last, the sign that the Son of Man is coming will appear in the heavens, and there will be deep mourning among all the peoples of the earth. And they will see the Son of Man coming on the clouds of heaven with power and great glory. And he will send out his angels with the mighty blast of a trumpet, and they will gather his chosen ones from all over the world—from the farthest ends of the earth and heaven.

Matthew 24:30–31 NLT

You've probably heard that all good things must come to an end. Sometimes that sounds a bit dismal. Say you're celebrating a special birthday and it's been so amazing—the best day ever—and you really, really don't want it to be over. Unfortunately, there's not a thing you can do to stop the day from ending. When midnight comes, that's it. When it's over, it's over. The end.

Maybe it's kind of like that when you think about the earth coming to an end. Maybe the thought of this planet's last day leaves you feeling a little concerned—or even totally freaked out. After all, there are some pretty cool things about the earth—hopefully you appreciate and enjoy them. Maybe you love a particular snowy mountain that's great for snowboarding. Or you might love the ocean, the sound of the waves tumbling in one after the next. Or perhaps there's a particular tree that means a lot to you, or you like the way the grass smells after it's been cut. You can't picture all of that just coming to a screeching halt—end of story.

Can you remember how you felt as a little kid? Maybe you didn't want your childhood to end; you didn't want to grow up. But time passes . . . and suddenly you're old enough to drive and do some other pretty cool things, and you realize you wouldn't go back to being a five-year-old for anything. The ending of one good thing led to the beginning of something far better.

God's plan for the earth to end is so there can be a new beginning. And God's new beginning will be way better than what has just ended—far greater than anything you can imagine!

My Prayer

Dear God,
I'm so glad I can trust you with endings and beginnings. Help me not only to be ready but also to eagerly anticipate whatever you're bringing my way.
Amen.

Final Word

Now it is God who has made us for this very purpose and has given us the Spirit as a deposit, guaranteeing what is to come.

2 Corinthians 5:5 NIV

Stone for the Journey

When God ends something, he begins something even better.

325

Day 3 · Our Example

Words from the Rock

When that happens, remember this: Servants don't get better treatment than their masters. If they beat on me, they will certainly beat on you. If they did what I told them, they will do what you tell them.

John 15:20 Message

The unknown can be scary. Whether it's an imagined monster that lurked beneath your bed when you were seven, or the first day at a new high school in a new town, something about not knowing what's around the next corner can be a little freaky. Maybe that's why Jesus spent so many of his last days with his disciples preparing them for what was coming. He knew that his friends were going to face challenges unlike anything they ever had before. He wanted them to be informed and ready.

One of the warnings Jesus gave is in regard to how his followers would be treated. It's kind of like having a big brother who tips you off about the bullies who live down the street, cautioning that he got attacked by them and that you should be on your guard too. He's our example. In other words, if someone doesn't like Jesus, they probably won't like you either.

On the other hand, if people respect Jesus, you can expect them to respect you too. His friends are your friends. Jesus has a lot of friends, which means you do too. He knows that when times get tough—and they will—you'll be comforted by having these kinds of friends around you. And by the same token, Jesus wants you to be the kind of friend that others can lean on during their hard times. He wants you to follow his example and to be as loyal and kind and loving to your friends as he has been to you.

My Prayer

Dear God,

Thanks for giving me a heads-up sometimes. Please teach me to be the kind of friend that others can trust to stand by them. Amen.

Final Word ·

This is how we know what love is: Jesus Christ laid down his life for us. And we ought to lay down our lives for our brothers.

1 John 3:16 NIV

Stone for the Journey ·

Jesus shows me how to love others.

Day 4 • Be Aware

Words from the Rock ·

Now learn this lesson from the fig tree: As soon as its twigs get tender and its leaves come out, you know that summer is near. Even so, when you see all these things, you know that it is near, right at the door. I tell you the truth, this generation will certainly not pass away until all these things have happened. Heaven and earth will pass away, but my words will never pass away.

Matthew 24:32–35 NIV

If you look up at the sky and see ominous, dark clouds rolling in, you might suspect that the weather is changing. Perhaps there's a major thunderstorm coming, and if you're outside, you might even want to make a plan to go somewhere to escape the elements. That's just common sense.

God gave us the physical abilities to see and hear and think in order to avoid perils like tornadoes or hurricanes. But he also gave us a spiritual ability to perceive other kinds of dangers. You are designed to listen with spiritual ears and to see with spiritual eyes. Unlike your physical ears and eyes, your spiritual senses can become dull if they're not used. Jesus wants you to keep them sharp and ready. In the same way you can see storm clouds gathering overhead, you can discern when a spiritual situation is risky. Like you might need to be careful around someone who tries to put words in God's mouth, or a "friend" who encourages you to do something you know is wrong.

The way you can keep your spiritual senses in top form is by spending time with Jesus. The more you keep your spiritual eyes on him and the more you tune your spiritual ears to his voice, the less likely you'll be blindsided. Even if it seems you're surrounded by storms and other threats that Jesus says will come your way—even if everything around you appears to be falling apart— you will remain safe when you're close to Jesus. He has promised to be with you and to protect you through anything.

My Prayer

> *Dear God,*
>
> *Help me to remain connected to you, and teach me to tune my spiritual senses in to you. Thank you for keeping me safe in times of trouble.*
>
> *Amen.*

Final Word

> Letting your sinful nature control your mind leads to death. But letting the Spirit control your mind leads to life and peace.
>
> Romans 8:6 NLT

Stone for the Journey

> God will help me keep my spiritual senses sharp.

 # Day 5 · No Excuses

Words from the Rock

> They will do all this to you because of me, for they have rejected the One who sent me. They would not be guilty if I had not come and spoken to them. But now they have no excuse for their sin. Anyone who hates me also hates my Father. If I hadn't done such miraculous signs among them that no one else could do, they would not be guilty. But as it is, they have seen everything

I did, yet they still hate me and my Father. This fulfills what is written in their Scriptures: "They hated me without cause."

John 15:21-25 NLT

You may have heard that ignorance of the law is no excuse to break it. Imagine you're driving down the highway and don't see a speed limit sign anywhere. Maybe it's a remote area, or maybe a strong windstorm blew all the signs down. You're not really sure how fast you should go, so you decide to drive ninety miles per hour.

Before long you see flashing blue lights in your rearview mirror. You pull over and say to the officer, "Sorry, man, I didn't know what the speed limit was right here." Do you think he'll smile and say, "No problem," then close his little book and walk away? Don't count on it. If you're a licensed driver, you should know what the speed limits are on certain kinds of roads in your state. You should know you need to respect those laws even if a speed limit sign isn't around.

That's kind of like what Jesus is saying here. He's been out in the open in his teachings about God. His listeners aren't ignorant about the coming Messiah. They know about the old prophecies, and they're aware that Jesus has fulfilled many of them by doing miracles (healing people, feeding thousands, raising the dead). Jesus has done everything possible to show everyone that he is God's Son, and the news of his power and authority and influence has spread across the land.

Yet there are those who absolutely refuse to believe him. Like children covering their eyes and ears, some stubbornly choose to reject Jesus, deciding to hate him. Despite the fact that Jesus did everything possible to win them over, they won't listen. Don't be like them. Take Jesus's words to heart—knowing who he is becomes your excuse to love him.

My Prayer

Dear God,

Thank you for showing yourself to me so I have no excuse for not following you. Help me to remember all you've done so my faith remains firm.

Amen.

Final Word · · · · · · · · · · · · · · · · ·

Now there is no condemnation for those who belong to Christ Jesus. And because you belong to him, the power of the life-giving Spirit has freed you from the power of sin that leads to death.

Romans 8:1–2 NLT

Stone for the Journey ·

I have no excuse not to love Jesus.

Week 45

 ## Day 1 · Distractions

Words from the Rock ·

When the Son of Man returns, it will be like it was in Noah's day. In those days before the flood, the people were enjoying banquets and parties and weddings right up to the time Noah entered his boat. People didn't realize what was going to happen until the flood came and swept them all away. That is the way it will be when the Son of Man comes.

Matthew 24:37–39 NLT

Again Jesus is talking about the end of time and how vital it will be for us to remain connected to him and tuned in. Envision being on an elegant cruise ship out in the middle of the sea. It's one of those mega ships with everything anyone could possibly want to do—lots of swimming pools, a water park, rock climbing, wakeboarding, skeet shooting, golf, restaurants, shopping, theaters . . . and the list goes on. It's a floating party.

Then there's an announcement that something is wrong and that passengers should report to the lifeboat areas. Well, the ship seems solid enough, the sky is blue, and the music is still playing, so the fun continues, and most of the passengers just ignore the warning. They think, *What could possibly be wrong?*

Remember the *Titanic*?

Jesus says it will be somewhat like that in the last days. He warns us that many people will be so distracted with having a good time—partying to the max—that they'll be oblivious to what's really going on and the approaching danger. Like the passengers on the *Titanic*, who felt it was impossible for such a humongous ship to sink, they will ignore the warnings. Many will refuse to get into the lifeboats . . . until it's too late. That's why Jesus wants you to keep tuned in to him. He wants your spiritual ears to be listening and your spiritual eyes to be wide open so you'll know what's coming, so you'll be ready and eagerly waiting. Don't be distracted!

My Prayer

Dear God,

I always want to stay tuned in to you. Help me to realize when something in my life is trying to distract me from you. Keep me connected to you.

Amen.

Final Word

You have faith in God, whose power will protect you until the last day. Then he will save you, just as he has always planned to do.

1 Peter 1:5 CEV

Stone for the Journey

When my eyes are on God, I can't be distracted.

Day 2 · Forever Friend

Words from the Rock ·

> When the Friend I plan to send you from the Father comes—the Spirit of Truth issuing from the Father—he will confirm everything about me. You, too, from your side must give your confirming evidence, since you are in this with me from the start.
>
> John 15:26–27 Message

Sometimes life is just plain hard. Like when everything seems to be going wrong and you're not sure how much more you can take. Maybe your family is dysfunctional—having serious problems and just really messed up. Maybe something at school is making you crazy. Or maybe someone has broken your heart. Is there anything that can make you feel better?

How about a friend? What if you had a really good friend to turn to—someone who was a great listener and knew you better than anyone? What if this friend loved you no matter what and cared deeply about you? What if this person was ubersmart and gave excellent advice? Do you think that would help you feel better? Would it help you through a hard time?

Jesus promises you a friend like that in his Spirit—who is actually part of Jesus. God's Spirit is ready to be an amazing friend and is able to guide you through all kinds of tough situations. Unlike human friends, who sometimes let you down, he will be loyal, sticking with you through everything.

As with human friends, this relationship is a two-way street. You need to be a friend in return. You need to invest some of yourself—your time, your energy, your attention—in order to strengthen this friendship with God's Spirit. As with a human friendship, the payoff is worth it. With the Spirit as your constant companion, you might feel lonely sometimes, but you will never be alone.

My Prayer ·

> *Dear God,*
>
> *I welcome your Spirit into my life. Please show me how I can be a better friend to your Spirit and solidify this relationship.*
>
> *Amen.*

Final Word · · · · · · · · · · · · · · · · ·

His Spirit joins with our spirit to affirm that we are God's children. And since we are his children, we are his heirs. In fact, together with Christ we are heirs of God's glory. But if we are to share his glory, we must also share his suffering.

Romans 8:16–17 NLT

Stone for the Journey · · · · · · · · · · · · · · · ·

God's Spirit is an amazing friend.

 ## Day 3 • Be Prepared

Words from the Rock · · · · · · · · · · · · · ·

Two men will be in the field. One will be taken, and the other will be left. Two women will be grinding grain with a mill. One will be taken, and the other will be left.

Matthew 24:40–41 NCV

The Boy Scout motto is "Be prepared." You might wonder, *How exactly? And be prepared for what?* A well-trained scout would answer, "Be prepared for anything." Is that even possible? If you're taking a hike in the woods, you'd probably want to pack things like a compass or a tracking device, drinking water, energy food, proper clothing, and maybe matches. A cell phone might come in handy too. But that's only enough preparation for a day hike. What about preparing for a life?

That calls for a different kind of preparedness, one that's even more important—spiritual preparedness. Let's face it, someone might be all ready for an earthquake or hurricane. But even with a well-stocked pantry, a generator, a tank of drinking water, medicine and first-aid items, candles, blankets, and other emergency supplies, that person could still be caught off guard if, instead of a natural disaster, there was a spiritual disaster.

Jesus says he will come to earth in the last days to gather up those who believe in him—the ones whose hearts are ready for his return—and take them back to heaven with him. But the ones who don't believe—even if they have everything necessary to survive floods and famines—will be left in the lurch when they realize their lack of spiritual preparedness.

While it's good to be prepared for any kind of emergency, it's even better to be prepared to hear and respond to Jesus when he calls out to you. When he says it's time to go, be ready.

My Prayer

> Dear God,
>
> Help me to be spiritually prepared. I know that means I need to stay connected to you. Thank you for your promise to see me through whatever comes my way.
>
> Amen.

Final Word

> We do not lose heart. Though our outer self is wasting away, our inner self is being renewed day by day.
>
> 2 Corinthians 4:16 ESV

Stone for the Journey

> God prepares me for what lies ahead.

 # Day 4 · Hold On!

Words from the Rock

> I have told you these things so that you won't abandon your faith. For you will be expelled from the synagogues, and the time is coming when those who kill you will think they are doing a holy service for God. This is because they have never known the Father or me. Yes, I'm telling you these things now, so that when they happen, you will remember my warning. I didn't tell you earlier because I was going to be with you for a while longer.
>
> John 16:1-4 NLT

Jesus knew that his disciples were going to go through a kind of living hell after he was gone. His beloved followers would be beaten and tortured and imprisoned and even killed because of their relationship with him. In essence, they would be brutally terrorized in an attempt to completely shut down Christianity. Some evil leaders wanted Jesus's message stopped in its tracks, and they mistakenly thought they could accomplish their diabolical plan by persecuting and eliminating anyone who followed Jesus. Of course, they were wrong.

Jesus never tried to hide these frightening facts from his followers. He was blunt with them—so much so that if their faith had been weak, some of them might have slunk away like dogs with their tails between their legs. Really, how appealing would it be to hear that not only were you going to be bullied, tortured, and possibly murdered, but as a result, your loved ones would probably suffer as well? The forecast was grim.

Perhaps some might have preferred not to know what was coming—they might have thought ignorance was bliss. But Jesus wanted them to know so that they wouldn't be surprised or taken aback and they could hold tight to their faith. He knew that, more than anything, their faith was what would see them through.

It's no different for you. While you probably will never be treated as badly as his disciples were, you will go through tough times. Sometimes you might even suffer for your beliefs, but ultimately, if you hold on to Jesus, you will make it through. When you get hit with something hard, see it as a reminder to cling to your faith—and hold on tight!

My Prayer ·

> Dear God,
>   Instead of getting rattled and worried when hard times come my way, please remind me that I need to hold on to you more tightly.
>   Amen.

Final Word ·

> Don't blame God when you are tempted! God cannot be tempted by evil, and he doesn't use evil to tempt others.
>
> James 1:13 CEV

Stone for the Journey ·

Tough challenges call for tough faith.

 ## Day 5 • Always Ready

Words from the Rock · · · · · · · · · · · · · · · · · · ·

Be on your guard! You don't know when your Lord will come.
Homeowners never know when a thief is coming, and they are
always on guard to keep one from breaking in. Always be ready!
You don't know when the Son of Man will come.

Matthew 24:42–44 CEV

No one ever plans to be robbed. Even if you hear that there's a thief in
the neighborhood, you can't predict if he'll hit your house tonight or
tomorrow night or next week. In most burglaries, the victims are caught un-
awares and taken completely by surprise. So a lot of homeowners use home
security systems for protection, because even if it's the middle of the night
and you're sleeping and unaware of a break-in, a security system is on top of
it. A security system never sleeps. That is, unless someone forgets to turn it
on. Then there's a problem.

Here Jesus is reminding you to make sure you keep your spiritual security
system up and running and in good shape. That means you don't neglect
things like prayer or reading your Bible or spending time with other believers.
To neglect those habits is to neglect your spiritual security system—and that
leaves you vulnerable.

When you're doing what you should—maintaining your spiritual security system—you are ready for anything. And that brings a special sense of
peace—the kind of peace that lets you enjoy a good night's sleep without
worrying about a break-in. You can rest easy because you know you've done
what needs to be done.

Jesus wants you to be ready—not just for when he comes back to get you,
but for every good thing he has for you until then. Be ready!

My Prayer

Dear God,

Help me to take responsibility for maintaining my spiritual security system by obeying you. I want to be ready for everything and anything, especially for you.

Amen.

Final Word

You must learn to endure everything, so that you will be completely mature and not lacking in anything.

James 1:4 CEV

Stone for the Journey

God wants me to be ready for whatever comes my way.

Week 46

 Day 1 • Change Is Good

Words from the Rock

Now I am going to him who sent me, yet none of you asks me, "Where are you going?" Because I have said these things, you are filled with grief. But I tell you the truth: It is for your good that I am going away. Unless I go away, the Counselor will not come to you; but if I go, I will send him to you.

John 16:5–7 NIV

Some people don't like change. They resist anything different and want everything to remain the same—status quo, leave it be, don't rock the boat. . . . But change is inevitable. Like it or not, change happens. For the most part, it's a good thing, even if you can't understand it at the time.

However, as the end of Jesus's earthly life drew closer, his disciples were not eager for change. They did not want to lose Jesus—they felt they needed him and that he still had work to do with them and others. And they most certainly did not want to see him die. What possible good could come of that? No, Jesus's followers longed for him to remain with them on earth indefinitely. They loved him and knew that life had never been as wonderful or exciting or fulfilling as it was with Jesus around. If his disciples had called the shots, Jesus never would have left them. Fortunately for everyone, God had other plans.

If Jesus had remained with his disciples and all had stayed the same, God's plan for forgiveness and redemption would have been thwarted. Jesus had to die on the cross and come back to life in order to change things. That was God's intention all along, and Jesus knew it. He also knew that he couldn't send his Spirit back to help his believers unless he first left. They were going to need his Spirit so they could be changed and mature.

Jesus wants the same for you. He wants his Spirit to change you—to help you grow and become more like him. Change really is good!

My Prayer

> Dear God,
>
> Thank you for your perfect plan. Thank you for sending your Spirit to change me. Please help me to be more like you.
>
> Amen.

Final Word

Come on, let's leave the preschool fingerpainting exercises on Christ and get on with the grand work of art. Grow up in Christ.

Hebrews 6:1 Message

Stone for the Journey

God's changes in me are good.

Day 2 • When No One's Looking

Words from the Rock ·

Who then is the faithful and wise servant, whom the master has put in charge of the servants in his household to give them their food at the proper time? It will be good for that servant whose master finds him doing so when he returns. I tell you the truth, he will put him in charge of all his possessions.

Matthew 24:45–47 NIV

Have you ever walked into a fast-food restaurant or small business and seen that the employees are slacking? Maybe someone is talking on a cell phone and someone else is sitting on a counter, and you wait for them to come help you, but it's like they don't care. Maybe they're thinking, *We only make minimum wage—what's the big deal?* But what would happen if the owner of the business walked in? They'd probably snap right to it. Well, unless they wanted to get fired.

Some people act differently based on who is watching them. For instance, students don't usually cheat if the teacher has her eyes on them. Children don't sneak candy if Mom is nearby. But what happens when no one is looking?

Jesus describes an employee who does what's expected even though the employer is far away. This is a worker who knows what needs doing and enjoys doing it. This employee probably gets satisfaction from doing things right. And when the employer returns, he's pleasantly surprised. He feels fortunate to have such a good worker and rewards him or her for a job well done.

How do you behave when you think no one is looking? Do you slack off, break rules, or do what you know you shouldn't? Or do you get satisfaction from doing things right even if it seems like no one but you can see? And how does it feel to remember that God is always watching? He misses nothing. God wants you to grow up so that you'll do what's right no matter who's looking. Why is that? Because he knows that is what's best for you and will make you happiest, and he plans to reward you for it.

My Prayer

Dear God,

> *Please teach me to do what's right no matter who is watching me. Help me to remember that it's really in my best interest to obey you. Amen.*

Final Word

Then you will not become spiritually dull and indifferent. Instead, you will follow the example of those who are going to inherit God's promises because of their faith and endurance.

Hebrews 6:12 NLT

Stone for the Journey

God knows and rewards when I obey.

 ## Day 3 • Perceptions

Words from the Rock

When he comes, he'll expose the error of the godless world's view of sin, righteousness, and judgment: He'll show them that their refusal to believe in me is their basic sin; that righteousness comes from above, where I am with the Father, out of their sight and control; that judgment takes place as the ruler of this godless world is brought to trial and convicted.

John 16:8–11 Message

Most of the human race shares a common flaw in the area of perception—we think our point of view is correct. As a result, we can be quick to jump to wrong conclusions and make false assumptions. We form opinions on things we don't understand. We pass judgment without knowledge. It's just the human way. But it's not God's way.

A great part of Jesus's earthly mission was to show us a different way to think and reason. He basically wanted to shake things up. Whether because of old, preconceived notions about religion or a misunderstanding of the nature of God, Jesus wanted to reform our hearts and minds.

Before Jesus came to earth, much of the religious community attempted to keep God in a box. They allowed their own human restrictions to limit their perception of him. But Jesus broke that box wide open. He showed people different sides of God—like forgiveness, compassion, mercy, and love. Jesus's life revealed that God was a lot different than many had assumed.

Unfortunately, we sometimes fall back to our old human ways—making wrong assumptions about God. Maybe we decide God is angry or mean. Or we conclude that he can't possibly love everyone—what about serial killers? Or we deduce that God's forgiveness is something we can earn or deserve. That's when we need to return to Jesus—we need to focus on his words and his teaching and allow him to transform our earthly minds so we can think and reason more like him.

My Prayer · · · · · · · · · · · · · · · · · ·

Dear God,
I confess that sometimes I make snap judgments and come to
wrong conclusions. Please change my thinking to be more like
yours.
Amen.

Final Word · · · · · · · · · · · · · · · · · ·

Don't be like the people of this world, but let God change the way you think. Then you will know how to do everything that is good and pleasing to him.

Romans 12:2 CEV

Stone for the Journey · · · · · · · · · · · · · · · ·

God can transform my thinking.

Day 4 · Timing Is Everything

Words from the Rock ·

> I have much more to say to you, but right now it would be more
> than you could understand. The Spirit shows what is true and
> will come and guide you into the full truth. The Spirit doesn't
> speak on his own. He will tell you only what he has heard from
> me, and he will let you know what is going to happen.
>
> John 16:12–13 CEV

It's easy to get in a hurry, to feel rushed—like you're racing the clock. With "help" from instant messaging, high-speed internet service, fast-food chains . . . it almost seems like the world is spinning faster and faster. As a result, we can get into the habit of expecting things to move quickly, and we become irritated when something takes longer than we think it should. We want what we want, and we want it now!

But there can be good reasons to wait. For instance, if you're baking a cake, it won't do any good to rush the cooking time. Taking it out of the oven too soon will ruin it.

Spiritual things can be like that too. Jesus has a lot to tell you, to teach you, and to show you, but he knows you can handle only so much at once. To dump everything on you would totally overwhelm you. That's why Jesus wants his Spirit to dwell in you. The Spirit knows when it's time to show you certain things. He knows when it's the opportune moment to push you in a particular direction, and when it's just the right instant to warn you to avoid something.

Hopefully you're tuned in and your spiritual watch isn't running too fast or too slow. With God's Spirit, timing is everything. To rush the Spirit isn't just futile, it's foolish—not to mention impossible since you can't hurry God. Waiting on God diligently and patiently will accomplish far more than trying to speed things up. Trust God enough to slow down and listen.

My Prayer ·

Dear God,

I know I can be impatient and want to hurry things up. Show me how to align my spiritual clock with yours. Teach me to tune in to your Spirit.

Amen.

Final Word ·

He will keep you strong to the end so that you will be free from all blame on the day when our Lord Jesus Christ returns.

1 Corinthians 1:8 NLT

Stone for the Journey ·

God's timing is perfect.

Day 5 · Full Disclosure

Words from the Rock ·

The Spirit of truth will bring glory to me, because he will take what I have to say and tell it to you. All that the Father has is mine. That is why I said that the Spirit will take what I have to say and tell it to you.

John 16:14–15 NCV

Everyone has seen news flashes. Maybe they're text messages or blurbs on TV or headlines on the internet. They might be something shocking or sensational, like a jetliner went down, a rock star died, or there's been a shooting. You're given just enough information to pique your interest. Naturally, you want to find out more, and as you investigate, you might discover that the news event is so recent that you can't get to the bottom of it. You might even be getting false information. Or you could find out that the story's been way overblown just to get you to tune in to some irresponsible news source.

It's not like that with Jesus. Because God has made everything known to him, he likewise wants to make everything known to you. Jesus wants you to understand things like God's love and forgiveness, how important it is to obey him, and God's plan for your life. He can do this through his Spirit. Of course, he won't do it all at once since that would blow your mind. But he will inform you of what you need when you need it. You can trust that his revelations will be honest and accurate.

Your responsibility is to stay tuned in to him. Instead of listening to unreliable sources—ones that may or may not be right—you need to make sure you're getting your information from God's sources, via things like the Bible, God's Spirit, or wise and trusted counsel. You can trust that, in the right timing—when you stay connected and obedient—what you need to know will be made known to you. You will not be misled or left in the dark because Jesus promises to give you full disclosure.

My Prayer

Dear God,

I want to know your plans for my life. Thank you for promising to reveal to me what I need to know. Help me to stay tuned in to your Spirit.

Amen.

Final Word

God was kind and decided that Christ would choose us to be God's own adopted children.

Ephesians 1:5 CEV

Stone for the Journey

God's Spirit keeps me informed so I can follow him.

Week 47

Day 1 • Before the Dawn

Words from the Rock ·

Are you trying to figure out among yourselves what I meant when I said, "In a day or so you're not going to see me, but then in another day or so you will see me"? Then fix this firmly in your minds: You're going to be in deep mourning while the godless world throws a party. You'll be sad, very sad, but your sadness will develop into gladness.

John 16:19–20 Message

You've probably heard the saying, "It's darkest right before the dawn." It's true—the world can seem like a cold, black place when you're in the midst of a really difficult time. Whether you're grieving a lost friendship, a broken heart, or even a death, the world can feel hopeless and bleak.

Jesus knew his disciples were about to go through a rough period like that. He knew they would feel lost, deserted, even in despair. But he wanted them to understand it would only be temporary, that their overwhelming sadness would be replaced with joy and gladness. He didn't want them to lose hope.

Jesus knows you'll have times like that in your life. Maybe they will never be as dark and discouraging as the three days his disciples spent thinking that the world as they knew it had ended, that the hope of the world had died on the cross. Still, Jesus is aware that your life won't always be smooth and easy. That's not how it is for anyone who chooses to follow him. He knows there will be ups and downs. There will be sad times and happy times. But the sun will always rise after a night of darkness and despair. In time, your joy will return . . . and someday you'll experience sunlight and joy forever.

My Prayer ·

> *Dear God,*
>
> *I realize my earthly life isn't supposed to be nonstop sunshine and gladness. When times are dark, please remind me it won't always be like that.*
>
> *Amen.*

Final Word ·

> If we live in the light, as God does, we share in life with each other. And the blood of his Son Jesus washes all our sins away.
>
> 1 John 1:7 CEV

Stone for the Journey ·

> God replaces my darkness with light.

 ## Day 2 · Pain to Joy

Words from the Rock ·

> Whenever a woman is in labor she has pain, because her hour has come; but when she gives birth to the child, she no longer remembers the anguish because of the joy that a child has been born into the world. Therefore you too have grief now; but I will see you again, and your heart will rejoice, and no one will take your joy away from you.
>
> John 16:21-22 NASB

There's nothing that Jesus doesn't understand. Although he never had a baby, he perfectly describes how a mother feels after giving birth to a child. Labor, no matter how short it is (and it's usually not), feels like it will never end. In fact, the actual birthing process is one of the most physically painful experiences a human can endure. Yet most mothers will tell you that as soon as the baby is safely delivered and nestled in her arms, she forgets all about the pain she just endured. It's like her brain is temporarily wiped clean. Even when she does remember it later, it's as if the memory has been softened or diminished somehow. Otherwise there would be a lot fewer children in this world.

Jesus uses the childbirth metaphor to describe the enormous suffering his disciples will experience when he's temporarily removed from their world. Their grief will be excruciating—as painful as childbirth. But, he points out, it won't last long. When they reunite with Jesus, all that suffering will be forgotten.

Being separated from Jesus is supposed to hurt. It's God's way of reminding you to stay connected. If you experience that kind of intense spiritual anguish, the kind that aches deep inside, you need to do everything you can to reconnect yourself to Jesus. Once that relationship is restored, all sense of pain will fade away—it will be replaced with real joy!

My Prayer

> *Dear God,*
> *I don't want anything to separate me from you. If something does, help me to recognize it and repair it quickly.*
> *Amen.*

Final Word

> Those who plant in tears will harvest with shouts of joy.
>
> Psalm 126:5 NLT

Stone for the Journey

> I find joy in Jesus.

Day 3 • Love in Action

Words from the Rock

> The King will say . . . , "I was hungry, and you gave me food. I was thirsty, and you gave me something to drink. I was alone

and away from home, and you invited me into your house. I was without clothes, and you gave me something to wear. I was sick, and you cared for me. I was in prison, and you visited me."

Then the good people will answer, "Lord, when did we see you hungry ... thirsty ... away from home ... without clothes ... sick or in prison?" ...

Then the King will answer, "I tell you the truth, anything you did for even the least of my people here, you also did for me."

Matthew 25:34–40 NCV

It's not difficult to say the words "I love you." In fact, some people say these words rather carelessly, not really considering the meaning. There are others who say them insincerely, when they actually feel no love whatsoever. Some people even use them manipulatively, in order to get something from someone.

God wants your love for him to be genuine, and one way to show that love is real is by putting it into action. When you love someone, you're willing to go the distance to help them. If they're in need, you give. If they're lonely, you comfort. That's the way love acts.

Jesus takes this to an ever deeper level. He says we show our love to him in the way we love others. When we feed a hungry person, we feed Jesus. We give a poor person clothes, and it's like we clothed Jesus. We invite a homeless person into our home, and Jesus is there too. We visit an inmate, and Jesus feels we have visited him.

Nothing pleases Jesus more than when you go out of your way to love others selflessly and wholeheartedly like that. His Spirit will lead you and guide you in loving that way—if you're tuned in. Instead of just telling Jesus you love him, why not put it into action!

My Prayer ·

> *Dear God,*
>
> *I do love you and want to show it by loving others. Please help me to see those in need and how I can help them.*
>
> *Amen.*

Final Word ·

> Dear children, let's not merely say that we love each other; let us show the truth by our actions.
>
> 1 John 3:18 NLT

Stone for the Journey · · · · · · · · · · · · · · ·

> Love for others equals love for Jesus.

Day 4 • Just Ask

Words from the Rock · · · · · · · · · · · · · · ·

> At that time you won't need to ask me for anything. I tell you the truth, you will ask the Father directly, and he will grant your request because you use my name. You haven't done this before. Ask, using my name, and you will receive, and you will have abundant joy.
>
> John 16:23–24 NLT

Sometimes you'll hear someone say, "Just call me if you need anything." Sure, it sounds sweet and nice, and they might even mean it—or maybe they're just being polite. Would that friend sound as generous and kind if you called at three in the morning and asked him or her to come plunge your toilet? Probably not.

Jesus is not like that. And God never sleeps. When you are promised that you can ask for anything at any time—and that you will be heard and answered—you can believe it. Jesus gives you that kind of access to the Father because he's like your hotline to God. Does that mean you have a spiritual genie? That if you ask for something, your wish is his command and he'll give you whatever you want, like a new car or a million dollars or a singing career? If you think that, you're missing the point.

It's all about being connected to Jesus. When you're tight with Jesus, his Spirit will guide you so that you understand how to ask for what you need. You will know how to pray about what really matters—like helping people to know God better, ways you can grow in your faith, or anything else God wants to do in your life. As you get closer to Jesus, your prayers become more on target with what God wants.

My Prayer

Dear God,

Thank you for always being there and for hearing my prayers 24-7. I want to get closer to Jesus so I can pray the way you want me to.

Amen.

Final Word

We ought always to give thanks to God for you . . . because your faith is growing abundantly, and the love of every one of you for one another is increasing.

2 Thessalonians 1:3 ESV

Stone for the Journey

Jesus teaches me to pray.

Day 5 · Love Connection

Words from the Rock

God the Father loves you because you love me, and you believe that I have come from him. I came from the Father into the world, but I am leaving the world and returning to the Father.

John 16:27-28 CEV

Jesus can't make things any clearer than he does here. This is plain-speak at its best. This clear statement is all about love and connection. Jesus's love connects us to the Father's love—and then Jesus returns to the Father. Can it get any simpler than that? Yet if you know anything about religion and history and humankind, you know that it's still possible for people to mess up this truth.

In fact, in the two thousand years since Jesus gave this statement, many religious leaders have tried to complicate its simple message. Some have tried to make it seem that this love relationship must be earned or that forgiveness must be purchased. Others have portrayed Jesus's love as exclusive—like it's a special club with a secret handshake—and that it's okay to push others away. Some have twisted Jesus's message, completely deleting the love part, in order to hurt and even kill others.

Jesus's message of love and acceptance is so simple and straightforward, so accessible and pure . . . yet some still manage to mangle it. What can you do to keep that from happening to you? What can you do to ensure that you don't get pulled down the wrong trail? How about writing Jesus's words on your heart? Memorize some Bible verses that are meaningful to you so that you can take them with you wherever you go. That way if you run into someone who wants to point you in another direction, you won't be misled. Perhaps you can even help them return to the truth!

My Prayer

Dear God,

Thanks for the simplicity of the love connection. Help me to keep that connection alive and vital and to write your words on my heart.

Amen.

Final Word

You are the body of Christ, and each one of you is a part of it.

1 Corinthians 12:27 NIV

Stone for the Journey

Jesus's love connects me to God.

Week 48

 ## Day 1 · Coming Back

Words from the Rock ·

> Do you finally believe? In fact, you're about to make a run for it—saving your own skins and abandoning me. But I'm not abandoned. The Father is with me. I've told you all this so that trusting me, you will be unshakable and assured, deeply at peace. In this godless world you will continue to experience difficulties. But take heart! I've conquered the world.
>
> John 16:31–33 Message

People don't always do what is right. They don't always act like they know they should. Jesus's disciples—the same men who later founded the original Christian church, shared the gospel with thousands, even gave up their lives for their faith—were no different. When the going got tough . . . they actually ran the other direction.

Frightened and confused, these men cowered in dark corners, considered abandoning their faith, and even denied knowing Jesus, just as he had predicted they would do. That's why he told them ahead of time what would happen—to reassure them that it would be okay.

Jesus understands your human weakness. He knows you can't possibly live the "perfect Christian life" day in and day out. He knows you'll blow it. But he wants you to realize that, even when you do blow it, he's ready to welcome you back. Because of who he is (he never blew it), he has made up for all your shortcomings, and he is able to forgive you and get you back on track.

Even though you'll feel sad and discouraged when you turn your back on Jesus, you shouldn't beat yourself up too much. Remember that Jesus understands. Most of all he wants you to return to him—to confess you blew it, to receive his forgiveness, and to believe he is able to restore your relationship with him. He wants to bring you back to that place of peace.

My Prayer ·

Dear God,

I'm relieved that you know I'm not perfect and that I'll blow it sometimes. Help me to be quick to turn back to you. Thank you for welcoming me with open arms!

Amen.

Final Word ·

Therefore confess your sins to each other and pray for each other so that you may be healed. The prayer of a righteous man is powerful and effective.

James 5:16 NIV

Stone for the Journey ·

God's love always welcomes me back.

 Day 2 • Like a River

Words from the Rock ·

"I was hungry, and you gave me nothing to eat. I was thirsty, and you gave me nothing to drink. I was alone and away from home, and you did not invite me into your house. I was without clothes, and you gave me nothing to wear. I was sick and in prison, and you did not care for me."

Then those people will answer, "Lord, when did we see you hungry or thirsty or alone and away from home or without clothes or sick or in prison? When did we see these things and not help you?" . . .

"Anything you refused to do for even the least of my people here, you refused to do for me."

Matthew 25:42–45 NCV

Some people think that the more they keep for themselves, the richer they will be. Maybe that makes sense on some levels. But have you ever seen hoarders—people who refuse to get rid of anything? Their houses fill up until they can barely walk through the rooms or use the furniture. Yet many of them will go out and get even more stuff—hauling it in and piling it up until it's truly a health hazard and firetrap. This kind of behavior seems crazy to most people, but a hoarder thinks it's normal.

There are a lot of explanations for hoarders. Some reasons are complicated, but others are common—like insecurity, fear of poverty, or anxiety that they'll run out of something or need something they've given away. In a way, it's like not believing that God can and will provide for them. Instead of relying on God's generosity, they are grabbing as much as they can and stuffing it into their homes. Not only is it impairing and dysfunctional, it's exactly the opposite of how God wants us to live.

God generously gives us what we need, and he wants us to be just as generous to those around us—especially to those in need. God knows that when we give, we open ourselves up to receive. Like a river that needs to flow freely to stay healthy, we need to give freely to stay healthy. When we bless others with our generosity, it's like we're blessing Jesus.

My Prayer

> *Dear God,*
>
> *Please show me ways I can be generous. Whether it's with my time or my money or my friendship, let me give to others like I'm giving to you.*
>
> *Amen.*

Final Word

> [If one's gift] is contributing to the needs of others, let him give generously . . . let him do it cheerfully.
>
> Romans 12:8 NIV

Stone for the Journey

> God wants his generosity to flow through me.

Day 3 • With Open Arms

Words from the Rock · · · · · · · · · · · · · · · · · · ·

Father, the time has come for you to bring glory to your Son, in order that he may bring glory to you. And you gave him power over all people, so that he would give eternal life to everyone you give him.

John 17:1–2 CEV

Before Jesus came to earth, most religions were extremely exclusive. Remember how the scribes and Pharisees and religious leaders seemed to do everything possible to keep ordinary people from getting close to God? It was as if they felt it was their job to build a giant wall around God, posting signs that said "Keep Out" or "No Trespassing" or "Stay Away." There were other religions that weren't much different, as if religion was a private club—for members only. They had to pay their dues, be born in a certain family, obey certain rules, act a certain way, or live in a certain neighborhood just to be good enough to belong.

But Jesus said, "Enough!" Fed up with man-made efforts to separate people from God, Jesus was done with exclusivity. He opened his arms wide, inviting anyone and everyone to come and receive him. Then with arms still spread wide, he died on the cross so that God would welcome all believers into his kingdom. Unlike the other uptight religions, Jesus's rules were simple—love God and love others, and come on along!

When Jesus said he came for "all people" and for "everyone," he meant it. His love is not limited, and his mercy is endless. And he wants you to be an extension of his love and mercy to everyone around you. No walls. No barriers. No cliques. No exclusions. This is a party where everyone is invited. All are welcome. The way you show that you belong to Jesus is by inviting others into your life—with open arms!

My Prayer ·

Dear God,

Thank you for welcoming me into your family. Help me to be warm and inviting to everyone around me. I don't want to exclude anyone.

Amen.

Final Word ·

Love each other with genuine affection, and take delight in honoring each other.

Romans 12:10 NLT

Stone for the Journey ·

God welcomes me so I can welcome others.

 ## Day 4 · Attention!

Words from the Rock ·

As you know, the Passover is two days away—and the Son of Man will be handed over to be crucified.

Matthew 26:2 NIV

There was a time in Jesus's ministry when even his closest followers had no idea that his life would end so tragically. Maybe if they'd known that he was going to be sentenced to death like a common criminal, they would have hung their heads and slunk away. Perhaps Jesus knew this, and that was why he waited until his arrest and death were only hours away to speak so explicitly to his disciples. He knew they could bear only so much. He wanted to protect them from what he knew could be their undoing.

From the disciples' perspective, death was a permanent state of being. Jesus knew his friends would see this as his final exit—the end of the story, that's all there is. Yet he understood they needed to know what was coming—they needed to be privy to this shocking news so that, in time, they would understand.

Death is hard for anyone to grasp. Even if we believe in Jesus's promise of heaven and life after death, it's still painful and sad to see someone die. It cuts us to the core—and it really does feel final. Nothing on earth is more extreme than death. To experience that kind of a loss is like the ultimate wake-up call. No matter our state of mind, death always gets our attention.

Jesus knew that his death would get a lot of attention too, and when he rose from the dead, he would get even more. His victory over death would be one more thing to separate him from every other religion's leaders, one more thing to show that he was truly from God—the real deal. He died and rose so we can live. It's an amazing gift that should hold our attention for all of eternity.

My Prayer

> *Dear God,*
>
> *Death does get my attention. Thank you for giving up everything so I can live. Help me to appreciate this today.*
>
> *Amen.*

Final Word

> We believe that Jesus died and rose again and so we believe that God will bring with Jesus those who have fallen asleep in him.
>
> 1 Thessalonians 4:14 NIV

Stone for the Journey

> Jesus's death gave me life.

Day 5 • Jesus's Gift

Words from the Rock

> This is eternal life: that people know you, the only true God, and that they know Jesus Christ, the One you sent.
>
> John 17:3 NCV

Nothing was more important to Jesus than for everyone to know his Father God. Nothing. And Jesus was willing to do anything to bring this message to everyone on earth. Anything.

Imagine it's a thousand years ago and you live in a fabulous kingdom with your wonderful father, and life is extremely good. You are surrounded by dear friends, and there is amazing food, beautiful gardens, swimming pools, horses to ride . . . It's the best place in the world. But this kingdom is surrounded by a moat of toxic liquid that will dissolve anything that touches it. This liquid was put there by people who dwell outside of the kingdom. Because you have a telescope, you know that the people on the other side are sick and starving, and thanks to earthquakes their land is being destroyed. You tell your father you want to rescue them, so he lets you build a bridge over the moat.

You get to the other side and begin telling the people about your father. But their reactions are mixed. Some don't believe you—they say it's impossible to cross that moat. Some say your father is evil. Some ignore you or laugh at you. Finally, as their world is falling apart, you convince some to follow you back across the bridge, but as you get there you see the bridge is starting to dissolve. Quickly you stretch yourself across the bridge and tell people to just walk over you—and hurry to the other side. They make it, but in the process you fall into the toxic liquid and die.

That's kind of like what Jesus did for you. He gave up everything when he left his Father's kingdom. Then he laid down his life so you could meet his Father. That was his mission—his gift for all mankind. What is your response to that gift?

My Prayer

Dear God,

Thank you so much for sending Jesus. Thank you that Jesus was willing to die for me. Please help me to never take that gift for granted.

Amen.

Final Word

Christ Jesus, who died—more than that, who was raised to life—is at the right hand of God and is also interceding for us.

Romans 8:34 NIV

Stone for the Journey

Jesus gave all for me to know God.

Week 49

Day 1 • Incomprehensible

Words from the Rock ·

> I glorified You on the earth, having accomplished the work which You have given Me to do. Now, Father, glorify Me together with Yourself, with the glory which I had with You before the world was.
>
> John 17:4–5 NASB

It's hard to envision someplace you've never been before. Especially if you don't have photos or videos or some other kind of description. Even if someone tells you about this distant place, unless you have an astonishing imagination, you probably won't get it right.

When it comes to imagining how fantastic heaven is, no one on earth can possibly get it right. You could take all the very best things on earth (gorgeous mountains, white sandy beaches, majestic rain forests, stunning canyons, rolling fields of wildflowers, sapphire blue lakes—anything you think is beautiful), and even if you multiplied those wonders a thousand times, you'd still probably miss how incredible heaven really is. It's incomprehensible.

Even more incomprehensible is Jesus's willingness to leave heaven—and to leave his Father behind—in order to come to earth and complete the work God had set before him. Yet he did it—cheerfully, wholeheartedly, and selflessly. He threw everything he had into getting out the good news that God loved everyone and that he wanted a relationship with them. When Jesus's work was done, he took it a step further and gave up his own life in a brutal and humiliating death. What more could he do?

He did all this because of his love for his Father . . . and because of his love for you. With his mission complete, Jesus returned to heaven and was reunited with his Father. His reward for a job well done is to celebrate with everyone who's now welcome in heaven—including you! And if heaven was totally awesome before Jesus left, how much better it will be now!

My Prayer

Dear God,

Heaven really is incomprehensible, but I know it will be the best experience imaginable. I'm so thankful I'll get to participate in it. Amen.

Final Word

Then I saw a new heaven and a new earth, for the first heaven and the first earth had passed away, and there was no longer any sea.

Revelation 21:1 NIV

Stone for the Journey

I cannot begin to imagine how fantastic heaven is.

 ## Day 2 · All-Out Love

Words from the Rock

Why are you bothering this woman? She has done a beautiful thing to me. The poor you will always have with you, but you will not always have me. When she poured this perfume on my body, she did it to prepare me for burial. I tell you the truth, wherever this gospel is preached throughout the world, what she has done will also be told, in memory of her.

Matthew 26:10–13 NIV

One of Jesus's disciples appears to put more faith in money than he does in Jesus. Judas, the bookkeeper for the disciples, rants about a woman after she's emptied a very expensive bottle of perfume on Jesus. "Why this waste?" Judas demands. "We could've sold that perfume for a lot of money . . . and we could've even given the money to the poor."

Jesus knows this woman has done this extravagant thing out of pure self-lessness. It's her way of expressing her love and gratitude to Jesus, who, as

God's Son, isn't worried about something as insignificant as money. The most important thing here is that this woman understands who Jesus is—that he is part of God and that nothing is too good, too expensive, or too fine for him. Her gift is a form of true worship, and Jesus receives it as such. He even goes so far as to mention that this woman's gift will be used as an example of worship for years to come—and now, two thousand years later, we're reading about it!

How do you worship Jesus? Are you a cheapskate worshiper? Are you miserly in your praise? Do you hold back in fear that it costs too much to love him? Or do you realize that Jesus is King of Kings—and nothing is too good for him? Do you grasp that no matter how much praise and worship and love you lavish on him, it is no more than his due? Jesus invites you to pour yourself out like the woman with the perfume—holding nothing back!

My Prayer

Dear God,

I want to be like the woman with the perfume. I want to pour myself out on you. Please teach me how to do that—to give my all like you did.

Amen.

Final Word

Now we can rejoice in our wonderful new relationship with God because our Lord Jesus Christ has made us friends of God.

Romans 5:11 NLT

Stone for the Journey

I will pour out my love for Jesus.

Day 3 · Family Ties

Words from the Rock ·

> I have revealed you to the ones you gave me from this world.
> They were always yours. You gave them to me, and they have
> kept your word. Now they know that everything I have is a gift
> from you, for I have passed on to them the message you gave
> me. They accepted it and know that I came from you, and they
> believe you sent me.
>
> John 17:6–8 NLT

Everyone has an innate longing to be part of a supportive, loving family. A few people are fortunate enough to enjoy a real sense of that kind of family here on earth. Maybe they're born into one, or they're adopted somewhere along the line. Or perhaps they figure out how to put together a family of their own making—a family of dear friends who are as close as blood relatives. Anyone who's included in a loving family appreciates its value and importance. Even those with slightly dysfunctional families probably wouldn't trade them in.

Yet for many people, and for many reasons, being part of a loving family is just a dream—an impossible dream. Some people live their entire lives feeling like they're on the outside looking in, and they experience loneliness whenever they see what appears to be a healthy and loving family.

God understands this. That's why it was so important for Jesus to come to earth and to accomplish his mission of introducing everyone to God. This was God's way to ensure that we all have a chance to be part of an incredibly, amazingly, miraculously loving family—his family. He gathers up all his children and welcomes us into his phenomenal family, and when the time is right, he brings us home to live with him and with Jesus throughout eternity. One great big happy family!

But it's even better than that—you can actually experience this sense of family right here and now. Once you become God's child, you're automatically linked to millions of spiritual brothers and sisters here on earth. You're no longer on the outside looking in—you are part of God's amazing family right now!

My Prayer ·

Dear God,

Thank you for adopting me into your incredible family. Help me to love my spiritual brothers and sisters the way you have loved me. Amen.

Final Word · · · · · · · · · · · · · · · · · ·

By faith we have been made acceptable to God. And now, because of our Lord Jesus Christ, we live at peace with God.

Romans 5:1 CEV

Stone for the Journey · · · · · · · · · · · · · · · · · ·

I am part of God's family.

 # Day 4 • Prayer Power

Words from the Rock · · · · · · · · · · · · · · · · · ·

I pray for them. I am not praying for the world, but for those you have given me, for they are yours. All I have is yours, and all you have is mine. And glory has come to me through them.

John 17:9–10 NIV

Sometimes it's hard to pray. We make all kinds of excuses. Like maybe you don't know quite what to say or how to say it. Maybe you wonder how long you should pray—is two minutes too short; is two hours too long? Perhaps you assume you need to get yourself to the right place to pray properly, like on a church pew or on your knees or on a mountaintop. Maybe you think you should read a book about prayer—just to make sure you're doing it correctly. It's even possible you've convinced yourself that you don't have the right kind of words to use in your prayers, that you need a special "spiritual" vocabulary that will make God sit up and listen.

Of course, that's all pretty ridiculous—because there are no rules for how to pray. Mostly God wants you to do it—just do it. Prayer is how you communicate with God. It's the way you express how you feel, what you need, what worries you. It's how you confess a problem or ask for help. It's how you thank God or tell him you love him. Prayer is like talking to a friend, and anytime is the right time to do it; anywhere is the right place. You don't even have to close your eyes or fold your hands or say, "Amen." In other words, prayer is quite simple. It's beneficial and something you need to do for your own health and well-being on a regular basis.

That's a lot to know about praying, but did you know that Jesus prays for you? Even though Jesus is God's Son and one with God, he still cares so much about you and loves you so much that he prays for you. That alone should convince you that prayer is vital. So what's stopping you from praying right now?

My Prayer

> *Dear God,*
> *Show me how to pray to you. Remind me there are no rules.*
> *Help me to see that prayer is simply having a conversation with you.*
> *Amen.*

Final Word

> I thank my God every time I remember you. In all my prayers for all of you, I always pray with joy.
>
> Philippians 1:3-4 NIV

Stone for the Journey

> God wants to hear from me today.

Day 5 • Lifetime Membership

Words from the Rock ·

> I am no longer in the world; and yet they themselves are in
> the world, and I come to You. Holy Father, keep them in Your
> name, the name which You have given Me, that they may be
> one even as We are.
>
> John 17:11 NASB

God designed us in a way that makes us long to be part of something big-ger than ourselves. We desire a connected oneness—something that joins us into a larger community. Although some mistakenly assume that kind of connection can be accomplished through electronic means like text messaging, email, blogs, chat rooms, social networks, cell phones . . . what we actually want is something more—much, much more.

Maybe you've heard someone say, "It feels like something is missing in my life." Perhaps you've felt like that too—isolated, lonely, left out. Some people might become members of clubs or churches or cliques to find that connected-ness. Others might gather at sports events or concerts, getting lost in the crowd and hoping that will substitute for belonging—until it's time to go home. A few might even take the dark route and join a gang. It's all about wanting to be included, to be a member of something, to belong.

Jesus knows about oneness because of his tight relationship with his Fa-ther—and all of heaven. He knows how important it is for everyone to partici-pate in this kind of connection. He spent all of his earthly life trying to help us understand how much we need to unite ourselves to him and his Father. This doesn't mean you shouldn't belong to any other type of group. It simply means your most important membership—the one that will last for eternity—is in being connected to God. Jesus already paid your dues, so you might as well enjoy the privileges of membership.

My Prayer ·

> *Dear God,*
>
> *Thank you for including me. Whenever I feel lonely or left out,*
> *please remind me that I belong to you.*
>
> *Amen.*

Final Word ·

May our Lord Jesus Christ himself and God our Father, who loved us and by his grace gave us eternal encouragement and good hope, encourage your hearts and strengthen you in every good deed and word.

2 Thessalonians 2:16–17 NIV

Stone for the Journey ·

I have a lifetime membership with God.

Week 50

 ## Day 1 · Communion

Words from the Rock ·

Jesus . . . blessed the bread and broke it . . . and said, "Take this and eat it. This is my body."

Jesus picked up a cup of wine and gave thanks to God . . . and said, "Take this and drink it. This is my blood, and with it God makes his agreement with you. It will be poured out, so that many people will have their sins forgiven. From now on I am not going to drink any wine, until I drink new wine with you in my Father's kingdom."

Matthew 26:26–29 CEV

Some call this event the Last Supper, and it's the final meal that Jesus ate before his death. What he says to his disciples during that meal is not only surprisingly graphic but also slightly disturbing on some levels. He tells them that they are eating his body and drinking his blood. But what does that mean? Certainly he's not endorsing cannibalism or vampirism.

The point Jesus is making is that he wants his followers to be so much a part of him, so connected to him, that it's as if his being (his flesh and blood) is actually inside each one of them—like his blood is flowing through their veins. That is real oneness. It's not easy to grasp, but Jesus knows it will take this kind of oneness for his followers to stick with him through all the trials and challenges that will soon be hurled at them. As graphic as the idea of eating his body and drinking his blood is, he wants to drive this concept home.

Jesus wants everyone to understand that his body will be beaten and broken and his blood will be spilled—in other words, he will die—in order to give us this kind of oneness with him. If we're repulsed by this truth, if we try to shove this gift away, we will miss out. As abhorrent as it might seem, it's only when we embrace Jesus's torturous death that we get to enjoy his forgiveness.

My Prayer

Dear God,

Thank you for dying on the cross, for being broken, and for spilling your blood so I can be one with you and receive your forgiveness and eternal life.

Amen.

Final Word

Since we have now been justified by his blood, how much more shall we be saved from God's wrath through him!

Romans 5:9 NIV

Stone for the Journey

Jesus's blood buys my forgiveness.

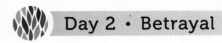

Day 2 • Betrayal

Words from the Rock · · · · · · · · · · · · · · ·

> While I was with them, I kept them safe by the power you have
> given me. I guarded them, and not one of them was lost, except
> the one who had to be lost. This happened so that what the
> Scriptures say would come true.
>
> John 17:12 CEV

You probably know by now that one of Jesus's disciples is a betrayer. Judas Iscariot, the same man who was anxious about finances, sells Jesus out. He reveals Jesus's whereabouts for thirty pieces of silver. While this sounds diabolical and malicious, it's something that must happen in order to fulfill an old prophecy about Jesus. In order for people to understand that Jesus is truly the Messiah, the Son of God, all of the Old Testament prophecies must be fulfilled during Jesus's time on earth—and they are.

Jesus knows in advance he will be betrayed, and he's well aware that Judas will be responsible for turning him over to the authorities, after which Jesus will be beaten, interrogated, tortured, humiliated, and eventually killed. Yet Jesus loves Judas. He treats this betrayer as a dear friend. Right up until the end, when Judas reveals Jesus's identity with a kiss, Jesus never says a harsh word against him. We don't hear much about Judas after that—except that he is so grieved by his actions that he hangs himself.

We don't know whether or not Judas cried out to Jesus in his final breath, if he confessed his sin and begged for forgiveness . . . but it's possible that when we get to heaven we'll be surprised. We'll probably be surprised by a lot of things in heaven. But because we do know Jesus is all about mercy, love, and forgiveness, we can assume that Jesus would have reached out his hand to Judas.

In the same way, you can be assured that Jesus will forgive you when you betray him. And you will. Everyone betrays Jesus at some point in life. Whether it's briefly turning your back and pretending not to know him, or totally walking away from him for a while, you will betray him. The important thing is that you turn back to him, tell him you're sorry, and accept his forgiveness.

My Prayer ·

Dear God,

I don't ever want to betray you. If I do, please remind me that your forgiveness is there for me. Let me hurry back to you and confess that I blew it.

Amen.

Final Word ·

God treats us much better than we deserve, and because of Christ Jesus, he freely accepts us and sets us free from our sins.

Romans 3:24 CEV

Stone for the Journey · · · · · · · · · · · · · · · · · ·

God forgives the worst in me.

Day 3 · Wake Up!

Words from the Rock · · · · · · · · · · · · · · · · · · ·

[Jesus] prayed, saying, "My Father, if it is possible, let this cup pass from Me; yet not as I will, but as You will." And He came to the disciples and found them sleeping, and said to Peter, "So, you men could not keep watch with Me for one hour? Keep watching and praying that you may not enter into temptation; the spirit is willing, but the flesh is weak." He went away again a second time and prayed, saying, "My Father, if this cannot pass away unless I drink it, Your will be done."

Matthew 26:39–42 NASB

On the most difficult night of Jesus's life—which is about to end—at a time when he wants and needs his best friends (his beloved disciples) to surround him with their love and support . . . they are asleep. Jesus is desperately praying to his Father—confessing his concerns, expressing his deepest emotions, even to the point where he sweats drops of blood—and his buddies are snoozing.

It's as if the weight of the world . . . the entire universe . . . is resting on Jesus's shoulders tonight. He knows that his earthly mission (to save the human race) is nearly over. He's done everything possible to show them God's love and mercy—but is it enough? Time is running out, and his death is imminent. Because of his love for all mankind (then and now), he suffers great agony as he prays to the Father about what lies ahead. Then he submits his will to his Father, saying, "Do it your way, not mine." And throughout his torment, while he struggles, his friends are fast asleep.

It's tempting to take a nap when times get hard. It's like sleep is the great escape. While Jesus understands your humanity, he still warns you to be careful. He doesn't want your human weakness to cause you to fall flat on your face. Instead of dozing off when the going gets rough, why not go to Jesus and ask him for help? Wake up!

My Prayer

Dear God,

I confess that sometimes I want to hide from my problems. Remind me that you handle things differently. Help me to come to you for help.

Amen.

Final Word

We can rejoice, too, when we run into problems and trials, for we know that they help us develop endurance.

Romans 5:3 NLT

Stone for the Journey

God wants me to face my troubles.

Day 4 • Complete Joy

Words from the Rock · · · · · · · · · · · · · · · · ·

> Now I'm returning to you. I'm saying these things in the world's hearing so my people can experience my joy completed in them.
>
> John 17:13 Message

Jesus is talking to his Father about his friends and all the people who will follow him in the centuries to come—including you. Knowing his earthly time is nearly over, Jesus prays to his Father about what's to come. What will happen to his friends when he's gone? Although Jesus knows he's about to be killed, he's not even thinking about that. His primary concern is for his followers.

On a night when he knows that his earthly life is pretty much over, that he won't get to be with his friends anymore, that he won't get to heal and teach and do miracles, and that he is about to endure an excruciating form of death . . . he asks his Father to make sure his followers experience his joy.

Joy? On a dark, dismal night, when his buddies are fast asleep, while he is alone and suffering and in deep spiritual anguish, Jesus asks God to make sure his friends have joy? Yes. He's not only asking God to give them joy, he's asking God to *complete* his joy within them—in other words, to finish the work Jesus began.

He is entrusting his loved ones into his Father's hands because he knows that only God can finish this impossible mission. Only God can bring joy after what will soon become the darkest day in the history of the world. Jesus's faith in his Father convinces him that this is possible. Even now, Jesus knows that if his work is complete and full in you, it is because his Father has linked your life to his—which results in real joy.

My Prayer · · · · · · · · · · · · · · · · · · ·

> *Dear God,*
>
> *Please complete Jesus's work in me so his joy will be part of my life. When I feel my joy is lacking, remind me to come to you.*
>
> *Amen.*

Final Word · · · · · · · · · ·

Because of our faith, Christ has brought us into this place of undeserved privilege where we now stand, and we confidently and joyfully look forward to sharing God's glory.

Romans 5:2 NLT

Stone for the Journey · · · · · · · · · · · ·

Jesus's joy in me means God is at work.

 ## Day 5 · Safekeeping

Words from the Rock · · · · · · · · · ·

I have given them your word. And the world hates them because they do not belong to the world, just as I do not belong to the world. I'm not asking you to take them out of the world, but to keep them safe from the evil one. They do not belong to this world any more than I do.

John 17:14–16 NLT

More than anyone, Jesus understands that this world is a dangerous place. In fact, the eve of his murder is when he prays specifically for the safety of his friends. Their association with him puts them at serious risk. He already told them that if someone hated him, they will hate his disciples too—danger by association.

Jesus knows that this kind of danger and hatred will continue through the future—those who hate Jesus will hate anyone who belongs to him. That includes you—your association puts you at risk. Because Jesus loves you just as much as he loved his disciples, he wants you to remain safe too.

Now, being that Jesus is the Son of God, you'd think he could do whatever it takes to keep you safe. If he wanted, he could probably design a special escape route, a secret passageway, that would swoosh you away from this earth to a secure location. But he doesn't want to do that. He would rather keep you safe in the midst of danger because he knows that's where you can be most effective.

Jesus doesn't want you to live an anxious, cautious, sheltered life. He doesn't want you cowering in corners, shivering in fear. Instead, he wants you to trust him and be assured of his ability to protect you as you face whatever comes your way. That kind of confidence gets attention—people see Jesus's power at work in you. That's when they want to find out how they can have this power for themselves.

My Prayer

> *Dear God,*
>
> *I confess this world sometimes scares me, but I know you'll keep me safe. Help me to walk in that kind of confidence so others will see you in me.*
>
> *Amen.*

Final Word

> Something even greater than friendship is ours. Now that we are at peace with God, we will be saved by his Son's life.
>
> Romans 5:10 CEV

Stone for the Journey

> God will keep me safe.

Week 51

Day 1 • Rags to Riches

Words from the Rock

> Soon you will see the Son of Man sitting at the right side of God All-Powerful and coming on the clouds of heaven.
>
> Matthew 26:64 CEV

Everyone enjoys a rags-to-riches story. Like when a homeless guy wins the lottery. Or someone rises up from the projects to stardom. Experiences like that get our attention and warm our hearts.

Jesus's life is the ultimate rags-to-riches tale. Actually, it's more like a riches-to-rags-to-riches story. First of all, he leaves all the riches and wonders and beauty of heaven to come to earth as a helpless baby. And he's not born in a hospital or even a house—no, Jesus is born in a lowly stable with farm animals watching.

Then, after Jesus spends his whole life serving others and doing God's will, he is captured and beaten and ridiculed and subjected to a brutal execution. Really, can a man's life end more miserably than that? Nailed to a cross between a couple of thieves while his executioners throw dice for his clothing, Jesus reaches an all-time low. Even though he trusts his Father, it must be difficult . . . and excruciatingly painful. And then he dies.

But here's the good part—the happy twist in the story that Jesus tells his disciples to anticipate. He wants them to realize that shortly after his death, he'll be alive again, and he'll be reunited with his Father. Jesus will have beaten death, and he will sit at God's right side. He will emerge from the depths of despair and rise up to join all the glories of heaven. There Jesus will rule and reign with his Father God. From rags to riches. And because of him, you will experience the same thing—your relationship with Jesus will transform your life from rags to riches!

My Prayer

Dear God,

I'm so thankful that no one and nothing could hold Jesus down. I know that his victory is my victory; his story is mine. I can go from rags to riches too.

Amen.

Final Word

Could it be any clearer? Our old way of life was nailed to the cross with Christ, a decisive end to that sin-miserable life—no longer at sin's every beck and call!

Romans 6:6 Message

Stone for the Journey

God can turn my life around.

Day 2 • The Mission

Words from the Rock · · · · · · · · · · · · · · · · · ·

> Make them holy—consecrated—with the truth; your word is consecrating truth. In the same way that you gave me a mission in the world, I give them a mission in the world. I'm consecrating myself for their sakes so they'll be truth-consecrated in their mission.
>
> John 17:17–19 Message

Jesus's earthly mission is to spread the Good News—to communicate to the world that God loves everyone and wants them to be part of his family. Jesus passes that mission on to each of his friends. He invites every follower to imitate him in the mission of sharing that Good News. If you love Jesus, you won't want to let him down.

If you're like most people, though, you might find that mission a little overwhelming. How do you do it? Where do you begin? What if you fail? It's a big assignment, and it's pretty intimidating. Do you need some kind of special training? A college degree? Do you need to memorize the Bible from cover to cover first? What if someone questions your qualifications to do this mission?

Jesus doesn't ask you to do something he doesn't intend to help you with. He knows it's not easy. That's why he promises to send his Spirit to teach you. His Spirit of truth will show you how to share the Good News—he will guide you in how to tell others God loves them. Remember the two commandments Jesus gave you? Love God with all you are, and love your neighbor as yourself. If you do those two things, you will fulfill Jesus's mission, and others will notice you're living a life that stands out.

My Prayer ·

Dear God,

Thank you for giving me a mission. Thank you for sending your Spirit. Help me to keep your two commandments so I can fulfill your mission.

Amen.

Final Word · · · · · · · · · · · ·

It is by believing in your heart that you are made right with God, and it is by confessing with your mouth that you are saved.

Romans 10:10 NLT

Stone for the Journey · · · · · · · · · · · · · · ·

My mission is to let God love others through me.

 ## Day 3 · Amazed by Grace

Words from the Rock · · · · · · · · · · · · · · ·

Jesus said, "Father, forgive them, for they do not know what they are doing." . . .

[A thief on the cross next to Jesus] said, "Jesus, remember me when you come into your kingdom."

Jesus answered him, "I tell you the truth, today you will be with me in paradise."

Luke 23:34, 42–43 NIV

Who would appreciate a hot meal more—a guy who just polished off a super-sized dinner or a guy on the street who hasn't eaten for days? The answer is obvious. By the same token, which person would appreciate being tossed a life preserver—the one standing onshore or the one drowning in the surf? Again, it's obvious. The ones who know they are in need of help are the ones who most appreciate it.

Now consider the two criminals nailed to the crosses on either side of Jesus. Both are being executed because they are guilty of serious crimes. Which one of these men appreciates Jesus's forgiveness? One man, despite being put to death, is still arrogant, and he dismisses and mocks Jesus. The other man knows he's being executed because he's a criminal, but he also knows who Jesus is. He understands that Jesus is the Son of God, and he respects that Jesus has the power to forgive sin. He's the man who knows he's in need, and he's the man Jesus promises to take to paradise with him.

Can you imagine how amazed the thief must have been in that moment? What had started out as a dark day suddenly turned promising—he received a second chance and an invitation to a brand-new life. All because he knew that he was a sinner and that Jesus was a forgiver—he understood that he had a need Jesus could meet.

How do you respond to Jesus's grace? Do you see your need of forgiveness? Do you welcome God's mercy like the guy on the cross did? Or do you think you're such a good person you don't need it?

My Prayer

Dear God,

I'm so thankful for your mercy and forgiveness. Help me to always be amazed by your grace toward me. I never want to take it for granted or push it away.

Amen.

Final Word

His Spirit lets us know that together with Christ we will be given what God has promised. We will also share in the glory of Christ, because we have suffered with him.

Romans 8:17 CEV

Stone for the Journey

I need God's grace 24-7.

Day 4 • Unity

Words from the Rock

I am not praying just for these followers. I am also praying for everyone else who will have faith because of what my followers will say about me. I want all of them to be one with each other, just as I am one with you and you are one with me. I also want them to be one with us. Then the people of this world will believe that you sent me.

John 17:20-21 CEV

Jesus had you specifically in mind when he prayed these words. He knew that generations of believers would come and go for ages and ages—and he knew that you would be one of them. As hard as it is to wrap your mind around this, nearly two thousand years before you were born, *Jesus prayed for you.* What was the focus of this prayer? Jesus's heartfelt request was that God would make his believers one. He wants us to be united, joined together in heart and purpose, bound together in love. Jesus wants his followers to be connected to each other the same way he is connected to his Father.

Is that what you observe when you look at Christians today? Do you sense a strong bond of oneness between different churches and denominations? Do the Baptists love the Presbyterians? Do the Methodists love the Lutherans? If these questions make you stop to wonder, you're not alone. Unfortunately, reports of church disputes, theological bickering, and Christians arguing among themselves tend to circulate. When outsiders hear these stories, they feel repulsed. Who wants to become part of a group that claims to love one another but treats each other like enemies? Isn't that a little hypocritical? And don't you think it must break Jesus's heart?

So what's your responsibility? Do you do your part in helping the Christian community to be united in love? Do you do your best to promote oneness? Do you love your Christian brothers and sisters? Jesus prayed that you would be one with fellow believers, but he knows you have a choice in the matter. He prays that you will choose love. How do you pray?

My Prayer

Dear God,

I want to echo Jesus's prayer—that all Christian believers would be one. Please show me how to help make this happen. Let your love flow through me.

Amen.

Final Word

Whoever loves his brother lives in the light, and there is nothing in him to make him stumble.

1 John 2:10 NIV

Stone for the Journey · · · · · · · · · · · · · · · · ·

God wants me to promote unity.

Day 5 • Reputation

Words from the Rock ·

I have given them the glory you gave me, so they may be one
as we are one. I am in them and you are in me. May they experience such perfect unity that the world will know that you sent
me and that you love them as much as you love me.

John 17:22–23 NLT

Imagine that you just arrived in a new town and you're really hungry. You
spot a nice-looking restaurant with a brightly lit sign that says, "Delicious
Food Served Here." Okay, no one needs to twist your arm. But you're barely
inside when a foul odor hits you. You glance in the kitchen and see the cook
pick a hamburger off the floor and slap it on a plate. The waitress, wearing a
stained apron, makes a hacking cough as she points you to a dirty table. Then
suddenly a green-faced guy leaves his half-eaten meal behind, and as he races
for the bathroom, he hurls right there on the filthy linoleum floor. Still hungry?

What if that's how nonbelievers feel about the church? What if someone
is spiritually hungry and sees a cheerful sign that lures him into some kind of
fellowship group, but once he's inside, he observes bickering and fighting and
hatred and jealousy? Would he stick around? Or would he have raced (like you
would have from the creepy restaurant) in the opposite direction?

Jesus knows that when his followers truly love each other, it naturally draws
outsiders in. Believers who forgive each other, practice kindness, and want to
help others can attract a positive kind of attention that reflects well on Jesus. In
other words, people recognize that Jesus is loving and forgiving when believers
practice love and forgiveness on a regular basis. His reputation is established
by us. It seems simple enough, but sometimes Christians lose sight of this.

What kind of reputation are you giving Jesus? What do others see when
they look at you?

My Prayer

Dear God,

I want to reflect your goodness by the way I live. I want my actions to point others toward you. Please show me practical ways to express your love.

Amen.

Final Word

May you always be filled with the fruit of your salvation—the righteous character produced in your life by Jesus Christ—for this will bring much glory and praise to God.

Philippians 1:11 NLT

Stone for the Journey

God's love is reflected in me.

Week 52

Day 1 · Heavenly Hopes

Words from the Rock

Father, I want everyone you have given me to be with me, wherever I am. Then they will see the glory that you have given me, because you loved me before the world was created.

John 17:24 CEV

What if you were just going about your day with nothing much to do because it's a Saturday, and you're broke, so you don't have any plans? You pass by this new amusement park, which is supposed to be awesome, and you see that they're running a special introductory offer—free admission, free rides, and even free food for a limited time only. What would you do? If you're like most people, you'd go inside, get on your phone, and call your best friends to come join you, because something that great needs to be shared!

Maybe that's a tiny bit how Jesus feels as he prays this prayer. He's asking his Father to make sure all his followers will join him in heaven. Jesus is still on earth when he makes this request, and it's been a while since he was in heaven. But he knows heaven well since he was with his Father at the beginning of time and they created it together. Chances are he's been missing it. And because he knows how absolutely fabulous that kingdom is, he wants all his friends to enjoy the amazing experience with him!

Can you imagine Jesus's anticipation? It's not easy to envision heaven because it's so far outside the realm of our earthly experience, but Jesus must have been incredibly excited at the prospect of gathering all his friends around him in the most spectacular, most incredible, most wonderful place in the entire universe.

How do you feel when you think about heaven? Hopeful? Excited? Do you want to talk to others about heaven?

My Prayer

Dear God,

I admit that heaven boggles my mind. Please give me glimpses of how fantastic it will be so I can be as enthusiastic about your kingdom as you are.

Amen.

Final Word

Above all, you must live as citizens of heaven, conducting yourselves in a manner worthy of the Good News about Christ.

Philippians 1:27 NLT

Stone for the Journey

Heaven is beyond my wildest expectations.

Day 2 · Love Letter

Words from the Rock· ·

Righteous Father, the world has never known you, but I have
known you, and these disciples know that you sent me on this
mission. I have made your very being known to them—who
you are and what you do—and continue to make it known, so
that your love for me might be in them exactly as I am in them.

John 17:25-26 Message

What if you really, really loved someone, but they lived in an extremely
remote place on the other side of the planet—a location so removed
that there was no internet and no phones, and it was too far for you to travel
there? What if your only hope of communicating your love to them was through
the postal service, which only delivered mail once in a while? Of course, you
would write that person a letter. A very carefully worded letter in which you'd
represent all of your thoughts, dreams, hopes, desires . . . and love for them.
You would want to write the perfect love letter.

That's kind of how God felt—only his love letter came in the form of his Son.
Jesus came to earth to express every loving thought, dream, hope, and desire
that God has for you. All of this was written on Jesus's heart and delivered to
earth so you could understand how much God loves you. A perfect love letter.

In the same way, Jesus wants you to be his love letter. You are the way that
Jesus, now in heaven, can communicate with the people around you. Your
kindness, your helpfulness, your caring, your generosity, your love . . . all convey
the love that Jesus wants to share with others. You are his love letter.

My Prayer· ·

Dear God,
    Thank you for sending Jesus as your love letter. Please help me
to be a better message of love to the people around me.
    Amen.

Final Word ·

If we can encourage others, we should encourage them. If we can give, we should be generous. If we are leaders, we should do our best. If we are good to others, we should do it cheerfully.

Romans 12:8 CEV

Stone for the Journey · · · · · · · · · · · · · · · · · · ·

Jesus sends his love through me.

Day 3 · No Secrets

Words from the Rock ·

Everyone knows what I teach. I have preached regularly in the synagogues and the Temple, where the people gather. I have not spoken in secret. Why are you asking me this question? Ask those who heard me. They know what I said.

John 18:20–21 NLT

After Jesus's arrest, he is taken to the high priest and questioned. The point of the religious leaders' questions is to arrive at something they can actually charge him with—something worthy of execution. They want him dead, and the sooner the better, since the festivities for their biggest holiday (Passover) are about to begin.

When confronted, Jesus answers them honestly. He reminds them that he hasn't hidden anything from them. He's always been out in the open about everything. They know who he is. They know what he's taught. He has no secrets. Of course, this only aggravates them more.

The priests' biggest problem is that Jesus is guilty of nothing. Although the hypocritical religious leaders are guilty of all kinds of things, they still love the law and would never want to be accused of breaking it themselves. They must come up with some other way to get rid of Jesus. With news of his ministry growing, his numbers increasing daily, and so many gathered in Jerusalem to celebrate Passover, the priests fear Jesus is a real threat to their corrupt way of life.

As evil as these religious leaders sound, sometimes Christians are no different. How do we often react when we're caught doing something wrong? Don't we immediately try to dismiss or shove away whatever is attempting to reveal our embarrassment? Sometimes we even push Jesus away from us—we don't want him to come in and shine his light of truth on the mess we've made. We'd rather hide it. But there are no secrets with Jesus. Just as he makes himself known to you, he knows everything about you. Instead of blowing him off next time you mess up, why not fess up and tell him you're sorry.

My Prayer

Dear God,

Thank you for having no secrets from me. Help me to realize how silly it is for me to think I can keep anything from you.
Amen.

Final Word

God has now revealed to us his mysterious plan regarding Christ, a plan to fulfill his own good pleasure.

Ephesians 1:9 NLT

Stone for the Journey

I will live honestly before God.

 ## Day 4 • Forgiveness

Words from the Rock

"Peace to you. Just as the Father sent me, I send you." Then [Jesus] took a deep breath and breathed into them. "Receive the Holy Spirit.... If you forgive someone's sins, they're gone for good. If you don't forgive sins, what are you going to do with them?"

John 20:21–23 Message

After Jesus suffers an excruciatingly painful death on the cross, he is quickly taken down (before the Sabbath) and laid to rest in a rich man's tomb. For three dark days, his disciples endure the most depressing and hopeless hours of all eternity. Not only is their best friend gone, but in their minds, the hope of the world and the Son of God is dead. As far as they know, they're next. And all for what? From what they can see . . . nothing.

Then, on the third day, *Jesus returns to life!* He appears to numerous friends and disciples, who are amazed and beside themselves with joy. He tells his followers to gather and wait for him to give them some last words of encouragement. When he shows up, he greets them and then breathes his Spirit into them—his Holy Spirit, the one he promised was coming. The one who will finish all that Jesus has begun.

Is it surprising that some of Jesus's last earthly words are telling us to forgive others? He had just died a brutal death in order to offer everyone forgiveness and a new relationship with God. Forgiveness is at the front of his mind . . . and rooted deeply in his heart.

Jesus knows that forgiveness is the only way humans can live together. First we desperately need forgiveness from God. Then we need forgiveness from each other. We need to pour out forgiveness with the same generosity that Jesus poured it out to us. As he said, what good will it do to hang on to someone else's sins? Follow his example and forgive freely!

My Prayer

> Dear God,
>
> Thank you for forgiving me even before I knew I needed to be forgiven. Help me to forgive others quickly, even if they don't know they've hurt me.
>
> Amen.

Final Word

> If we live in the light, as God does, we share in life with each other. And the blood of his Son Jesus washes all our sins away.
>
> 1 John 1:7 CEV

Stone for the Journey

> Forgiveness changes me.

Day 5 · Always!

Words from the Rock · · · · · · · · · · · · · · · · · · ·

> I have been given all authority in heaven and on earth! Go to the people of all nations and make them my disciples. Baptize them in the name of the Father, the Son, and the Holy Spirit, and teach them to do everything I have told you. I will be with you always, even until the end of the world.
>
> Matthew 28:18–20 CEV

This is Jesus's last earthly commandment to all his followers. While it seems almost overwhelming in its enormity, it's also empowering. Basically Jesus is asking you to follow the example of how he lived on earth—with the additional promise that all the power of heaven will be backing you.

You have Jesus and God and the Holy Spirit in your corner now—as well as all of Jesus's disciples and followers who are cheering you on from heaven. In fact, all of heaven is urging and encouraging you to be everything God wants you to be. And you can be assured that God won't call you to do anything that's too difficult—he will equip you for whatever challenges come your way.

Perhaps the best part of this last word is Jesus's promise to be with you always—even until the end of this world. And always after that too. No one else can make and keep a promise like that. But Jesus can. Anytime you feel like you're alone, or that you've been betrayed or forgotten or hurt . . . Jesus is right there saying, "I am with you always, even until the end of time." That's a promise you can hold on to—always!

My Prayer ·

Dear God,

Thank you for your promise to always stick with me no matter what comes my way. Help me to never forget this promise and to cling to it when times are hard.

Amen.

Final Word ·

We know that Jesus Christ the Son of God has come and has shown us the true God. And because of Jesus, we now belong to the true God who gives eternal life.

1 John 5:20 CEV

Stone for the Journey ·

Jesus is with me always.

Melody Carlson is the award-winning author of around two hundred books, many of them for teens, including the Diary of a Teenage Girl series, the TrueColors series, and the Carter House Girls series. She and her husband met years ago while volunteering as Young Life counselors. Visit Melody's website at www.melodycarlson.com.

What if beauty is more than just
skin deep?

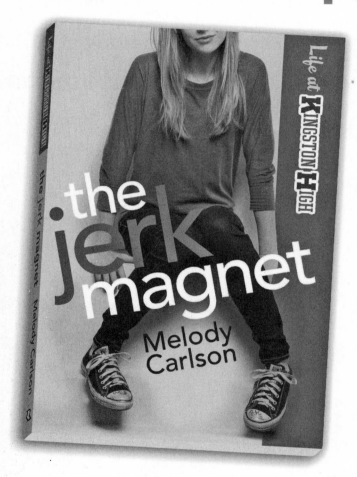

Don't miss the first book in the
Life at Kingston High series!

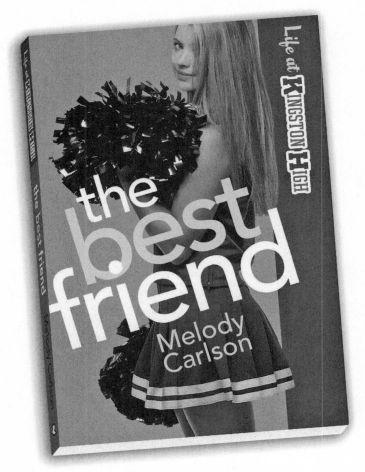

What do you do when your life's not all it's cracked up to be?
Get a new one.

Worlds collide when a Manhattan socialite and a simple
Amish girl meet and decide to switch places.

New School = New Chance
for That First Kiss

Just when it seems Elise is on top of the world, everything comes crashing down. Could one bad choice derail her future?

Girls know all about keeping secrets,
but Sophie's is a really big one.

Visit Melody Carlson at www.melodycarlson.com.

Aster Flynn Wants a Life of Her Own . . .

But will her family get in her way?

Revell
a division of Baker Publishing Group
www.RevellBooks.com